Lawrence W. Tyree Library
Santa Fe College
3000 NW 83rd Street
Gainesville, FL 32606

DATE DUE

IN U.S.A.

D1600397

DEMOCRATIC ROYALISM

STUDIES IN MODERN HISTORY

General Editor: J. C. D. Clark, Joyce and Elizabeth Hall Distinguished
Professor of British History, University of Kansas

Published titles include:

Doron Ben-Atar
THE ORIGINS OF JEFFERSONIAN COMMERCIAL POLICY AND
DIPLOMACY

Conal Condren
THE LANGUAGE OF POLITICAL THEORY IN SEVENTEENTH-
CENTURY ENGLAND

William M. Kuhn
DEMOCRATIC ROYALISM: The Transformation of the British
Monarchy, 1861–1914

C. D. A. Leighton
CATHOLICISM IN A PROTESTANT KINGDOM: A Study of the Irish
Ancien Régime

Cecilia Miller
GIAMBATTISTA VICO: Imagination and Historical Knowledge

Marjorie Morgan
MANNERS, MORALS AND CLASS IN ENGLAND, 1774–1858

W. D. Rubinstein
A HISTORY OF THE JEWS IN THE ENGLISH-SPEAKING WORLD:
Great Britain

Jim Smyth
THE MEN OF NO PROPERTY: Irish Radicals and Popular Politics in
the Late Eighteenth Century

Democratic Royalism

The Transformation of the British Monarchy, 1861–1914

William M. Kuhn
Assistant Professor of History
Carthage College
Wisconsin

palgrave

Published by
PALGRAVE
Houndmills, Basingstoke, Hampshire RG21 6XS and
175 Fifth Avenue, New York, N. Y. 10010
Companies and representatives throughout the world

PALGRAVE is the new global academic imprint of
St. Martin's Press LLC Scholarly and Reference Division and
Palgrave Publishers Ltd (formerly Macmillan Press Ltd).

ISBN 978-0-333-65813-0

This book is printed on paper suitable for recycling and made from fully managed and sustained forest sources.

A catalogue record for this book is available from the British Library.

Transferred to digital printing 2001

For Albert J. Kuhn
and in memory of Roberta Marshall Kuhn

Contents

List of Illustrations		viii
Acknowledgements		ix
Abbreviations		xi
Introduction		1
1	Walter Bagehot: Male Efficiency and Female Dignity	15
2	William Ewart Gladstone: National Acts of Religion	32
3	Lord Esher: Empire Theater	57
4	Randall Davidson: Quietness, Compromise, Comprehension	82
5	The Duke of Norfolk: Authenticity, Eccentricity, Absurdity	112
Conclusion		140
Notes		144
Bibliography		163
Index		172

List of Illustrations

1. King George III at St Paul's in 1789, *The Illustrated London News*, 24 Feb. 1872, 184.
2. 'The Crowd Illuminated', *The Graphic*, 6 Mar. 1872, 19.
3. 'The Thanksgiving Day: A Rough Corner', *The Illustrated London News*, 9 Mar. 1872, 240.
4. Rehearsal for the Diamond Jubilee in front of St Paul's, *The Illustrated London News*, 19 Jun. 1897, 839.
5. Queen Victoria's Diamond Jubilee Thanksgiving Service in front of St Paul's Cathedral, 22 Jun. 1897, The Royal Archives.
6. The Nave, Westminster Abbey, arranged for the Coronation of King Edward VII, 1902, The Royal Archives.
7. Davidson's sketch of Divine Service at Osborne, 1883, Lambeth Palace Library.
8. Queen Victoria's Funeral Procession through London, January 1901, The Royal Archives.
9. 'His Majesty assisting Dr Temple to rise from his knees after paying fealty', *The Illustrated London News*, 16 Aug. 1902, 235.
10. F. Temple, Archbishop of Canterbury, R. Davidson, Bishop of Winchester, and W. Maclagan, Archbishop of York, 1902, The Royal Archives.
11. Procession in Whitehall to the Lying in State of King Edward VII, *The Illustrated London News*, 21 May 1910, 778.
12. Lying in State of King Edward VII, Westminster Hall, *The Illustrated London News*, 21 May 1910.
13. Lying in State of King Edward VII, Westminster Hall, May 1910, The Royal Archives.
14. 'Bouverie King of Arms', *Punch*, 25 Jun. 1902, 455.
15. 'Mr Punch holding a Court of Overflow Claims', *Punch*, 25 Jun. 1902, 455.

Acknowledgements

I would like to thank Her Majesty Queen Elizabeth II for gracious permission to use material and reproduce photographs from the Royal Archives at Windsor.

For allowing me to consult papers held privately or to quote from documents of which they own the copyright, I would like to thank Viscount Esher, Sir William Gladstone, David McGill on behalf of *The Economist*, His Grace the Duke of Norfolk and the Marquess of Salisbury.

For permission to reproduce photographs, my thanks to His Grace the Archbishop of Canterbury, *The Illustrated London News* Picture Library and the *Punch* Library.

For facilities to see manuscripts in their care, I am equally grateful to the following individuals and institutions: the Bodleian Library, the Trustees of the British Library, the Master and Fellows of Churchill College, Cambridge, the Guildhall Library, Kent Record Office, the Trustees of Lambeth Palace Library, the Public Record Office, Sterling Memorial Library at Yale University and the Library of Westminster Abbey.

The resources and atmosphere of a number of other libraries contributed to the completion of this work and the calm of its author. I would like to thank the staffs of the Milton S. Eisenhower Library at Johns Hopkins, the Library of Congress, the Institute of Historical Research at the University of London and the London Library.

This book is a revised version of a doctoral dissertation, which itself began as a BA paper. Financial support for research and revision came from a number of sources, above all from my parents, but also from a Frederic C. Lane Fellowship and from the Atlantic Committee at Johns Hopkins, from a fellowship in Western European Studies awarded by the Social Science Research Council, from the National Endowment for the Humanities, and from the Quality of Life Committee as well as Dean Donald Michie at Carthage.

My undergraduate teachers at Chicago were models of enthusiasm and encouragement. I would like to thank Bernard S. Cohn, Mark Kishlansky and Diana Postlethwaite. In graduate school, Robert Forster, John Higham, J. G. A. Pocock and Katherine Verdery all gave me much useful advice. Of all my teachers, my greatest debt is to David Spring. He supervised my thesis, read patiently through many drafts, gave careful criticism and sustained the project over many years.

A number of other scholars and experts read the manuscript or were

generous with their advice. In particular I would like to thank Richard
Altick, Walter Arnstein, Vernon Bogdanor, John Burrow, Jonathan Clark,
Pamela Clark, Joseph Hamburger, Philip Hicks, Marilyn Morris, Thomas
Noer, Katherine Penovich, Richard Price, John Martin Robinson, Kenneth
Rose and James Sack. Peter Stansky deserves a special mention for help
above and beyond the call of duty.

For satire, sympathy, skepticism and coffee, warm thanks to Sheila de
Bellaigue, Allison Derrett, Frances Dimond, Maude Eburne, Megan Gent,
Jenny Hurley, Jill Kelsey, Julia Melvin, Elizabeth Pearce, Helen Taylor
and Pat West.

Other British friends put me up and put up with me. I would like to
thank Jonathan Boardman, Jane Bond, George Dickson and Michael
Holland.

Fritz Kohn made republican remarks on the progress and Jane Graham
supported, assisted and cajoled at nearly every step along the way.

For any good ideas in this book, these people are responsible; the rest
is unmistakably my own.

My greatest debt is acknowledged in the dedication.

WILLIAM M. KUHN

List of Abbreviations

The following abbreviations and short forms appear in the notes:

AC	Arundel Castle
Add	Additional Manuscripts, British Library
Bell	Bell, George K. A., *Randall Davidson: Archbishop of Canterbury*, 3rd edn, London, 1952.
BL	British Library
CAB	Cabinet Letters to the Crown, Public Record Office
DP	Randall Davidson, First Lord Davidson of Lambeth Papers, Lambeth Palace Library
EM	Earl Marshal Papers, Arundel Castle
ESHR	Reginald Brett, Second Viscount Esher Papers, Churchill College, Cambridge
G & G	*The Political Correspondence of Mr Gladstone and Lord Granville 1868–76*, edited by Agatha Ramm, Camden 3rd ser., vols 81–2, London, 1952.
GD	*The Gladstone Diaries, 1825–39*, edited by M. R. D. Foot, 2 vols, *1840–54*, edited by M. R. D. Foot and H. C. G. Matthew, 2 vols, *1855–96*, edited by H. C. G. Matthew, 10 vols, Oxford, 1968–94.
Gleanings	Gladstone, William E., *Gleanings of Past Years, 1875–78*, 7 vols, New York, 1879.
HHM	Hatfield House Muniments
HJ	*Historical Journal*
J & L	*Journals and Letters of Reginald Viscount Esher*, edited by Maurice V. Brett and Oliver, 3rd Viscount Esher, 4 vols, London, 1934–38.
LC	Lord Chamberlain Papers, Public Record Office
Lees-Milne	Lees-Milne, James, *The Enigmatic Edwardian: The Life of Reginald 2nd Viscount Esher*, London, 1986.
LQV	*The Letters of Queen Victoria, 1837–1861*, edited by Arthur C. Benson and Viscount Esher, 1st ser., 3 vols, London, 1907. *1862–85*, edited by George E. Buckle, 2nd ser., 3 vols, London, 1926–28. *1886–1901*, edited by George E. Buckle, 3rd ser., 3 vols, London, 1930–32.
Notebook	Norfolk, Gwendolen, duchess of, *A Duke of Norfolk Notebook*, London, 1917.

PD	*Parliamentary Debates*, Hansard
PRO	Public Record Office
Q & G	Guedalla, Philip, *The Queen and Mr Gladstone*, 2 vols, 1934, reprint (2 vols in 1), London, 1969.
RA	Royal Archives, Windsor Castle
Robinson	Robinson, John Martin, *The Dukes of Norfolk*, Oxford, 1983.
T	Treasury Papers, Public Record Office
WAM	Westminster Abbey Muniments
WORK	Office of Works Papers, Public Record Office
Works	*The Collected Works of Walter Bagehot*, edited by Norman St John-Stevas, 15 vols, London, 1965–86.

Introduction

In a film made to commemorate the fortieth anniversary of her accession the queen danced a reel with her family in a bare pine ballroom. In another Scottish scene she and John Major sat in chintz-covered chairs while discussing Russia. The dance, the chintz, the Highland location and the Russian discussion – all of them were eerily indistinguishable from descriptions of the court in Queen Victoria's day. Victoria and Albert bought the Balmoral estate and rebuilt the house in the 1850s. The film showed their entwined initials V and A in a weathered stone cornice while the queen's voice could be heard saying 'There is I suppose a certain fascination in keeping the place as Queen Victoria had it. Nothing very much has changed.'[1] The Victorian inheritance plays a vital role in the modern British monarchy. The queen's houses in Scotland and Norfolk are both Victorian; statues of Queen Victoria dominate the approaches to Buckingham Palace and Windsor Castle. The film, the houses and the monuments all emphasize the continuities between the modern monarchy and the monarchy of Queen Victoria's day.

Recent scholarship, however, has taken a decidedly different view of the monarchy's Victorian past. In the most attention-getting remarks since John Grigg criticized the queen's advisers in the 1950s for making her sound like a priggish schoolgirl, David Cannadine has questioned the monarchy's claims to historical continuity. Royal ceremonies which appear to be ancient were actually, Cannadine said, 'invented traditions' dating from no earlier than the widowhood of Queen Victoria.[2] But unlike Grigg, who was assaulted in the street and received unpleasant packages in the mail from persons outraged by what he had said, Cannadine's argument has met with unusual approbation, especially for a specialized, scholarly work. Indeed, his argument has been so successful that he has been sought out by newspapers, television and radio, both in the USA and the UK for his expertise on the monarchy. For example, *The Economist*, in a surprising cover story, reversed its long-held position and argued in favor of abolishing the monarchy. The authors cited Cannadine as the primary scholarly support for their position.[3]

One of the reasons why the 'invented tradition' argument received such widespread attention was that it both coincided with and contributed to a phase of royal unpopularity that began in Britain during the late 1980s. Another reason was its novelty: it either replaced, revised or overturned both academic and popular views of the monarchy that had been accepted

1

for a long time. To understand the attractiveness of the argument it is necessary to know a little about its origins, its underpinnings, its affinities with
and its flat rejection of other scholarly work on the monarchy.

Cannadine's essay appeared in a collection of essays called *The Invention of Tradition*, edited by Eric Hobsbawm, one of Britain's most
important Marxist historians. In his contribution to the collection, Hobsbawm described a pattern of traditions all over Europe and in America that
were 'invented' between 1870 and 1914.[4] This phenomenon resulted partly
from the spread of electoral democracy and the fear that the newly-
enfranchised might not follow their masters, partly from a felt need for
social cohesion in an era of industrial dislocation. Invented traditions also
appeared in movements traditionally hostile to religious and symbolic ritual,
such as the socialist and labor movements, which celebrated May Day for
the first time in 1890. The most successful examples of manipulated traditions, according to Hobsbawm, were those which struck a receptive chord
in the audiences they were designed either to unify, pacify or control.

Hobsbawm argued that the inventions were 'more deliberate and sys-
tematic where, as in Britain, the revival of royal ritualism was seen as a
necessary counterweight to the dangers of popular democracy'.[5] He
pointed to Bagehot and Disraeli, who both recognized the value of the
monarchy in supporting deference and allying the poor to a system of
spoils in which they could not share. In essence, for Hobsbawm, British
royal ceremonial was a form of social control used by an anti-democratic
elite to mollify and stupefy the public.

Cannadine examined royal ceremonial and its cultural context over a
period stretching from the 1820s to the 1970s. He detected four phases in
the evolution of royal ceremonial. In the first phase, between the 1820s
and the 1870s, British sovereigns were often unpopular and their ceremonies
were disorganized, attracting little attention outside of court circles in
London. The next phase, from the 1870s until 1914, Cannadine called 'the
heyday of invented tradition'. This was the most startling part of his thesis.
Irritated by commentators who attributed the precision and timing of royal
ceremonies to 'centuries of precedent', he argued that the majority of the
royal ceremonies we in the twentieth century regard as ancient, were actually created for the first time at the end of the nineteenth century.[6] Class
conflict and industrial unrest were both the backdrop and motive force
behind these inventions: 'the deliberate ceremonial presentation of an im-
potent but venerated monarch as a unifying symbol of permanence and
national community became both possible and necessary' in the third quarter
of the nineteenth century.[7] Cannadine sometimes wavered about the age
of the monarchy and its ceremonies, as the next quote shows. However, he

always stuck to the notion that ceremonial was useful to politicians, even if he hid their identity by his use of the passive voice. His phase II had two new developments: 'the novelty of a mass society at home was reflected in the newness of formal empire abroad. And, once more, the originality of the development was concealed and rendered acceptable by associating it with the oldest national institution, the monarchy.'[8] In the third phase, from World War I to the 1950s, these newly-created royal traditions became routine. They were especially useful at times of social tension, during the General Strike and the Great Depression for example, when 'a politically neutral and personally admirable monarchy was presented, with great success, as "the rallying-point of stability in a distracted age"'.[9] In the final period, since the 1950s, Cannadine speculated on the importance of television for shaping the current era of royal ceremonial. His conclusion was clear: 'the continuity which the invented traditions of the late nineteenth century seek to establish with' earlier centuries 'is largely illusory'.[10]

Cannadine's subsequent journalism on the topic made the same point with greater drama and less subtlety. The Victorian monarchy, he believed, was an obstacle to progress in Britain. 'In a country frequently described as rational, capitalist and democratic, the monarchy remained – along with many others – a secretive, unaccountable, self-perpetuating and arguably corrupt institution.'[11] Queen Victoria and Prince Albert, contrary to the accepted image of their having been friendly to middle-class entrepreneurs, were 'snobbish' and hostile to self-improvement. 'Those who believe that nineteenth-century Britain witnessed the destruction of the industrial spirit might begin their search for the culprit at the very top of the tree.'[12] If the monarchy helped kill off industrial enterprise, it gave birth to nostalgia for a false, pre-industrial England that never was. He described the National Trust in the same words he used to discuss royal ceremonial. The National Trust generates 'not so much history as establishment mysterification [sic], in which there is no room (and no need) for dissent, opposition or an altern-ative point of view . . . the result is a neo-nostalgic, pseudo-pastoral world of manufactured make-believe, a picture-postcard version of Britain and its past, titillating the tourist with tinsel "traditions"'.[13]

Linda Colley, though working on an earlier period, did much to promote her husband's argument. She did this even though her own work often undermined his 'tinsel traditions' view of the monarchy. She examined the rise of a new sort of national consciousness late in the reign of George III, part of which centered on large, ritual celebrations of the king.[14] The gov-ernment, according to Colley, was wary of sponsoring mass appeals; min-isters approved of popular demonstrations in support of the monarchy, but initiatives from the royal family and support from those outside governing circles were of greater consequence in bringing these demonstrations about than official sponsorship. 'Only after the 1870s did Britain's governing elite commit itself to a patriotic, blatantly nationalist appeal.'[15] There were significant gaps between the rise of affection for Farmer George and the apotheosis of the widowed Queen Victoria. Colley noted that the rise of respect for the monarchy was a fluctuating process. If much prestige had accumulated under George III, there were lapses under George IV, William IV, and in the early years of Queen Victoria, until an upward trend began again in the latter part of the nineteenth century.[16] However, because an earlier generation of politicians was cautious about manipulating the monarchy for political gain, and because large royal ceremonies were as characteristic of the late eighteenth as of the late nineteenth century, the cumulative effect of Colley's work is to make us suspicious of the notion that royal ceremonies were 'invented' about 1870.[17]

A recent Cambridge dissertation points to similar conclusions. P. R. Williams studied perceptions of the monarchy in the press between 1837 and 1887. He found that throughout his period there were always two sorts of treatment of the monarchy, one tending to praise and the other to criticism, the former surpassing the latter by the late 1880s. Although Williams agrees with Cannadine that the 1870s and 1880s marked a period when 'royal ceremonial became more public and imposing – and did so in a calculated manner', he also stresses that the monarchy had been seen as an emollient of class tensions throughout the century and its ceremonies had been centers of large, loyal celebration since the beginning of the reign.[18] In short at the end of the reign continuities may have outweighed inventions, a position that even Cannadine himself appears to have recently endorsed.[19]

One of the sources of the difficulty and confusion is that Cannadine was inspired by and wished to ally himself with Geertzian cultural anthropology. Geertz saw the anthropologist's job as akin to that of the literary critic or the intellectual historian; he wanted to treat cultural artifacts as texts and probe them for their meaning. Geertz and Cannadine, however, were never a very good match. Cannadine's sympathies inclined more to 1960s social history than to intellectual history or literary criticism. Ceremonies were for him instruments in the hands of the powerful to abuse the ignorance of the powerless. In contrast Geertz imagined ritual to be creative, meaningful, and subconsciously consensual activity. Ceremonies in Geertz's model did not necessarily serve a useful purpose any more than poetry, or opera, or fiction serve a useful purpose: for Geertz ritual communicated and affirmed fundamental cultural beliefs. Cannadine's theoretical framework of society inclined to a conflict between haves and have nots, while Geertz's inclined to an implicit social agreement between different groups within a society on certain broad values and ethical themes. Furthermore, Geertz specifically rejected the view of ceremony that saw it as merely a tool in the hands of a scheming elite. He deplored those who would reduce the symbolic dimensions of authority 'to a command-and-obedience conception of political life'. He ridiculed those who refused to see symbols as powerful engines of both social stability and change in their own right.[20]

If the alliance between Geertz and Cannadine was uneasy, there were others who found the invented tradition perfectly to their liking, if not irresistible. These were more polemical writers who wanted the monarchy abolished. For them the late Victorian monarchy was a giant 'political confidence trick' dreamed up by elites to keep the working classes in line.[21] For example, Tom Nairn wondered why no credible republican alternative to the monarchy emerged in Britain during the last two centuries. Cannadine provided part of the answer. Nairn suggested that unprecedentedly splendid and well-organized late Victorian ceremonies should be thought of as imports from a more reactionary continental dynasty:

> The new, phoney Hapsburgism was imposed upon a country hitherto notorious for the squalor and incompetence of its public ritual. At least until the later 1860s the keynote of most public Royal occasions had been (as Cannadine puts it) somewhere between farce and fiasco.[22]

Similarly, Christopher Hitchens argued that if the monarchy were abolished Britons could become citizens rather than subjects and cease to believe in invented traditions. Ceremonies are for women and children, for the uneducated, unwashed and unclean. Myths have no place in a manly, rational, forward-looking and enlightened society. 'Illusions, of course, cannot be abolished. But they can and must be outgrown.'[23]

What the invented tradition argument revised, replaced or rejected was a more balanced, less showy, high politics account of the monarchy. Frank Hardie, for example, investigated the erosion of the monarchy's political prerogatives over the last century and a half.[24] John Cannon produced a number of important studies on how the monarchy adapted itself to a reduced role in a changed political environment.[25] In addition there is a tradition of sympathetic biography that has sought to show how individual kings and queens devoted themselves to the smooth running of constitutional monarchy.[26] The overall effect of the invented tradition approach was to suggest that monarchs were more troublesome and less dutiful than has been thought; that their advisers were less interested in adapting to changed circumstances than in trying to obstruct change; that if formal political prerogatives had dwindled away, the monarchy still had secret supplies of sham ceremonies that it could use to reclaim its political influence.

Some of the problems in the invented tradition argument will already be apparent from this summary of it. There are at least five other reasons why the influence of Cannadine on the way we think about the Victorian monarchy is unhelpful. First, although he claimed to be providing an anthropological account of the meaning of ceremonial, Cannadine actually derives from an old and honorable tradition of a different sort. This tradition has long attacked monarchical government as hostile to liberty, rationality and common sense. Cannadine descends from Tom Paine. Note the similarities between Cannadine's argument and Paine's criticism of the two forms of government whose irrationality and evil Paine most wished to expose. The first 'was a government of Priestcraft' founded on superstition, 'the second of Conquerors', founded on power. 'That they might avail themselves of every engine in their favour', England's conquerors, Paine wrote,

> united fraud to force, and set up an idol which they called *Divine Right*, and which, in imitation of the Pope, who affects to be spiritual and temporal, and in contradiction to the Founder of the Christian religion, twisted itself afterward into an idol of another shape, called *Church and State*. The key of St Peter and the key of the Treasury became quartered on one another, and the wondering cheated multitude worshipped the invention.[27]

The crown and its trappings were set up, in this account, by devious men who were out to defraud the public by asking them to believe in fictions. Compare this with Cannadine's point that ceremonies are 'inventions' hence impostures. It is impossible to take ritual seriously when approached from the tradition of the radical enlightenment; ceremonial cannot reflect a set of beliefs shared, however partially, by both actors and audience. It can only be a tool to enslave the powerless.

The Marxist bent of the invented tradition argument is a second serious difficulty. It amounts to a failure to try to understand the past on its own terms. The most important royal ceremonies were always religious acts. The historian who begins from the assumption that religion is a form of deception, or an opiate, will find in ritual 'neither joy, nor love, nor light, nor certitude, nor peace, nor help for pain', all of which the participants in late Victorian ceremonial may well have found there. The creation of symbols and the articulation of ritual is creative, intellectual, even artistic activity and it cannot be fully appreciated from a materialist angle. Cannadine attempted to come at the meaning of ritual by looking at transport technology, coins and the structure of the press; he never looked at the individuals who believed they were assisting at sacred acts. Neither he nor Colley was comfortable with the notion of art or symbolism living lives of their own, divorced from the world of political calculation, or at least possessed of their own logic and referents. For Colley royal portraiture was simply the propaganda of the powerful.[28] Cannadine put the materialist point more bluntly. Britain's aristocracy were never cultivated amateurs, they were just the crass, power-hungry, super-rich of yesterday. 'Ultimately, taste and culture are a function of economic relations: art follows cash.'[29] Thus, even if art, or portraiture, or royal ceremonial meant something completely different to the people who were present, for Cannadine all these have a way of merging into the dreary class struggle of the capitalist world.

If its affinities to Marx and Paine make the invented tradition argument fundamentally unsympathetic to ritual, a third problem is that the argument does not even work as a conspiracy of the political right. Certainly the monarchy's enormous increase in popularity and prestige toward the end of the nineteenth century depended on successful and extraordinary ceremonies in the capital. Bagehot, however, had his doubts about the dignified parts of the constitution. Moreover, Disraeli had nothing to do with any of these ceremonial events. He did persuade the queen to open Parliament a few more times in the 1870s than she would have otherwise, but these were fairly routine events.[30] They had none of the impact of major ceremonies like the thanksgiving of 1872 or the jubilee of 1897. Disraeli did make attention-getting speeches about the connections between monarchy and empire at Manchester and the Crystal Palace in 1872. Still, the monarchy's transformation depended on nonpartisan support. It would never have worked if it had been seen as the possession and pride of Disraelian Conservatives alone. Further, Disraeli's one symbolic act in support of the monarchy was, at least in the short term, a failure. He gave in to the queen's demand for the new title 'Empress of India'. Prominent Liberals attacked the necessary legislation for the title in both Houses and Bagehot, who had been thinking hard about the place of the monarchy in the constitution, scoffed at it in *The Economist*. Neither Disraeli nor the queen could count the new title an unequivocal success. When the imperial theme caught on later in the century, it was far more attributable to young radicals who had begun by opposing Disraeli, for example, Dilke, Chamberlain and Lord Esher, than to Disraeli himself.

Disraeli certainly brought an increased showiness to political life that coincided with the rise of commercial and industrial wealth late in the century. This showiness was indirectly reflected in the more grandiose public displays of the monarchy. Disraeli's influence on the transformation of the monarchy, however, has been exaggerated on the whole. The monarchy's success depended far more on the attachment or silence of its potential critics, on the acquiescence or conversion of young radicals than on Disraeli and its other natural friends among late-Victorian conservatives.

The other conspiratorial politician usually wheeled out by partisans of the invention of tradition is Lloyd George. He has been connected with the investiture of the Prince of Wales at Caernarvon in 1911, a ceremony which, because it had never been performed before in precisely the way planned for 1911, is often taken as a prime example of an invented tradition. Lloyd George hardly works though as an enemy of democracy, at least in this stage of his career when he was a populist advocate of anti-establishment causes. He was in favor of reforming the House of Lords, providing state pensions to the elderly and infirm, championing the Welsh periphery against the wealth and power of the capital. Members of the royal family, though certainly wary of him, were receptive and responsive to his suggestions that the Welsh connection should be emphasized in the ritual recognition of the heir to the throne's coming of age. In any case, the idea for the Welsh ceremony originated not with Lloyd George but with Queen Victoria's eldest daughter, the Empress Frederick in discussion with A. G. Edwards, bishop of St Asaph.[31] As Edwards pointed out in his memoirs, the ceremony was based on legitimate medieval and seventeenth-century precedents. Further, as will become clear from the chapter on the duke of Norfolk in this book, politicians were specifically excluded from the committee appointed to plan the investiture as a way of combatting any ulterior motives.

If the conspiracy of the political right argument did not fall down when some of the conspirators were looked at in detail, it would certainly be undermined by remembering that Britain in this period and afterwards was emphatically a successful, democratic nation. Surer, more advanced steps toward widening the basis of the constitution were being taken with each passing year in late nineteenth-century Britain than in any of its continental neighbors. Democracy survived and prospered along side of monarchy in Britain, as it was apparently impossible for it to do in either Germany, Austria or Russia. Students of royal ritual in these other countries have often welcomed Cannadine's work because it appeared to show that Britain's political elite was, like their own, rigidly conservative and fearful.[32] But surely the most important thing about Britain's monarchy was that it was not abolished in the cataclysm of the First World War. Instead, to large numbers of British people, the monarchy appeared to be allied and not opposed to Britain's democratic system.

Another serious objection to the invented tradition argument is its tele-ology. Cannadine wrote as if the large-scale media monarchy of the late twentieth-century were the natural destination of the monarchy in earlier centuries. Thus, cultural developments and technological innovations could be seized on by courtiers and politicians either to further their conspira-torial designs or to make the monarchy more like the one we know in the latter half of the twentieth century. Thus, the monarchy of the period between the death of George IV and the advent of Disraeli was a failure because the royal family had not discovered what we know now, which is that it is compelling theatre for the royal family to ride in carriages when the rest of us ride in cars. 'The prevailing state of transport technology', Cannadine said of the early nineteenth-century monarchy, 'served further to contain the monarchy within society rather than to elevate it above. For there was nothing particularly anachronistic, romantic or splendid about the way in which English royalty travelled.'[33] The trouble here is that if royal transport was not anachronistic, Cannadine's argument certainly is.

The final flaw in the invented tradition argument can be seen by com-paring it with the similar project of disinheriting the colonial past, popular among many scholarly camps in the late twentieth century. For example, Christopher Columbus was raised to mythological proportions of imposs-ible goodness in the late nineteenth century. Now many scholars feel it necessary to demonize him: they claim that he practiced genocide, had no respect for the environment and inspired generations of racial prejudice against native Americans. Significantly, Cannadine saw the apotheosis of Columbus as happening at the same time as the apotheosis of Queen Victoria.[34] Just as the anti-Columbus, anti-colonial school now sees Columbus as culpable for much of the evil that Europe has imposed on the rest of the world, so Cannadine set out to debunk the myth of the late Victorian monarchy and to connect it with much that is wrong in Britain today. What neither the anti-colonial nor the invented tradition schools will do is treat the late nineteenth-century myth – of either Columbus or Queen Victoria – as a meaningful story to the people who created it. Nor can they conceive how myths might play an important and not necessarily pernicious role in the everyday lives of rational and intelligent people.

For all its problems, the one clear contribution of the invented tra-dition argument was to show that the monarchy of the First World War was a good deal more secure, more popular and more prestigious than it had been a hundred years earlier; and that ceremony contributed to the change. As deeply flawed as the invented tradition position is, it still raises useful questions about the late Victorian monarchy. What exactly were the people up to who had some responsibility for managing late Victorian royal ceremonies? Why did they think the monarchy was an institution that was worth keeping? Surely the monarchy could not have survived as long as it has if it were just a plot: what factors can we attribute to its survival? Above all, what did it *mean* to those who were responsible for staging the ceremonial displays that came to be so key to its public appearance in the years before the First World War?

The purpose of this book is to consider the ideas and plans of those who acquired and exercised the greatest influence during a crucial period in the shaping of the modern ceremonial monarchy. Surprisingly, there were more Liberals among them than Conservatives. Sincere, attached to parliamentary government as much as to monarchy, they were, on the whole, statesmen devising pragmatic solutions to problems as they arose. They had visions of what the monarchy might become in the future, but in the short term they were much more concerned with forging legitimate ceremonial links to the past. The ceremonies they devised helped transform the monarchy from an institution with dwindling political power into a tremendously attractive centerpiece of national identity. More than speeches or political subterfuge, it was the ceremonies that won over people of different political stripes and class loyalties. Moreover the success of the ceremonies contributed to the long-term enhancement of the monarchy's status, even though the short-term political plans individuals sometimes tied to those ceremonies often failed.

The critical juncture for the transition from a politically powerful monarchy to a monarchy that derived its power from the hold it had on people in the streets came with the death of the Prince Consort in 1861. George IV and William IV both had the ambition and the power to influence political events. Their time on the throne was too brief, while their ceremonies were either too grandiose (George IV) or too haphazard (William IV) to capture the public imagination. Prince Albert also wished to influence political events, although he was prepared to exercise this influence in a less public, more quiet, apparently neutral way. He also wanted the court to adopt middle-class ideals of domesticity, piety and earnestness, partly because he believed in them himself and partly because he knew this might augment the royal family's popularity with a wide constituency. He hoped as a result to increase his power behind the scenes. He was initially successful, but his time was also too brief to bring about a lasting settlement.

These men's political ambitions did not preclude the monarchy from having a ceremonial role, but it taught politicians that the monarchy was still a force to be reckoned with, and sometimes competed with, in the political world. Queen Victoria intended to influence political events after her husband's death, but she was less able, her concentration more diffused, her absences from London more prolonged, and gradually opinion grew up in the period after 1861, aided by the men examined here, that the monarchy's chief power was to be exercised in realms other than the political world at Westminster. True, Queen Victoria was an obstructive and annoying thorn in the side of successive Liberal governments.[35] The fact that Gladstone felt it necessary to keep this a secret from many of his cabinet colleagues shows how little, by the 1880s, politicians were willing to tolerate interference from the sovereign in cabinet business.

The death of the Prince Consort provided opportunities for influential advisers to fill his place. Moreover, because Queen Victoria was on the throne for nearly twice as long as a widow as she had been as a wife, there were more opportunities to articulate a predictable and enduring statement of the monarchy's purpose in a changed era. In the 50 years after the Prince Consort's death a stable settlement emerged, a settlement not seriously threatened until the First World War. One characteristic of this settlement was a more reduced degree of royal influence behind the scenes than the prince would have liked. The other was a more enhanced ceremonial role than the prince could have imagined. Large royal ceremonies, widely reported and massively attended, took place with increasing frequency in the fifty years after his death.

During this period a number of royal ceremonies stand out in unusual prominence. They are the large-scale ceremonies that, taking place in either the Abbey or St Paul's, were conceived of as extraordinary opportunities to state the *raison d'être* of the monarchy. They attracted the greatest number of people to the capital and required the skills of the broadest range of officials behind the scenes. These were the events about which officials were most revealing of their aims, purposes and motivations. Among them are the thanksgiving for the recovery of the Prince of Wales in 1872, Queen Victoria's jubilees of 1887 and 1897, the coronations of Edward VII in 1902 and George V in 1911. Of course there were other smaller occasions and appearances, but because these were more routine, the people who arranged them were often silent about their purposes and plans. So what follows here pays more attention to the big, unusual ceremonies because they required more self-conscious commentary from the people involved.

From a survey of the papers of politicians, public departments, household officials, civil servants and clergymen, as well as from a close look at the ceremonies themselves, five notable persons appeared. These five all possessed exceptional influence over the way significant ceremonies were either conceived or arranged. Each of the five was also typical. Each possessed elements of a common outlook on the monarchy. Each had views on the value of royal ceremonial that were characteristic of the notions generally held by a wider range of public men who had responsibility for advising the monarch and charting a course for the monarchy.

Chapter 1 begins with a look at Walter Bagehot (1826–77), a journalist and intellectual whose published work had a decisive impact on the shaping of a powerful and enduring consensus on the monarchy. W. E. Gladstone (1809–98), the subject of Chapter 2, is better known as Queen Victoria's arch-enemy than as engineer of her apotheosis. Yet, he organized one of the biggest ceremonies of the second half of the century and quietly did more than Disraeli to enhance the monarchy's reputation.[36] The next chapter examines a courtier. Reginald Brett, second Viscount Esher (1852–1930) is much better known than Gladstone as an organizer of ceremonial. He is less well known as a publicist for the royal family and a careful editor of the documents that would be used to write the Victorian monarchy's history. Randall Davidson (1848–1930), archbishop of Canterbury from 1903 to 1928, is the subject of Chapter 4. Davidson was Esher's colleague and contemporary as an organizer of ceremonial. His sermons on the meaning of state occasions were widely distributed and widely read. The last chapter explores the career of Henry Fitzalan-Howard, fifteenth duke of Norfolk (1847–1917). Norfolk was hereditary earl marshal on state occasions. He engaged in a bizarre controversy in the first decade of the twentieth century that throws the attitudes of officials toward the monarchy into high relief.

I have tried to describe here a high politics of symbolic representation, to capture the way in which powerful people vied with one another and ultimately reached compromises on the official portrayal of the monarchy. They wanted to explain its purpose and defend its relationship to both the nation and the empire. Often they also wanted to enlist royal support for a desired political object. What emerged from all their activity – political, ceremonial, religious and intellectual – was a consistent and persuasive argument for the maintenance of the monarchy under modern – urban, industrial, democratic – conditions. I have called this argument *democratic royalism*.[37] The argument was articulated in speeches, sermons, press reports and works of history; but, above all the ceremonies themselves conveyed the argument. Using democratic royalism, officials attempted to persuade a newly-powerful public that monarchy was not opposed, but crucial to the success of an expanded democracy. Royal spectacles provided evidence that democracy was rooted in a stable and continuous political tradition. They raised the moral consciousness of the nation. They showed how faith, duty, service, and self-sacrifice were necessary to the success of a political system based on consent, trust and a wide degree of active public participation. They wove together diverse geographic and ethnic loyalties into a single sense of purpose and pride. Finally, democratic royalism, in both words and acts, showed how government could be entertaining to watch; the late Victorian monarchy could transform the dull duties of citizenship into moving lively, even amusing theatre.

Most of the men considered here were worried about the consequences of an expanded franchise and as they grew older they looked upon the future without much confidence. But they were certainly not inventing royal traditions to flummox the working classes. They respected precedent too much, sometimes they were enslaved by it, to treat tradition that lightly. They were too proud of parliamentary democracy in Britain, especially as a contrast with continental despotism, and too aware of the momentum of democratic constitutional change to try to resist it through the monarchy. They altered and adjusted traditions, they did not invent them. They saw the need to renovate the monarchy, to assess what had been handed down in order to find what was wisest and most relevant for their own age, to see it all anew through late-Victorian lenses. They grasped the potential of the monarchy to act as a double-edged sword. It kept a highly-stratified society aware of the fine gradations of rank; it also had the power, at rare moments, to bring people together.

This then, is both a political history and a cultural history. It explores what the monarchy meant to a political elite, and what that elite thought the monarchy meant to the rest of the nation. I have not looked directly at what the monarchy meant to people standing in the streets or to those who stayed at home. To a certain degree, however, large royal ceremonies in the capital captured fleeting moments of national consensus. If this were not the case, they would not have attracted the vast concourse of people that they did. Nor would newspapers have devoted such extensive coverage were they not certain of an immense readership ready to consume their reports. Cultural anthropologists have long known that in certain central rituals communities of people 'speak about themselves to themselves', that they are unusually communicative about the implicit beliefs that underlie their common social life. On these ritual occasions some members of society symbolize what they believe to be essential ideas in their cultural life both for their own benefit and the benefit of others.[38] That anthropological assumption underlies this study of royal ceremonial.

Put another way, as the sociologists Edward Shils and Michael Young said of the coronation of Queen Elizabeth II, 'a society is held together by its internal agreement aboxut the sacredness of certain fundamental moral standards.' Seldom explicitly discussed or even consciously perceived, these fundamental values are 'sacred' not in the conventional religious sense, but in the sense that they both attract and generate a large degree of unspoken reverence from different groups within a given society. 'The coronation', Shils and Young continued, speaking of 1953, 'provided at one time and for practically the entire society such an intensive contact with the sacred that . . . [it may be interpreted] as a great act of national communion'.[39] In short, this study inclines to a similar, consensual model of royal ritual because that was precisely what the organizers hoped to achieve, what the participants themselves considered remarkable and what Victorian commentators regarded as a mark of the ceremonies' success.

Even though the focus here is on the elite, the ceremonies studied here offer hints at what it meant to a much larger cross-section of the country to be English, and to profess feelings of loyalty to the Crown. So this is a cultural history too, in that it tries to relate ceremonial acts conceived by a small group of men to broader issues that were the subject of wider cultural debate. Among these issues were the expansion of democracy, the rootedness of religion in England's national history, the drama of empire and the necessity of a new restraining morality for an age that was too proud of its possessions. As we shall see, there were arguments about these ceremonies among those who planned them. No doubt there was disagreement too among those watching in the streets, who may well have been simply curious or complacent rather than loyal and enthusiastic. Nevertheless, to the degree that royal ceremonies did indicate something common, or shared, or agreed upon, it is hard not to conclude that these were eloquent events in a people's collective life. As such they must tell us what people were thinking in the quiet moments that took place at the center of state occasions in the half century after the death of the Prince Consort. Those who, late in the twentieth century, wonder about the monarchy's future, who wonder whether a new consensus for the twenty-first century is even possible, may see the way forward by knowing a little more about the late Victorian past.

1 Walter Bagehot: Male Efficiency and Female Dignity

No one has been of greater consequence for the modern British monarchy than Walter Bagehot. He is the one authority that both defenders and critics of the Crown make it their business to know. Further, Bagehot has now served as an authoritative source on the monarchy for more than a hundred years. His ideas about the monarchy appear primarily in his analysis of parliamentary government, *The English Constitution* published in 1867. Legal experts on the constitution began to refer to Bagehot's book from the 1880s onwards.[1] Oxford and Cambridge dons began to teach it around the turn of the century.[2] At around the same time civil servants began to cite Bagehot as an authority on royal finance and on the Crown's relationship to the House of Lords.[3] Every sovereign since George V has studied Bagehot. The current queen learned about Bagehot from the provost at Eton. The current heir to the throne has sought out Bagehot's modern editor for advice and further reading on Bagehot.[4] Even John Cannon and Tom Nairn, who have written very different histories of the modern British monarchy, agree that Bagehot remains the starting place for discussions of the monarchy. Nairn puts the case more vividly and less neutrally than Cannon. For Nairn *The English Constitution* is the 'chief malefactor' and Bagehot the 'guilty party' responsible for quashing reasonable republicanism in Britain and stamping out progressive criticism of the monarchy.[5] Clearly Bagehot is someone we need to get to know too.

Bagehot was born in Bank House, Langport, Somersetshire in 1826. His mother's family owned the bank. His father, who came from another prominent family in Langport, worked in the bank. He would one day grow up to manage the bank's affairs himself. Both sides of his family were prosperous and middle class. Although he came to be intimately connected with London society, as most of his ancestors were not, he died much as they had, a rich man of the commercial classes. Thus, one of the shrewdest commentators on Victorian social inequality knew something of life in the highest circles without exactly belonging to those circles himself.

Bagehot's upbringing contributed to this feeling of identity with the Victorian ruling classes at the same time as he stood apart and aloof from them. His father was a Unitarian. He had the dissenter's belief in discipline and the dissenter's skepticism about the establishment in Church and State. Bagehot's mother, on the other hand, was an Anglican. She looked askance at her husband's rationalizing faith. As a boy Bagehot attended services led by his father in the drawing room on Sunday mornings. In the afternoons he went with his mother to Church of England services in the town or one of the neighboring villages.[6] Bagehot's father had no formal schooling and was anxious to give his son a thorough and modern education. He sent the young Bagehot away to a school run by Unitarians in Bristol and in 1842 to University College in London. The elder Bagehot objected to the doctrinal tests necessary for Oxford and Cambridge. In Bristol and London young Bagehot learned science and political economy, topics excluded from the curriculum at the public schools and ancient universities. At University College he probably had a better, broader education than those of his contemporaries at Oxford and Cambridge, but he also missed out on the slight social advantage of those who were reared in the older universities. Still, he was cheerful about the schooling his father had planned for him and teased his mother in one letter about how much he would miss her when he went away to 'the *heretical* college' in London.[7]

As a student Bagehot was devoted to his studies and worked too hard. He was sometimes made fun of, not only by fellow schoolboys in Bristol, but also by the sons of dissenting ministers with whom he attended lectures in London. It is almost as if he feared something in himself that had to be chained down to strict habit and routine. There was a streak of madness in his family. He had a retarded half-brother and his mother suffered from periods of insanity that increased in frequency as she grew older. At University College Bagehot first began to write journal articles on literary and political topics. There is a direct link between the tensions in his family and one essential characteristic of his writing. His articles often divide the world into a sphere of passionate irrationality and a sphere of strict reason. One half of the world is childlike, female, sensual, bordering on madness, the other is responsible, masculine, and ultimately imposing its discipline on the opposite sphere in order to keep it from spinning out of control. One of his early references to the monarchy in his published work arises in precisely this context. He criticized Macaulay for failing to understand seventeenth-century Cavaliers, whose nature was sensual and hedonistic. Bagehot gave this explanation for the attraction of the monarchy to Cavaliers and Tories.

> As a riotous state tends to fall under martial tyranny, a passionate mind tends to subject itself to an extrinsic law – to enslave itself to an outward discipline . . . An hereditary monarchy is, indeed, the very embodiment

of this principle. The authority is so defined, so clearly vested, so evid-
ently intelligible; it descends so distinctly from the past, it is imposed
so conspicuously from without.[8]

For seventeenth-century Cavaliers the monarchy was the imposition of
discipline on sensuality.

Bagehot identified with Cavaliers, but he was also loyal to the progressive, reforming spirit of the constitution Macaulay celebrated. He adored
his half-mad Anglican mother; he was obedient to the critical rationality
of his dissenting father. His strategy was sometimes to build a playful or
ironic bridge between the two, to acknowledge his own conservative instincts, but to scrutinize them, often satirize them, at the same time. Here
for example is the twenty-five year old Bagehot writing to his mother
about the opening of the Crystal Palace Exhibition in 1851.

> I took a start yesterday and went to see the Queen open the Exhibition.
> It went off very well though her Majesty looked matronly and aged and
> the ladies in attendance on her were an affecting spectacle . . . The form
> of the building is that of a cross – the long stroke from an analogy to
> Church architecture being called the nave, and the short stroke the
> transept. The Queen sat in the centre with the crowd around and behind
> her, and I was lucky enough to get a place in the front row of one of
> the galleries immediately overlooking the chair of state . . . I fancied
> that I caught two or three words of the archbishop's grace or benediction
> but I am not sure: at any rate I heard a sermonic tone of voice which
> was a great satisfaction. I suppose the Archbishop was inserted in the
> programme to please the foreigners who are in the habit of consecrating
> railways and all sorts of secular places: otherwise I think he might as
> well have been left out as there was nothing in keeping with him, –
> nobody minded him and the Queen looked as if she wished that he
> would leave off.[9]

Already there are hints of the later Bagehot here. He loved to tease and
is out to shock his mother's devout sensibilities. There is the sovereign
looking her age, the archbishop's solemn words that cannot be heard, the
consecration that is really just a show put on for foreigners. However, his
very presence in a choice seat is at odds with his satirical tone. There was
an immense throng on opening day and an enormous demand for admission. Had he taken such trouble to get so desirable a spot simply to heap
ridicule on the proceedings? A close look at Bagehot's mature writing dem-
onstrates that this perversity, this tendency to deprecate and do homage at
the same time, runs right through Bagehot's attitude toward the monarchy.[10]

Grasping this is one of the most essential elements in understanding how he articulated a vision of the monarchy that was acceptable to persons on both ends of the political spectrum, and how the whole of the official class came to adopt his point of view.

After University College Bagehot thought of becoming a barrister, but he found the law too dull and gave it up. He continued to write for journals, indulging his one side by writing on literature and poetry, and yoking this to his other side by writing on politics and economics. Out of filial piety he left London for Somersetshire to work in the family bank and be closer to his mother. It was the experience in banking that led him to the position he would hold at the peak of his career. He proposed a series of articles in 1857 to James Wilson, founder and owner of *The Economist*. The two became friends and Bagehot next proposed marriage to Wilson's eldest daughter, Eliza. Then as now this was an effective way to a good job. But no one could have said how quickly this would happen: Wilson went out to fill an administrative post in the Indian administration in 1859 and left Bagehot in charge of *The Economist*. A year later he was dead and Bagehot assumed the editorship, a place he held until his own early death in 1877.

Wilson had launched *The Economist* in the heat of the battle between the landed interest and the commercial middle classes over the Corn Laws. *The Economist* was in favor of repeal. After the victory, Wilson devoted the journal to maintaining the principle of free trade. It was not exclusively devoted to economic topics, but also to politics, and to a lesser degree, reviews of literature. In the 1860s the journal had a great degree of influence; both Conservative and Liberal politicians looked to Bagehot for advice on economic issues, although a pamphlet he wrote on parliamentary reform also received favorable notice.

Bagehot must not have been satisfied with this quiet influence behind the scenes, because in the very era that he was composing *The English Constitution*, he tried and failed to get into Parliament. He stood as a Liberal, but he was a rather conservative Liberal who was not optimistic about further expansion of the electoral franchise. Bagehot wrote *The English Constitution* between 1865 and 1867 during a period of increasing agitation for a further reform of the constitution. The work bears the marks of someone who is witnessing a movement he does not like, but feels powerless to stop. Faint traces are also detectable of the failed parliamentary candidate who feels a little outside the political institutions he praises and, to a certain degree, romanticizes.

In *The English Constitution* Bagehot proceeded by juxtaposing paired opposite ideas.[11] He contrasted 'the paper description' of the constitution with 'the living reality' and observed that 'many refinements of the literary theory' could not be found in the 'rough practice'.[12] He wanted to treat the constitution in a simplified manner, different from the dull, academic discussions of legal experts.[13] He claimed that common notions about the constitution were in error. Its excellence lay neither in the separation of the legislative, executive and judicial powers, nor in the balanced union of the monarchical, aristocratic and democratic elements.[14] Instead, he argued that a true understanding of the English system lay in seeing its division into two parts: 'first, those which excite and preserve the reverence of the population – the *dignified* parts, if I may so call them; and next, the *efficient* parts, those by which it, in fact, works and rules'. The dignified parts, consisting of the monarchy and the House of Lords, '*gain* authority' while the efficient House of Commons and cabinet '*use* authority'. By the one, a constitution wins 'the loyalty and confidence of mankind'. By the other, it employs 'that homage in the work of government'.[15]

The monarchy appears in two separate chapters of *The English Constitution*. The first of these considers the monarchy in its dignified capacity and describes how it exerts power over people's imaginations. The next considers the monarchy in its business capacity – 'the real work the Queen does' – and describes the use of the queen at two of the three stages of representative government, when a ministry is appointed and during its continuance in office.[16] The use of the queen at the third stage of representative government, when a ministry ends, is considered separately.[17]

Bagehot set out five reasons why the monarchy was useful in its dignified capacity. 'The best reason why monarchy is a strong government is, that it is an intelligible government. The mass of mankind understand it, and they hardly anywhere in the world understand any other.'[18] Uneducated men, according to Bagehot, were unable to understand the complex interaction of political parties and public opinion through which the country was governed. 'The action of a single will, the fiat of a single mind', on the other hand, were 'easy ideas' that anyone could understand.[19] The unique advantage of England's constitutional monarchy was that it had 'a comprehensible element for the vacant many, as well as complex laws and notions for the inquiring few'.[20]

The social, intellectual and moral distance Bagehot perceived between educated and uneducated men is a theme that runs through the work. 'The lower orders, the middle orders, are still, when tried by what is the standard of the educated "ten thousand", narrow-minded, unintelligent, incurious.'[21] The great mass of uneducated Englishmen were, for him, primitive survivals. Their stupidity was a result of unequal rates of intellectual progress. He used a geological metaphor to convey his meaning.

Great communities are like great mountains – they have in them the primary, secondary, and tertiary strata of human progress; the characteristics of the lower regions resemble the life of old times rather than the present life of the higher regions.[22]

Bagehot returned to this theme in the conclusion. 'The change in the state of the higher classes since the middle ages is enormous, and it is all improvement; but the lower have varied little, and many argue that in some important respects they have got worse.'[23] The difficulty in so heterogeneous a community was to maintain order, to assure the rule of the wise over the rude and uncultivated. In *Physics and Politics*, where he aimed to set out the political prerequisites of human progress, Bagehot observed that even in progressive communities there was the chance of a sudden return to the savagery of barbarous ancestors. Such had been the case in the French Revolution, or in any large riot.[24] Order was only maintained in England by the deference of the ignorant to the spectacle of the great.

The second of the five ways in which Bagehot thought the monarchy acted on people's minds was that it lent a religious sanction to the proceedings of government.[25] Englishmen deferred to royal show because of the aura of sacred mystery that surrounded the throne. Far from being reasonable or easily intelligible, this aspect of the monarchy appeared to defy reason and was the more powerful for it.

That which is mystic in its claims; that which is occult in its mode of action; that which is brilliant to the eye; that which is seen vividly for a moment, and then is seen no more; that which is hidden and unhidden; that which is specious, and yet interesting, palpable in its seeming, and yet professing to be more than palpable in its results, this . . . is the sort of thing – the only sort – which yet comes home to the mass of men.[26]

The religious reverence which the mass of men held for the monarchy assured their continuing obedience to the *status quo*. For that reason, royal magic was not to be interfered with or it might be dispelled. 'When there is a select committee on the Queen, the charm of royalty will be gone. Its mystery is its life. We must not let in daylight upon magic.'[27] Bagehot elaborated on this point in a number of articles on the monarchy in *The Economist*. In 1867 and 1874 he again stressed that to meddle with royal magic would be to destroy it, to enquire too closely into the civil list would be to impair the dignity of the Crown and to threaten the reverence that so beneficially attached to it.[28] Bagehot was disturbed by Disraeli's proposal in 1876 that the queen should take the new title, Empress of India. He thought that it was a mistake to toy with the healthy magic of the throne, to add a new title to an institution whose essence was ancient associations.[29] Bagehot's monarchy was not the imperial, vaguely oriental monarchy envisioned by Disraeli. The religious magic of Bagehot's monarchy was indigenous, and it served as a focus of island history instead of colonial expansion.

Bagehot's anxiety about preserving the aura that surrounded the throne applied also to the other dignified institution, the House of Lords. When the House of Lords looked as if it might reject Gladstone's Irish Church Bill in 1869, and so strengthen the hand of those who wanted to reform the Lords, Bagehot warned that the prestige of a hereditary legislature could not withstand intimate enquiry and discussion.

> The prestige of a privileged order is like the credit of a bank: if you do but discuss whether a bank is bad or good the bank will stop, and so of an aristocracy: if you have to prove that it *ought* to be obeyed, it will not be obeyed.[30]

The prestige of the House of Lords, like that of the monarchy, rested on an irrational basis, on its traditional pre-eminence rather than logical and utilitarian assessments of its value. This was why Bagehot argued that reform or 'great change must be bad for an assembly which, whether it ought to or not, *in fact* rests on *prestige* and not on argument, on history not on reason'.[31]

The third and fourth ways monarchy lent strength to the ruling order show that Bagehot acknowledged the imaginative appeal of the Crown to more than just those at the lowest end of the social scale. The queen was both head of English society and head of English morality.[32] As the head of society, the queen prevented the chronic competition for social preferment that would re-open every few years if the premier and his wife were at the head of society. Social climbing and snobbery were inevitable; but, royalty at least had a mitigating influence. Because the sovereign always occupied the place at the pinnacle of society, no one in England could compete for it. In opposition to republicans Bagehot argued that one of the hazards of exchanging constitutional monarchy in England for a republic was that the competitive ostentation of new wealth would fill the vacuum left by the removal of old rank.[33] This is what had happened in the American republic, he claimed.

Bagehot spoke of the monarchy as having moral force as well. The domestic virtues of the queen allowed middle-class families to identify their own virtues with those of the royal family, as well as they elevated the value of those virtues. He spent, however, little time on this, the fourth of the monarchy's appeals to the imagination. It occupies only a single paragraph of the whole chapter. Further, he was not hopeful that the sovereign would always set a good moral example.

> A little experience and less thought show that royalty cannot take credit for domestic excellence. Neither George I, nor George II, nor William IV were patterns of family merit; George IV was a model of family demerit.[34]

George III set a good moral example, but kings and princes would ordinarily be tempted by all the seductions and unsuitable occupations available to persons of their rank.

> Grave and careful men may have domestic virtues on a constitutional throne, but even those fail sometimes, and to imagine that men of more eager temperaments will commonly produce them, is to expect grapes from thorns and figs from thistles.[35]

The fifth and final function that monarchy assumed in its dignified capacity, and the one Bagehot considered to be most important, was that it acted as a disguise. 'It enables our real rulers to change without heedless people knowing it. The masses of Englishmen are not fit for an elective government; if they knew how near they were to it, they would be surprised, and almost tremble.'[36] A calm national mind was one of the prerequisites of cabinet government. The excitement involved in ministerial change was prevented by the disguise or artifice of an apparently unchanging ruler.

> The mass of uneducated men could not now in England be told 'go to, choose your rulers;' they would go wild; their imaginations would fancy unreal dangers, and the attempt at election would issue in some forcible usurpation. The incalculable advantage of august institutions in a free state is, that they prevent this collapse. The excitement of choosing our rulers is prevented by the apparent existence of an unchosen ruler.[37]

After setting out these reasons why the monarchy was useful in its dignified capacity, Bagehot turned to consider the use of the monarchy in its business capacity. He thought this use was practically nil. After examining the utility of the Crown at the three stages of representative government, he concluded that the Crown was generally of very little use at all. Bagehot showed that at each of the three stages a wise king would be of considerable use and could exert considerable influence for good, but that in the ordinary course of affairs hereditary kings were not wise. To acquire wisdom, a king had to work. Too often the sovereign came to the throne without the necessary discipline for work.

Why should he work? It is true he will lose the quiet and secret influence which in the course of years industry would gain for him; but an eager young man, on whom the world is squandering its luxuries and its temptations, will not be much attracted by the distant prospect of a moderate influence over dull matters.[38]

Bagehot was aware of the opportunities of high station, but he was not hopeful that those opportunities would be grasped. Like a young king, a young peer had great power to do good if he had a taste for parliamentary business. It was not likely that he would acquire such a taste: 'A young lord just come into £30,000 a year will not, as a rule, care much for the law of patents, for the law of "passing tolls", or the law of prisons.'[39]

Thus, one reading of Bagehot is that the key to understanding the place of royalty and aristocracy in the English constitution is not in any residual utility they may have had in the business of ruling the nation, but in the spectacle they provided for the ruled.

However, there are some intriguing inconsistencies in Bagehot about the spectacle provided by the dignified parts of the constitution.[40] Toward the nobility he was at once cynical about others' reverence and, if not reverential himself, perhaps slightly wistful. At one point in *The English Constitution* he maintained that the mind of a nobleman was likely to be of no more than an ordinary character. In fact, it was likely to be of less than an ordinary character. Several paragraphs later, however, he showed appreciation for aristocratic style and manner.

As the world has gone, manner has been half hereditary in certain castes, and manner is one of the fine arts. It is the *style* of society; it is in the daily-spoken intercourse of human beings what the art of literary expression is in their occasional written intercourse.[41]

He argued in *The English Constitution* that noblemen were likely to be of use only in their showy capacity. They were unlikely to be of use in a business capacity. But in journalism published a decade earlier he argued that this was not so. He urged his readers to recognize that aristocratic statesmen possessed abilities necessary to the conduct of governmental business. Tact, taste, cultivation and discretion were necessary qualities that unaristocratic statesmen did not have.[42]

Bagehot could identify both with cynical philosophers who deprecated spectacle, as well as with poets who could enjoy aristocratic pageantry without any bitterness.

It is not given to the children of men to be philosophers without envy. Lookers-on can hardly bear the spectacle of the great world. If you watch

the carriages rolling down to the House of Lords, you will try to deprecate the House of Lords. Idleness is cynical. Both Béranger and Horace
are exceptions to this. Both enjoy the roll of the wheels; both love the
glitter of the carriages; neither is angry at the sun.[43]

Bagehot also appreciated pageantry in prose. In this passage on Gibbon he
both praised and poked fun at the historian.

Grave, tranquil, decorous pageantry is a part, as it were, of the essence
of the last age. There is nothing more characteristic of Gibbon. A kind
of pomp pervades him. He is never out of livery. He ever selects for
narration those themes which look most like a levee; grave chamber-
lains seem to stand throughout; life is a vast ceremony, the historian at
once the dignitary and the scribe.[44]

In both these passages Bagehot shows a latent liking for dignified spectacle at odds with the strong first impression given by his work that such
spectacle was suited only for the uneducated.

It may be well to remember that one of the uses of the monarchy in its
dignified capacity was that it prevented competition for the leadership of
society, that it mitigated natural reverence for wealth by occupying a
position money could not buy. Bagehot thought the same was true of the
aristocracy. Reverence for rank mitigated the idolization of wealth.[45] It was
not only the very mean who idolized wealth: the astute men of business
for whom he edited *The Economist* were also worshippers. After the
passage of the Second Reform Bill, Bagehot argued that it was necessary
for the House of Lords, representing aristocracy, and the Commons,
representing the new trading wealth or plutocracy, to band together in
guiding the electors of the new constituencies. He argued that the aristocracy
ought to lead this pact because new wealth in England naturally deferred
to old wealth. The men who populated the House of Commons were not
uncultivated, but they were in their way deferential and worshipful.

Of course there have been many countries in which certain old families,
whether rich or poor, were worshipped by whole populations with a
more intense and poetic homage; but I doubt if there has ever been any
in which all old families and all titled families received more ready
obedience from those who were their equals, perhaps their superiors, in
wealth, their equals in culture, and their inferiors only in descent and
rank.[46]

The worship for rank was thus more widespread than one might imagine
from other passages in Bagehot. In fact, Bagehot thought, quoting Gladstone,

that every man had a 'sneaking kindness for a lord' but was a little afraid that it might be found out, so kept it quiet.[47]

Sometimes Bagehot admitted quite openly that even the most intelligent men's beliefs were made up of both rational and irrational elements.[48] The fortunes of the financial magnates who did their business in Lombard Street were occasionally ruined by crises and bad management at the Bank of England. 'But still there is a faith in the Bank, contrary to experience, and despising evidence.'[49] Similarly, in *The English Constitution* Bagehot argued that there was a 'traditional part of human nature', that 'most easily impressed and acted on by what is handed down', which was very strong. 'The most intellectual of men are moved quite as much by the circumstances which they are used to as by their own will.'[50] Because this large part of human nature was sleepy and habitual rather than active and voluntary, a certain authority had been conceded to old institutions simply because they were old.

There is something more here than sleepy acquiescence in ancient institutions. Bagehot wrote of Englishmen in Lord Eldon's day that they did not naturally idolize the *status quo*, as Lord Eldon did. They were not naturally illiberal, although 'there is or was a strong feeling of loyalty, of attachment to what is old, love for what is ancestral, belief in what has been tried'.[51] Attachment to what was old was an imaginative sentiment. If the first Edinburgh Reviewers rightly resisted blind Eldonite defense of the *status quo*, they made a mistake by going too far in the other direction. They ignored the power of what was imaginative and mystical. The 'clear, precise, discriminating' intellects of the Edinburgh Reviewers shrank 'at once from the symbolic, the unbounded, the indefinite'; but, insisted Bagehot, 'the misfortune is, that mysticism is true'.[52] Many things that possessed ancient associations also possessed a mystical charm appealing even to the most enlightened of men.

Bagehot's religious views provide us with more material that suggests that he too may have participated in the irrational reverence for ancient institutions characteristic of those he sometimes seemed to despise.[53] The Church of England makes no appearance in *The English Constitution*. It is clear from Bagehot's discussion of the Public Worship Regulation Act in 1874, however, that he regarded the Church as among the country's dignified institutions. He spoke of reforming the Church in terms identical to those he had used in discussing reform of the monarchy and House of Lords. As usual he has trouble keeping the irony out of his voice.

The English Church is one of those among our institutions which, if it is to be preserved at all, should be touched most anxiously. It is one of our oldest institutions. Every part of it has a history, which few of us thoroughly understand, but which we all know to be long and important.[54]

In this and another article which followed later the same year, Bagehot worried about preserving not only the established Church, but also the supply of first-rate men who were to be ordained in the Church.[55] He thought intelligent men who were considering ordination would be discouraged from doing so by the ecclesiastical legislation of that year. This would lead in turn to a decline in intellectual quality and independent judgement of the clergy. His desire to preserve the high caliber of clergymen and the comprehensiveness of the Church provide telling contrasts with his more cynical assessments of the usefulness of the other dignified institutions. The Church was no mere spectacle for the vulgar, it was a repository of toleration and intelligence as well as tradition.

Bagehot was less suspicious of the designs of Anglican clergymen than of Roman Catholic priests. Yet, he still possessed some admiration for the Roman Catholic Church. Bagehot's friend, Richard Holt Hutton, wrote that

> What attracted Bagehot in the Church of Rome was the historical pres-
> tige and social authority which she had accumulated in believing and
> uncritical ages for use in the unbelieving and critical age in which we
> live – while what he condemned and dreaded in her was her tendency
> to use her power over the multitude for purposes of a low ambition.[56]

Shortly after Bagehot's death Hutton wrote a memoir in which he noted that Bagehot possessed a 'double vein'. He sympathized 'with the works of high imagination' at the same time as he had 'clear insight into that busy life which does not and cannot take note of works of high imagination'.[57] It is important to keep this double vein in mind when considering Bagehot on the monarchy. It shows that, despite all he tells us about the gullibility of the vulgar, he could be a reverent and sincere believer himself. Bagehot's appreciation for what was old, for that which possessed imaginative and mystic appeal, suggests some embarrassment in the posi-
tion of an educated man who argued for the maintenance of the monarchy as a necessary way of calming the vulgar and uninitiated.

Every one of the men who had some share in transforming the monarchy before the First World War, and who are considered in succeeding chapters, read Bagehot and showed signs of having accepted his argument. They all show signs too of his embarrassment. It is important to see, however, that some of the most prominent and experienced politicians of Bagehot's own day were far from his point of view on the monarchy; and that *The English*

Constitution really did pave the way to quite a new official attitude toward the Crown.

It is usual to disregard Disraeli's comment on Prince Albert – that, had he lived, his power would have been 'despotic' – as a characteristically flamboyant exaggeration. However, men of all parties had grown, perhaps grudgingly, to respect the Prince Consort's judgement in the years before his death. It is not unlikely that his influence would have increased as the older generation of politicians died out and younger men came in. Nor was it outrageous for a good deal of real power to be conceded to hereditary monarchs in the 1860s. There was the example of the queen's uncle, King Leopold of the Belgians, who was widely credited with both intelligence and political discernment. There was also the less reputable example of Louis Napoleon in France, with whom the queen and Prince Albert had a fairly close relationship in the later 1850s.

When Prince Albert died in 1861, not all ministers were of Bagehot's opinion that the monarchy was principally for show and that the sovereign's political will mattered little. The reverse is true. Lord Clarendon, a former minister and diplomat, who was in touch with all the most powerful members of the cabinet, noted that the prince's death made everyone in the ministry uneasy. It was possible for him to indicate in 1861, as Whig politicians had throughout the eighteenth century, that ministers owed their places as much to the confidence of the sovereign as to their power in the House of Commons. Clarendon told the duchess of Manchester that in the general wariness following the prince's death, ministers were watching each other 'as cats do mice' lest one of them should improve his standing with the queen at the expense of the others. Clarendon was a Whig and a moderate reformer. He was not particularly royalist. Unlike Bagehot, he believed the queen had serious political responsibilities and important business to transact with ministers. He thought that attention to these responsibilities was the only way the queen could overcome her grief.[58]

Later in the 1860s the queen's retirement from public life and her heir's having nothing to do began to attract adverse comment. Bagehot surprised many by describing 'the actions of a retired widow and an unemployed youth' as being enormously important for the constitution.[59] Lord Robert Cecil, destined to be premier as third marquess of Salisbury, thought otherwise. In the pages of *The Saturday Review* he argued that loyalty to the throne, when stimulated by external display, was an important barrier against disorder.

Hereditary monarchy is upheld, in spite of many inconveniences which attach to it, because the emotion of loyalty has been ascertained by

experience to be not only a cheap defence of order, but one for which
no substitute, even tolerably effective, can be found.[60]

The queen's continuing seclusion was harming her popularity and dimin-
ishing the effectiveness of the throne as a barrier against disorder. 'Seclusion', wrote Cecil, 'is one of the few luxuries in which Royal personages
may not indulge. The power which is derived from affection or from
loyalty needs a life of almost unintermitted publicity to sustain it.'[61] He
thought that one of the weaknesses of constitutional monarchy was that
the personal popularity of the sovereign was bound up with estimation of
the Crown as an institution. Queen Victoria's unpopularity endangered
constitutional monarchy. It was especially important that the queen return
to public life and provide visible support of strength and stability in the
unstable times he anticipated from the coming arguments about parliamentary reform.[62]

John Vincent has commented on the diaries of another important mid-
Victorian political figure, Lord Stanley, later 15th earl of Derby, that during
the 1860s

> Constant anxiety is shown by politicians about the Queen. While Bagehot
> was praising the Queen as an 'elegant facade', the London crowd was
> expressing very different opinions; the ruling few, knowing this, feared
> for the discredit it might bring upon themselves.[63]

Stanley thought that the queen was being selfish and irresponsible in re-
fusing to resume her public duties. He recorded in his diary in 1864 that
'Two years and a half have sufficed to destroy the popularity which Albert
took twenty years to build up.'[64]

In the 1870s Bagehot would concede that the queen was taking her
retirement a little too far and that Albert would never have allowed such
self-indulgence. But it is important to see how *The English Constitution*
responded directly to these politicians' anxieties and to a certain degree
changed their minds about the monarchy. Bagehot wanted men like
Clarendon to see that the monarchy's usefulness was no longer mainly in
the realm of business but in the realm of theatre; he wanted men like
Stanley and Cecil to see that, to a certain extent, idleness was a part of the
queen's appeal and hence a part of her job. He spoke of the monarchy and
the other dignified parts of the constitution using words that would have been
recognizable to mid-Victorians as appropriate to a middle-class wife. The
monarchy was one of the 'comely' or 'theatrical' part of government.[65] Just
as a wife's conspicuous and comfortable idleness supported her husband's

status, so did the monarchy, as one of the 'ornamental' or 'showy' elements of the English constitution help to prop up the state.[66]

Nineteenth-century ideas about the social roles of men and women were more rigid and patriarchal than those of either the century preceding or following. Mid-Victorians believed in a strict opposition between the sexes: men warred with one another in the hard-headed world of business, retiring in the evening to the households presided over by their wives, which were domestic havens of love, comfort, spirituality and calm. Men were reasonable and logical; women were emotional and relied on their instincts.[67] Bagehot's innovation was to adopt this language in speaking about the monarchy. The Crown's 'apparent separation from business', Bagehot wrote,

> is that which removes it both from enmities and desecration, which preserves its mystery, which enables it to combine the affections of conflicting parties – to be a visible symbol of unity to those still so imperfectly educated as to need a symbol.[68]

The Crown was a beguiling woman, able to appeal to the emotions of politicians as well as working men.

Linda Colley has shown how, beginning with the death of Princess Charlotte in 1817, the monarchy underwent a process of feminization: there was increasing fascination with and glorification of royal women. Colley believes this may have been a Protestant substitute for a Marian cult, but that wherever it came from, the expansion of female symbolism connected with the monarchy tended to heighten the importance of private female roles usually underrated by a male-dominated society.[69]

Bagehot was the first to recognize this increased feminization of the monarchy and to articulate it in terms that confined the monarchy almost completely in the female sphere. But if this heightened the dignity of the role of mothers, wives and daughters, Bagehot also made the monarchy harmless and politically less threatening. Because 'The light nothings of the drawing room and the grave things of office are as different from one another as two human occupations can be',[70] it was better to remove any remaining political responsibility from the Crown. 'It is in truth childish to heap formal duties of business upon a person who has of necessity so many formal duties of society.'[71] The three political rights that Bagehot left to the monarchy – 'the right to be consulted, the right to encourage, the right to warn'[72] – were the rights not of a sovereign but of a wife. In a critical age when the monarchy was not popular and talk of reform was in the air, Bagehot helped secure the monarchy's future by describing the constitution as a perfectly-adapted marriage between masculine efficiency and feminine dignity.

Bagehot described himself as a 'moderate Liberal',[73] but his argument was essentially in favor of keeping things as they were. This is clear from the tone of resignation and defeat found in his introduction to the second edition of *The English Constitution*, published in 1872, following the passage of the Second Reform Bill. All was not lost, however. The same year also saw a surprisingly powerful return of the monarchy to popularity, crowned by huge demonstrations of loyalty at the thanksgiving for the recovery of the Prince of Wales in February 1872. If the monarchy could still attract popular affection, government as Bagehot knew it would hardly be swept away. Perhaps the Tory in Bagehot recalled the article on Macaulay he had written in 1856, where he showed that true conservatism rested less on well-constructed arguments than on pure sensual pleasure in old ceremonies, traditions and displays. 'The essence of Toryism', Bagehot had written, 'is enjoyment'. Distribute dull tracts if you will. They may do some good in preserving old institutions, but 'The way to keep up old customs is to enjoy old customs; the way to be satisfied with the present state of things is, to enjoy that state of things.'[74] Bagehot had tickets to St Paul's for the thanksgiving and went to London on the day, but his wife, who was at home sick, says that only her mother, sisters and brother-in-law attended.[75] Perhaps, though, unknown to her, he left *The Economist* at midday and joined the crowd to watch the retired widow and unemployed youth as they were carried by in procession back to the palace from St Paul's.

I have called Bagehot's defense of the monarchy 'democratic royalism' because the words capture the way in which he married the conservative, restraining elements of the constitution to the progressive and liberal elements. His rationale for maintaining the monarchy was persuasive because it was neither Tory nor Liberal: it gave the majority of power to the Commons and the cabinet while retaining only a sliver of influence for princes, lords and clergymen. Their sliver could either expand or contract depending on whether they were responsible and paid attention. In Bagehot's attitude toward government there is a national trait common among mid-Victorian Englishmen and not altogether absent from Englishmen in the latter part of the twentieth century. He wavered between cynicism and credulity, between a contemptuous dismissal of 'mere show' and a silent enjoyment of the pretty irony of retaining historical institutions. He spoke with a wry dismissal of imaginative sentiments he knew he possessed himself. He was both philosopher and poet, both banker and literary critic when it came to describing the hold of the monarchy on human affections. By employing language that made the sovereign into a perfect middle-class wife, Bagehot struck a chord in the minds of his readers. Having explicitly feminized the monarchy he disarmed critics for more than a generation by implying that it was ungenerous to attack a lady.

With *The English Constitution* Bagehot set the stage for the monarchy's transformation from awkward vestige of the old regime into a popular symbol of the modern British state. He did something more, though, than reassure politicians that the utility of Queen Victoria lay in her ability to perform occasional ceremonies rather than to transact everyday business. This was a reassurance that the queen herself was, in any case, often at pains to contradict. He laid the foundations for an enormous increase in power. Just as Sir Walter Scott, Bagehot's example of someone who understood that the essence of Toryism lay in the enjoyment of old customs, was among the century's most popular and best-selling novelists, so too did the monarchy in the second half of the century become the most riveting part of government, and, on ceremonial occasions like the thanksgiving or the jubilees, the motive force behind tremendous sales of books, newspapers and illustrated magazines. The key to this increase in power – not political power exactly, but a sort of prestige that commanded the attention and attendance of politicians – lay less in the publication of more tracts than it did in the management of royal ceremonial. If we are to understand the circumstances and the thinking that went into the performance of these ceremonies, we must turn first of all to the politician who, much more than Disraeli, must be considered the grandfather of the modern British monarchy: William Ewart Gladstone.

2 William Ewart Gladstone: National Acts of Religion

Shortly after his last premiership William Ewart Gladstone sat in his library at Hawarden assessing his life's work. He made lists of achievements and mistakes, credits and debits, rendered careful accounts of his triumphs and disappointments. He was preparing for death and these were his final reckonings. In the same season he dreamed about the queen. He analyzed this dream as dispassionately as he did his career. His purpose was to know himself better, hence better prepare himself to meet God. He wrote:

> We may sometimes obtain a morsel of self knowledge through the medium of a dream . . .
>
> Since my retirement I have dreamt sometimes of Parliament and sometimes (both of them very rarely) of the Court, but without much meaning. Last night I dreamed that I was at Windsor. There had been a sort of breakfast, fugitive and early, at which several attended, and the Queen appeared, but without incident. However it was conveyed to me through one of the 'pages' (servants out of livery?) that *I* of all people in the world was to breakfast alone with the Queen at ten o'clock: a circumstance which was not accordant with what is known as to HM's (very judicious) habits with reference to the early part of the day. Well, the time slid on, and the hour approached, and I was getting duly into what I may call a small perturbation as to the how and where of access. But the dream had lost its tail. The hour never came. And the sole force and effect of the incident is to show that the subject of my personal relation to the Queen, and all the unsatisfactory ending of my over half a century of service, had more hold upon me, down at the root, than I was aware.[1]

Here was the most important reforming premier of a reforming century, dwelling as he approached death not on his astonishing record of achievement, but on how bitterly he felt the queen's lack of gratitude. The dream hints at the strength of Gladstone's feelings about the monarchy. None of the queen's prime ministers revered the Crown as much as he did. None of them had as much cause to resent her as he did. Although everyone knows about how difficult Gladstone and the queen found it to get along, few have seen how the evolution of their relationship decisively affected the future course of constitutional monarchy in Britain.

Bagehot's wry remark on Gladstone was that he combined 'the soul of a martyr with the intellect of an advocate'.[2] Seldom ambivalent, Gladstone's was a mind that abhorred inconsistency, contradiction and doubt. Nevertheless, his attitude toward the monarchy shows marked similarities to Bagehot's. Gladstone the advocate and politician saw chances to manipulate the monarchy for political gain. At the same time, Gladstone the Christian martyr made his journeys to Windsor as prime minister keenly aware of the sacred associations of English kingship, anticipating the queen's distinct hostility and wearing an imaginary crown of thorns.

In 1838 when he was 27, a bright young MP of whom much was expected, Gladstone attended the coronation of Queen Victoria. He left for the Abbey at nine in the morning and did not return home until late in the afternoon. It was a long ceremony, but he was far from bored. He had studied and prepared for it by reading the printed service earlier in the week. He was profoundly impressed, although he thought an awkward compromise had been struck between high church ornamentation and low church simplicity. 'The service is noble', he wrote in his diary, 'The sight magnificent. Chanting greatly wanted. Details should be either many or none.' Several weeks later he said that the coronation 'afforded the finest sight I ever saw, and a service noble beyond description'.[3] He paid close attention to the arrangements of religious services. Great acts of national religion struck a special chord in his psyche.

In fact the ceremony may well have spurred Gladstone to write his first book, a book which in old age he placed on the list of his political mistakes. In *The State in its Relations with the Church*, which he began to write in the month following the coronation of Queen Victoria, he made an old-fashioned argument that the state should be involved in the spiritual cultivation of its citizens. Jonathan Clark has described the book as 'the swan song of the old society' and Thomas Babington Macaulay ridiculed it soon after its publication as a call to turn back the clock and reimpose religious uniformity.[4] Gladstone's political mentor, Sir Robert Peel, threw the book across the room in disgust, so thoroughly did it brand his young protégé with impossibly outmoded Tory ideas.

The young Gladstone did not see it that way. For him the coronation service was the symbol of the tie between the Anglican church and English state. 'The most vivid exemplification of the nationality of the Church, and of the character of its connection with the State in England', he wrote, 'is found in the noble and august ceremonial of the Coronation of the Sovereign'. He quoted at length from the coronation service and concluded 'that the gorgeous trappings, and even the magnificent pile within which it is performed, are far less imposing than the grandeur of its language, and the profound and affecting truth of its idea'.[5] This idea was that the coronation represented divine sanction for the authority of the state.

Why, he asked, does the State clothe all its proceedings in the outward forms of dignity or beauty? Why do we indulge in what has been termed the expensive luxury of monarchy? Why are buildings for the use of the legislature to be created on a scale of the greatest architectural magnificence? Why are imposing *insignia* employed in the discharge of the most solemn functions of government? It is not difficult to reply, that such an exterior most truly corresponds with, and best represents, the inward dignity of those functions, as they are connected with the realisation among men of grand but also true and practical ideas.

This was his answer to Whigs and utilitarians who thought that statecraft could be reduced to a science existing 'only for the ends of security to persons and property, or the growth of wealth'. He was equally critical of cynics who believed that symbols and ceremonies were merely 'external shows' imposed 'upon the uninstructed', in order to 'generate a sentiment of reverence, which, in the absence of thoroughly intellectual habits, is conducive to general respect for the laws and to the maintenance of public tranquillity'. There was more art and less science in Gladstone's account; more faith and less world weariness. For Gladstone the coronation represented the beauty, dignity and grace of a Christian people united for centuries in self-government.[6]

What irritated his political friends was not so much his interpretation of royal symbolism and his obvious attachment to the throne as his activist ideas about the role of government in distinguishing between religious right and wrong. To them this was preposterous and savored of seventeenth-century fanaticism. Indeed there was a certain fanatical element in Gladstone's character. His religious calling was intense. It was the zealot and fanatic in him who had seen only six years earlier 'the Antichrist' behind the first Reform Act.[7]

Few of his contemporaries found it reasonable, as Gladstone did, to draw on biblical support for the constitutional position of the monarchy in England. A memorandum, written in his usual cramped and tortured hand, shows that he thought 'the circumstance attending the appointment of Saul' in the Old Testament supported 'the argument in favour of monarchy as the scheme of government most nearly analogous to the Divine govt and most appropriate to human nature'.[8] In the same epoch that the young Queen Victoria was discovering that she liked brown beer, riding and

German princes in tight trousers, young Gladstone was confiding a political philosophy to his diary not far removed from the divine right of kings.

In 1842 the two came face to face for the first time. The day afterwards Gladstone confessed in his diary how frightened he had been. Riding in his carriage to the palace he had

> dreaded personal introduction to the Queen: in the same way as, at the different earlier stages of this pilgrimage, to my headmaster at school, & to the Duke of Newcastle when in 1832 I first went to Newark. The same relative position, with an altered absolute position, recurred and brought with it the same mood: and I could not help looking onwards and thinking, I now go to see the Sovereign face to face: the day is near when with mine eyes I shall behold the King of Kings, when I shall be introduced before Thee, O my Redeemer.[9]

When most people looked at Queen Victoria in the 1840s they saw a blooming young matron, high-spirited, red-cheeked, already tending to Hanoverian heaviness in the hips. When Gladstone looked at her he saw God. It was the same sort of extreme reaction he had at the coronation: to see her crowned made him think of a perfect union between church and state, all the religious reforms of the past twenty years forgotten. Although he would go through significant political changes in the next decades, casting off his rigid Toryism, committing himself to Liberalism and reform, this deeply religious regard for the monarchy would remain constant. The queen, although she would grow to appreciate the usefulness of Gladstone's royalism, could not help finding him a bit odd.[10]

In the 1840s ill-feeling between the two was still a long way in the future. In an age of earnestness and industry, the queen's husband saw in Gladstone a fellow soul. Both of them worked too hard and were slow to appreciate jokes. They were also alike in thinking that, like political office, royal blood imposed an obligation of energy and a standard of conduct people could admire. The Prince Consort's conscious attempts to make the court appear impartial toward vying political parties, his cultivation of an image of middle-class domesticity, were part of his plan to increase the monarchy's prestige by making it a popular institution. He was the first to see how dependent the royal couple's power was on broadly-diffused public good feeling toward them. He impressed Gladstone with the idea that princes had to seek and to deserve public trust if the monarchy were to be retained in a critical age. This was a lesson Gladstone did not forget. He combined it in an odd way with the other idea that the queen had a direct connection with on high. He combined a new nineteenth-century notion that the queen was a public servant, a very high grade clerk from whom one required value for money, with a vaguely medieval idea that her coronation had rendered her sacred.

The death of the Prince Consort in 1861 led to the breakdown in relations between Gladstone and the queen. The queen's grief was acute and prolonged. Gladstone and all the world grieved with her. However, when her black dresses and long faces extended over two, then three, then ten years, people ceased to feel sorry for her. They thought she was giving in to self-indulgence. In fact the queen was as obsessed with death and dying as Gladstone was with meeting his maker. Especially in later life she liked a good funeral and seldom missed a chance to visit the newly-bereaved. The consequence of her own husband's death was that she retired from public life and stimulated in the early 1870s a small republican movement.

It was not all her fault. Revolutions in Paris tended to strengthen radical ideas in Britain. In 1870 revolution had returned to the French capital. Napoleon III, the great Napoleon's ne'er-do-well nephew, was ignominiously taken captive at the battle of Sédan in the Franco-Prussian War. The establishment of a new republic in France after violent civil unrest in Paris coincided with a small controversy about the queen's civil list in England. Parliament had fixed the amount of her annual allowance before she had children. The government of the day asked Parliament to approve additional grants to her sons and daughters as they either married or came of age. Ordinarily these separate provisions were not controversial, but in a year when French republicanism was in the air and when the queen was seldom seen in public, even loyal politicians began to ask why the queen's civil list was insufficient to pay for her children. Surely, they claimed, there had been savings in the civil list since the death of the Prince Consort. These savings might be used for her children. Then as now, the civil list was the one issue that could cause the monarchy serious trouble.

In 1871 Gladstone was in the midst of his first and most productive premiership. The disestablishment of the Irish church, the secret ballot, reform in the Army and Civil Service – all these great legislative measures were before him. He was as determined to solve the monarchy's problems and, if possible to improve and strengthen the throne, as he was to improve these other institutions. Gladstone thought it was not only a question of defending the queen's civil list. The queen also had to be brought back into the public eye and her son had to stop getting involved in divorce and gambling scandals. He thought a comprehensive solution would have to involve the Prince of Wales in some public display of hard work. Accordingly he hit on the idea of sending the heir to the throne where nobody wanted to go: Ireland. Few were enthusiastic about this plan, least of all the Irish lord lieutenant, Lord Bessborough, who derided it as 'wild and visionary'.[11]

Still, Gladstone kept the Irish idea in the back of his mind as he attended to more pressing business first. He stood up in Parliament and defended the additional grants to the queen's children, which were passed by large, non-partisan majorities. He had the Home Office keep an eye on Charles Bradlaugh, an atheist who was touring the country giving a comic anti-monarchical lecture that summer.[12] He ordered an investigation of the charges made by a pseudonymous pamphleteer in *What Does She Do With It?* that large sums from the civil list had been transferred illegally to the queen's private fortune.[13]

Gladstone's problem was that much of the republican heat was coming from radicals in his own party. The author of *What Does She Do With It?* was a former member of the government, G. O. Trevelyan. Sir Charles Dilke, a talented Liberal M.P. on Gladstone's left, turned up the temperature even further by giving a speech to working men at Newcastle in November 1871. With a radical's sure instinct for alarming the rich and exciting the poor, Dilke painted lurid pictures of goings-on at court. The royal yachts absorbed untold thousands of the taxpayers' money, while the queen was herself the only person in the country who paid no tax. There were flunkies in gold brocade everywhere, many of them corrupt political supporters of the government. Further, he claimed the queen was illicitly hiding away sums of public money in her private bank accounts. These were all gross but entertaining exaggerations, represented as established facts to his audience. Dilke concluded, 'If you can show me a fair chance that a republic here will be free from the political corruption that hangs about the monarchy I say, for my part – and I believe the middle classes in general will say – let it come.'[14]

Gladstone and his chancellor of the Exchequer, the intellectual albino, Sir Robert Lowe, disagreed about how best to reply to Dilke. It was easy enough to point out that the queen had paid tax – about £300,000 of it since the income tax had been re-instituted in 1842. More difficult was the fact that she had, through legal economies and the sort of plain living that had earned her and the Prince Consort public respect, saved about £500,000 from the civil list since the beginning of the reign. Lowe wanted to make a speech giving both figures. Gladstone thought that, although the savings could be defended, a public uproar would follow the news that the queen had accumulated half a million since the beginning of the reign.[15] Gladstone was of two minds on the question. He was certainly prepared to point out that a sovereign who stood at the pinnacle of English society had to be supported in a state of some magnificence. But as a zealous guardian of the public purse he was shocked at how much the queen had managed to save from her public allowance.

The queen had no doubts about 'Sir C. Dilke's disgraceful conduct'. She was sick and tired of vacillation and indecision. It was only necessary, she told Gladstone, for 'the Govt. to take a firm stand against revolutionary and extreme views and hold a high tone to keep *all straight*'. Gladstone had to keep his own supporters in line: 'it will no longer do to try to *please* the radicals by going further and further in that direction or by appearing to *fear* the House of Commons'.[16] In the midst of Gladstone's careful deliberations with Lowe about how best to defend the monarchy, only reprimands arrived from Windsor.

A possible solution presented itself by pure chance. The Prince of Wales became ill and nearly died down in Norfolk. The press immediately took up the story, not by suggestion from Downing Street, not by command from Windsor, but with an unerring instinct, then as now, for building circulation. Public interest increased, which in turn redoubled coverage from the sickbed. The queen, whose relations with her son were not much better than those with her prime minister, took the train to Sandringham to see how she could help.

The newspapers were filled with tender stories of the royal family's anxious reunion. In fact the house was full of people unaccustomed to being at such close quarters with one another. The scene was as unlike the folksy, bourgeois family the papers were describing as possible. The queen's private secretary, Henry Ponsonby, took a dry and detached view of all the activity surrounding the sickbed. He wrote his wife that on a walk outdoors with another member of the Household

> we were suddenly nearly carried away by a stampede of royalties, headed by the Duke of Cambridge and brought up by Leopold, going as fast as they could. We thought it was a mad bull. But they cried out: 'The Queen, the Queen.' and we all dashed into the house again and waited behind the door till the road was clear.

Everyone sat around after dinner whispering in corners. The Victorians believed that foul odors caused disease. Princess Louise's room was declared to be uninhabitable because of an odd smell there. The duke of Cambridge

> thought there was a bad smell in the library ... and when F. Knollys came in and said he smelt it, the Duke jumped up and said 'By George, I won't sit here', and went about smelling in all the corners.[17]

By the thirteenth of December, the prince appeared to be on his deathbed. It was nearly the anniversary of the Prince Consort's death, a sad day the queen celebrated annually. Crowds gathered outside telegraph offices for the latest bulletins. Then, on the fourteenth, improvement began. By the fifteenth, the queen could write to Gladstone with relief that the sympathy 'of the whole Nation is most gratifying and if he recovers – it must be to become more and more valuable to the Country who have shown him such love'. Popular interest in the prince's illness also impressed Gladstone. He replied to the queen by hoping that the general sense of relief might 'not alter that temper of humble acknowledgement and trust, in which the nation has so earnestly sought by prayer for the Prince's recovery'.[18] In 1870 Bismarck unified the German nation using blood and steel. In 1871 the queen and Gladstone saw that the British nation was being unified, less by design than by default, though sentimental telegraphic reports from the sickbed at Sandringham. The notion of the nation dwelling upon a monarchical object reassured the queen; for her this was enough. Gladstone was also happy with the monarchy occupying the national mind, but he wanted something more, because he liked the notion of the nation at prayer. Subsequent events would bring these two ideas of the nation into conflict.

The day after the queen and Gladstone exchanged these letters, a hint reached the foreign secretary, Lord Granville, that a state thanksgiving for the prince's recovery had been proposed at Sandringham.[19] Ponsonby repeated the hint the next day in the postscript of a letter to Gladstone, but he told the prime minister to be careful, because 'if stress is laid upon its being a great state function where splendor and pomp hide the religion or heartfelt desire of returning thanks The Queen may possibly object to it'.[20] Here was a providential and political opportunity, just the sort that most appealed to the man whom one historian has described as combining 'ethical urges with tough, tactical, and partisan manoeuvre'.[21] It was a way of both crushing Dilke and answering the royalty question. Gladstone examined precedents, discovered that George III had gone in state to St Paul's on his recovery from illness in 1789, and mentioned both the proposal and the precedent in the cabinet. He then went to Windsor to recommend a public ceremony to the queen.[22]

Gladstone and the queen had a long and testy interview on 21 December. Afterwards Gladstone spent days writing a long memorandum of their conversation. What the queen thought of as a private audience, Gladstone thought of as a political debate. Gladstone sent his memorandum to Granville and confessed gaily that 'being my own Reporter, you will see that I give myself the best of it'.[23]

In the private audience chamber at Windsor, looked down upon by fifteen

Gainsborough portraits of the family of George III and nine Winterhalter portraits of her own children, the queen had an army of silent witnesses on her side. She tried to squelch talk of a public ceremony. She began by objecting to the idea of a state thanksgiving

> because she disliked in an extreme degree the Cathedral service. She objected still more because she thought such a display, in point of religion, false and hollow. She considered that no religious act ought ever to be allied with pomp or show. Nothing should induce her to be a party to it. It would be of no use to press her as this was her conviction with regard to the religious part of the subject.

Gladstone granted what the queen had said if such 'ceremonials' were 'to be considered merely as vehicles for the expression of the religious feelings of those who are to be the principal actors in them'. But the recent demonstration of public feeling toward the prince had been so extraordinary that 'nothing short of a great public act of this kind can form an adequate answer to it'. Further, he asked the queen whether those 'who are to appear as principal personages' might not forget themselves and think of 'the great religious importance of such an act for the people at large'. On them it would make a deep impression and the chance ought to be seized to do so: 'There are in these times but few occasions on which great national acts of religion can be performed; and this appears to be one of them, for which the opportunity had now been offered.' Gladstone admitted that the 'religious importance' of the proposed ceremony

> was that of a symbol, but it was not therefore to be accounted slight: Royalty was in one point of view a symbol, and one of great consequence: its character and duties had greatly changed among us in modern times but perhaps in the new forms they were not less important than in the old.

Gladstone emphasized the 'extreme solemnity of the occasion: not only for the Prince ... not only for the Queen and Royal Family, but for the future of the Monarchy and of the country as connected with it'. The illness had put a stop to Dilke and his whole movement. The queen stood up for herself here and put in that France had much to do with the English agitation. Gladstone conceded this point and expressed his fear that France might continue unstable for some time to come. He chose to dwell, however, on the need for the Prince of Wales to find

> some means of living worthily of his great position and greater prospects: but this brought out no direct response; only there was a hope

expressed by the Queen in some part of the conversation that the illness, and the display of feeling, would act directly in a beneficial manner on the Prince's character and conduct.

At one point the queen and the prime minister discussed 'the lowered tone of society in the highest rank'. Gladstone thought it was the moral influence of the court on the aristocracy during the Prince Consort's day which had done 'much to elevate and purify its tone during the earlier part of the reign'. The remark again implied a criticism of the queen, whose ceasing to appear in public Gladstone connected with 'the lowered tone' of upper-class society. She disagreed, replying that she and her husband had observed the decline in aristocratic morals before his death and that the Prince Consort 'was accustomed to attribute it to the augmented intercourse with France'.

The latter part of the conversation turned on details. The queen said it would be more 'convenient and appropriate' if the service were held at Westminster Abbey; more convenient because it was closer to the palace and would not require so long a drive, more appropriate because it was 'where they were crowned'. But the precedent of 1789 was clear on this point and Gladstone responded that it would be bad 'to go against the established tradition, as it provoked adverse remark'. The queen thought a day of thanksgiving might be set as a general holiday instead of a procession to St Paul's. Gladstone thought this might be taken by some as a hardship, and be regarded by others as forcing them to participate against their will. Whereas a procession would be generally well received and 'the observance would have the grace of being entirely voluntary'. The queen at last reduced her objection to the length of the proposed service. Gladstone agreed that it would have to be shortened, noting with relish that in 1789 King George III and Queen Charlotte set out for St Paul's at ten in the morning and did not return to the palace until half past three in the afternoon.

The greatest point of contention in this conversation was religion. In fact many of the difficulties between Gladstone and the queen during that first ministry can be traced to religious differences between the two.[24] In the 1870s the queen thought of him as a high churchman and a ritualist with dangerous leanings toward Rome. In fact his religious ideas were composed of elements from different traditions. He was an evangelical in the importance he attached to public example and to conduct. But he had affinities with the high church tractarians as well in his emphasis on the solemnity and historical character of religious worship. 'He also shared the tractarian liking for ceremony and orderliness, but he disliked ritualism.'[25]

The queen felt more comfortable on religious matters with tolerant, non-dogmatic broad churchmen than with either high church or low church doctrinaires.[26] She hated the religious extremist she thought she saw in Gladstone.

In later life Gladstone recalled that the queen had once said to him 'You know I am not much of an Episcopalian.' He had replied 'No, Ma'am, I know that well.' He believed she was the first sovereign to have taken communion in the Scottish Kirk.[27] In worship the queen certainly preferred Presbyterian simplicity.[28] Her husband had been raised a Lutheran and he liked the Scottish Presbyterian service, which he and the queen attended in Balmoral, for its similarity to the Lutheran service.[29] The queen held his memory sacred and continued to attend the Kirk after his death. But even before her marriage she had developed an aversion to the august cathedral services Gladstone liked. The tradition of her Household before her accession had been short, plain, spoken worship. On her accession she had been required to change immediately to 'the solemn slow-moving grandeur of Anglican cathedral worship' characteristic of the Chapel Royal at St James's Palace or St George's Chapel in Windsor. The Prince Consort disliked this as much as she did and, in order to avoid the public solemnities associated with the Chapel Royal or St George's, they had a private chapel built inside their quarters at Windsor and attended a private chapel at Buckingham Palace when in London.[30]

These differences explain the disagreement between the queen and prime minister over the details of the thanksgiving. She was galled by his insisting on a stately service so foreign to her ordinary religious practice. He resented her insistence on simplicity and brevity, which he considered inappropriate to such an extraordinary and solemn occasion. 'The upshot of the whole', Gladstone concluded on Christmas Day, 1871, 'was that the Queen is in no way committed, and that the whole idea is subject to considerations of health, but it is entertained, and not unfavourably'.[31] The queen noted the meeting in her diary, but recorded nothing about St Paul's.[32]

Granville praised Gladstone's memorandum of his conversation with the queen, but knew instinctively that she would listen to the dean of Windsor more patiently on a religious question than she would to Gladstone.[33] The dean intervened and told the queen she would have to do the work. Gerald Valerian Wellesley, dean of Windsor, was one of the few clergymen prepared to be straight with her. He was a nephew of the duke of Wellington and had been at Eton with Gladstone. Both the queen and the prime minister liked him.[34] When he died in the 1880s Gladstone and the queen signed a truce for a short while to lament him. Soon after the beginning of the new year Wellesley wrote Gladstone that the queen had dropped her objections and agreed to go to St Paul's.[35]

She did not give in gracefully. She told one cabinet minister that she would go to St Paul's because it was necessary for the people to see her, but she made a point of saying that she hated 'pompous *official formal* displays of religion, so contrary to *true* Christianity and Protestantism'.[36] To Gladstone the queen wrote that

> while she unwillingly consents from her dislike to public religious displays – (her own growing inclination being more and more for the simplest form of worship) she is ready to go to St Paul's on this occasion, health permitting for she feels she is never sure of herself . . . The Queen herself has been suffering for 10 days from a cold and cough. The Dean of Windsor was strongly of opinion that the Thanksgiving Service shld *not* exceed 1/2 an hour or 3/4. The whole effect wld be spoilt by a long fatiguing service.[37]

Gladstone told Granville that his relations with the queen had become worse than ever 'as to combats in detail; and that accordingly it is more than ever desirable to think of some larger arrangement'.[38] Therefore, at the same time that he was writing to the dean of St Paul's and the lord chamberlain entrusting them with the planning of the ceremony at St Paul's,[39] he was also meeting with the queen's advisers, the cabinet, and aides to the prince to formulate a larger plan for the monarchy. The Irish residence was one option in this plan. All of the options were connected with putting forward the prince in the discharge of public duty.[40]

There was something slightly ridiculous about Gladstone's plans. The evidence was plain that it was hopeless to expect an Albertine restoration in Albert Edward. He was already overspending his income, he was seen with women not his wife, he made excuses not to attend committee meetings of the House of Lords and, when given confidential Foreign Office notes on the Franco-Prussian War, he passed them around at a dinner party. But Gladstone understood, as the prince did not, that in an increasingly democratic age, there was decreasing room for a purely private life among public figures, whether princes or politicians. Thus, it was impossible to lay plans for the prince's future aside.

Meanwhile Gladstone was up to his ears in the details of the approaching ceremony. When he learned that the queen proposed to go to St Paul's in informal dress and open carriages rather than formal robes and state coaches, he raised the matter in cabinet and informed the lord chamberlain of their collective disappointment.[41] The queen defended the plan of open carriages, which was 'to enable the *people* (for *whom this is*) to see' the royal family and reminded Gladstone of her religious objections to the proceedings. Gladstone returned a calm reply.[42] But to the lord chamberlain he wrote accepting the plan of 'half state' only under two conditions:

1. That the weather is fine, or at any rate such that the carriages may remain open.
2. That the procession proceed at a foot's pace.

But what if the day should be one of unmitigated rain? Let us hope not. Above all what if there should be any idea of going at a trot? It is better to be quiet now; but the Cabinet have seen so much, and think so strongly of the bad impression caused by hasty movement on these rare occasions that they will certainly interpose if need be.[43]

Nor did Gladstone allow the question of the service's length to drop. He saw the dean of St Paul's and learned that its length was estimated at between 35 and 40 minutes. Gladstone thought this was too short. He wrote sharply to the dean of Windsor, warning him 'that this is not a matter in which it would be impossible for a minister to interfere. There will be much comment and dissatisfaction, and all for the sake of a few minutes.'[44] Wellesley told him that the interference of ministers would greatly irritate the queen.[45] Several days later Wellesley was able to tell the prime minister that the service would certainly last three quarters of an hour, and with the time taken for the queen's coming in and going out, nearer an hour: 'We ecclesiastics at least think this is enough . . . When we get the Queen to St Paul's She will wait well enough, and it would be quite contrary to good management to discuss some minutes one way or other with Her before the time.'[46]

This was not all. In the days before the ceremony Gladstone also helped decide which members of the royal family were to ride in the queen's carriage.[47] He gave in to pressure, mainly from *The Times*, for more people to be allowed in St Paul's.[48] *The Illustrated London News*, an expensive weekly with a prosperous readership, also took an early interest in the ceremony. The paper prepared its readers for a grandiose ceremony on late eighteenth-century lines by printing an illustration of George III's thanksgiving in 1789. [See plate 1.] It also strengthened Gladstone's hand by referring to the precedent he had used to overrule the queen's objections. Gladstone ignored the queen's wishes again when he ordered that the speaker and the lord chancellor be added to the front of the procession, partly to conform to the 1789 precedent, partly to make sure that the queen's carriage could not proceed at a trot.[49] He also gave in to *The Times* on the route of the procession and advised that it should be lengthened.[50] He did all this while preparing for a busy parliamentary session and conducting delicate negotiations on damages owed to the United States arising from the civil war.

Shortly after noon on 27 February 1872 a procession of carriages emerged from Buckingham Palace and departed for St Paul's Cathedral.[51] Crowded into the last carriage were the queen's youngest daughter, Princess Beatrice, the Prince and Princess of Wales, their son, Prince Albert Victor, and the queen herself. The Prince of Wales appeared pale, thin and unwell. Standing absurdly on the palace balcony and bowing to the queen as she moved off down the Mall were the recently deposed French emperor, Napoleon III, and his empress, Eugénie. At Temple Bar during a temporary halt in the procession the queen held up her son's hand and, to the delight of the crowd, dramatically kissed it. She may have hated public appearances, but her theatrical instinct was sure and she played to her audience as skillfully as Dilke had to his.

The royal family reached St Paul's at 1 p.m. and entered a pavilion erected for the occasion on the western steps. Above the pavilion was an inscription: 'I was glad when they said unto me, We will go into the House of the Lord.' The queen was hardly glad, but ready to put up with it on this occasion. She did not foresee that she was renewing an old precedent and setting a new one; the occasions would multiply in future.

A congregation of just under 12 000 persons had been packed into the cathedral. The royal family took their places in a raised pew beneath the dome of the cathedral. Once they were seated a choir of 250 voices sang a *Te Deum*. A special form of thanksgiving was read:

> O Father of Mercies and God of all comfort, we thank Thee that Thou hast heard the prayers of this nation in the day of our trial: We praise and magnify Thy glorious name for that Thou hast raised Thy servant Albert Edward Prince of Wales from the bed of sickness: Thou castest down and Thou liftest up, and health and strength are Thy gifts: We pray Thee to perfect the recovery of Thy servant, and to crown him day by day with more abundant blessings both for body and soul; through Jesus Christ our Lord. Amen.

This was stately language that recorded a simple fact. The nation had prayed and the prince had recovered. There for a brief moment in the gaslight and the gloom, in the midst of the hoopla and newspaper sensationalism, was sincerity and thanksgiving. The queen, Gladstone and the congregation on their knees were as one.

The service ended at a few minutes before 2 p.m. The royal family retired to a little room where they had sandwiches, wine and biscuits. 'Very necessary for us all' said the queen.[52]

At night the occasion was marked by illuminations. Specially placed lanterns and gas jets lit up public buildings, arches along the route of the procession and the dome of St Paul's. As the convalescent prince lay stretched out on a sofa at Marlborough House, exhausted from the day's work, what the illuminations picked out most of all were the crowds still surging through the streets. *The Graphic*, a competitor of *The Illustrated London News* printed an engraving captioned 'The Crowd Illuminated'. [See plate 2.] Composed of different social classes, the facial expressions combine awe and menace, as if to say that the crowd itself was as remarkable and potentially destabilizing as the ceremony that had preceded the evenings's illuminations.

Both Gladstone and the queen commented in their diaries on the service inside the cathedral and the crowds along the route. The queen observed that 'The deafening cheers never ceased the whole way, and the most wonderful order was preserved. We seemed to be passing though a sea of people, as we went along the Mall.' Of St Paul's she wrote, 'the service appeared to me cold and too long'.[53] The prime minister, by contrast, described the service as 'short but impressive: the spectacle in and out of doors magnificent: the behaviour of the people admirable (to us very kind).' The ceremony lasted an hour.'[54]

The Illustrated London News also dwelled on the orderliness of the crowds, perhaps because much worse had been expected. The paper portrayed potential unruliness in its engraving 'The Thanksgiving Day: A Rough Corner'. [See plate 3.] Middle-class spectators sit calmly in a balcony while rough, raggedly-dressed men and women line the streets apparently pushing and shoving below. They seem to promise a riot much more than loyal and orderly cheering. The crowds stood for the nation and the nation, if not properly ministered to by royalties riding through the streets, might be whipped up by Dilke into the bloody excesses of the Paris commune. There were accidents and loss of life. Some persons were crushed in the press of the crowd; but these casualties had to be accepted as

> a stern necessity. The Queen and her people were engaged on Tuesday in the discharge of a sacred duty, that of a united acknowledgement of the great goodness of Providence, and to have omitted this duty would have been a national sin.[55]

The Illustrated London News was prepared to sacrifice a few spectators on the altar of national unity.

The skeptical and self-consciously intellectual *Saturday Review* agreed:

> Some accidents, of course, marred the serenity of the day and the success of the pageant. One or two persons were killed and many persons

were maimed or hurt. The recklessness of an English crowd is only equalled by its good humour.

Having dismissed the accidents in this offhand way, the anonymous writer noted that it had been a day 'not of conventional and strained, but of genuine, unbought loyalty' and concluded that the loyal 'multitude' had been the best part of the show.[56] The press thought the assembly of loyal and orderly crowds was as much a cause for rejoicing as the recovery of the Prince of Wales. Their smugness detracted from the spirit of unity and reconciliation that were the main impulses behind the ceremony. But the crowds surging through the streets were in the back of everyone's mind. No one, given the republican discontents of the past year, had been quite sure beforehand how they would act.

The success of the thanksgiving enabled the government to ignore Dilke. When in March Dilke moved his enquiry into the civil list in the House, he was heard with patience. But when Auberon Herbert rose to elaborate on Dilke's points, an uproar ensued. Dilke's motion was defeated by a vote of 276 to 2. The queen wrote Gladstone: 'Tho' the Scene was rather unseemly in some ways – the feeling shown in the House was most satisfactory.'[57]

This was a turning point in the history of the British monarchy. The prince's illness and the subsequent thanksgiving so thoroughly defeated Dilke that republicanism in Britain died out for several generations. Republicanism was hardly heard of again until the First World War. The success of the service and procession to St Paul's not only demoralized radicals. It also caught the attention of politicians and began to create a taste for such ceremonies among the public. Large-scale royal ceremonies in either the Abbey or St Paul's were far less frequent in the nineteenth century, even before the Prince Consort's death, than they have been in the twentieth century. The queen had not participated in such a cathedral service since the coronation of 1838. Aside from her religious objections to such services, she had come to the throne in an era when middle-class demands for constitutional change made old regime stateliness seem politically unwise. She had been trained by a whig premier who thought of aristocratic and ecclesiastical display as vulgar and in bad taste. This had kept her from paying too much attention to eighteenth-century ceremonial precedents.

Gladstone's insistence on her going to St Paul's contributed to the late Victorian revival of state and show. He renewed and reinvigorated a precedent the queen would have liked to forget. Just as Bagehot had predicted, a more democratic Britain demanded greater state and show from the monarchy. In 1887 and 1897 public demand for some commemoration of

the queen's long reign resulted in modified re-enactments of the thanksgiving of 1872. Had Queen Victoria had her way she would have left her
son a much quieter monarchy with more emphasis on private goodness (a
demand he would have found it difficult to meet in any case) than on
public display. However, Gladstone could have done a great deal more to
influence the future of the monarchy and the character of its public appearances had he not so antagonized the queen in the weeks leading up to the
thanksgiving. It was the remaining bitterness of these weeks that led the
queen to an icy and final rejection of Gladstone's plans for the Prince of
Wales to go to Ireland, that pushed her firmly in the direction of Disraeli,
that made Gladstone's view of the monarchy, a monarchy that merely
might have been. In the wake of his great and influential success on a
question of ceremonial, there were to come repeated political defeats on
questions of the monarchy's future. The national acts of religion he found
so moving were retained and repeated with increasing frequency in coming
years; but they came to be surrounded with imperial triumphalism he
loathed.

The first serious sign that the monarchy was going to take a course
Gladstone disliked came while the memory of the thanksgiving was still
fresh. In 1876 Disraeli, who two years since had replaced Gladstone as
prime minister, brought in the act by which the queen became Empress of
India. He introduced it reluctantly and at her insistence. She wanted the
new title because annoying continental royalties persisted in snubbing her
children, believing them to be out-ranked by the children of kaisers, tsars
and emperors. The Prince of Wales had been making a much-heralded tour
through India, where, she heard, she was sometimes referred to as an
empress. So she decided to have the additional title made official. Gladstone
opposed the new title in the Commons and forfeited whatever remaining
credit he had with her. Twice during March 1876 Gladstone spoke against
the Royal Titles Bill in the House.[58] He said the new title was an attempt
to glorify what was in fact a calamity: that England had not so far been
able to give India the 'benefit and blessings of free institutions'. Echoing
Bagehot, Gladstone said that everything connected with the Crown was
of the highest delicacy: it was the 'most sacred' portion of the power
Parliament was called upon to administer and ought only to be interfered with after careful thought. He disliked the title because he disliked
foreign novelties; English traditions and precedents were a safer basis for
legislation.[59]

Gladstone added that the act was somewhat less objectionable because
it was proposed for a lady, a queen who during four decades had exhibited
'a model of personal and domestic life', who had shown such a 'high and

loyal . . . sense of every engagement which the possession of her high station involves'. The ministry would never have dared to bring in the proposal under a man because Parliament would have been more sensitive to the authoritarian overtones of the title 'emperor'.[60]

Although the idea for the Titles Bill had originated with the queen, and although it caused the government more trouble than anticipated, it represented a victory for Disraeli. He had already begun to portray the conservative party in his speeches at the Crystal Palace and Manchester during 1872 as uniquely interested in the defense of the Crown, the Church and the empire.[61] The Royal Titles Bill represented an opportune and logical step along a path he had already taken. However, the step was offered purely by chance and was seen by the government at first as more of a liability than an opportunity.[62] Gladstone regarded the greater emphasis on the empire that went with the Titles Bill as a conscious and determined effort to win votes. In later life he dated a noticeable shift in the queen's political interests away from domestic issues toward continental and imperial affairs from her involvement with the Conservative ministry of 1874–80.[63]

Gladstone tried to counteract Disraeli's ministry with his pen. The appearance of the first volumes of Theodore Martin's biography of the Prince Consort offered him his chance. He wrote reviews of the first three volumes of the biography for a new tractarian publication, *The Church Quarterly Review*. The articles appeared anonymously in 1875, 1877 and 1878, and were later republished under his name in *Gleanings of Past Years*.[64] Against the efforts of Disraeli and the queen, who were projecting the image of a monarchy that was elevated, oriental and imperial, Gladstone recalled the monarchy of Victoria and Albert's young adulthood which had been humble and domestic, splendid yet frugal.

The palaces of England became shrines of domestic happiness; and the Court exhibited to the nation and the world a pattern of personal conduct, in all points most slippery and dangerous for a wealthy country, with a large leisured class, in a luxurious age. Idleness was rebuked by the unwearied labours of the highest persons in the land; vulgar ostentation grew pale in the face of a splendour everywhere associated with duty, and measured by its ends; impurity could not live in so clear an atmosphere; even thrift had its tribute of encouragement, where hospitalities truly regal and unwearied were so organised as not to put disdain upon the homely unattractive duty of living within an appointed income. All these personal excellences were seen and appreciated by the public; and they contributed, perhaps no less than wise legislation, and conduct inflexibly constitutional, to draw close the ties between the people and the throne.[65]

Gladstone wrote these reviews in one of the 'most Evangelical periods of his life'.[66] And the foregoing passage mirrors the ideas of the early evangelicals at the end of the eighteenth century. Hannah More had argued that people of rank provided patterns which were imitated by the rest of the world. Therefore, it was necessary for members of the upper classes to reform their behavior and set a more worthy moral example. Her *Thoughts on the Importance of the Manners of the Great to General Society* (1788) was meant to communicate this message to members of the nobility.[67] Just as Gladstone revived the precedent of George III's going to St Paul's in 1789, he would have liked the queen, Prince of Wales and all of their lords in waiting to sit in the library at Windsor reading Hannah More.

Gladstone looked at the upper classes in the 1870s and saw gamblers, spendthrifts, adulterers, *nouveaux riches* and unscrupulous Tories. In the golden age of his youth he remembered only aristocratic duty and purity. If the Household was not reading More, he could at least concur with Theodore Martin that the Prince Consort's life was a 'sermon made visible'.[68] It was a pity the queen was forgetting the prince and being carried away by Lord Beaconsfield.

The relationship of the sovereign's public conduct to the moral tone of upper-class society was a theme Gladstone never gave up. It led him to preserve a studied silence about the court, even when he was painfully aware how far things had drifted away from his Albertine ideal. This silence, especially on subjects which might have attracted a sympathetic hearing coming from him, did perhaps as much as the thanksgiving in 1872 to enhance the monarchy's popularity. Gladstone's second and third premierships did not improve his relations with the queen. After his introduction of the first Home Rule Bill in 1886, relations between the two were much worse. Nevertheless it was the royal family who approached Gladstone in 1889 when Lord Salisbury's government refused to move on a question of pressing financial concern to them. All the queen's children had been financially provided for by Parliament. Now some of her grandchildren were marrying and coming of age. The Prince of Wales had five children and, either through high spending or lack of adequate planning, did not have the money to provide for them.[69] The royal family hoped that Parliament could be persuaded to provide at least for the children of the heir, if not for all the queen's grandchildren. Francis Knollys, the prince's private secretary, approached Gladstone with the idea that a signal from him as leader of the Opposition might make the Government act.[70] Despite the fact that the prince was a gambler, a spendthrift and an adulterer, Gladstone rather liked him. Despite the fact that the queen had insulted him in a hundred small ways, most recently by not inviting him to her daughter's wedding when other political leaders had been included, Gladstone was prepared to help.

A parliamentary committee was appointed and, with Gladstone's agreement, approved a government proposal that an annual lump sum should be given the prince to provide for his children. Parliament was promised that it would not be asked to foot the bill for any of the queen's other grandchildren. Gladstone spoke in favor of the measure once it reached the full house. He kept to himself his conviction that a close look into the Prince of Wales's affairs would probably turn up 'a total absence of economical management'.[71] Instead he said he was

> averse to all economy which would not only affect the dignity, but which would impair the splendour of the Court. In a society constituted as this society is, the Court ought to be a splendid Court; and . . . a Court amply provided, but not extravagantly provided with means, worked in a genial spirit, and conforming to a high moral standard, is one of the most inestimable agencies which, in a country like this, you can bring to bear on the tone of society, and by means of which you can raise the standard of conduct from class to class throughout the kingdom.[72]

Gladstone had become isolated from general sentiment about the monarchy by the late 1880s. He was quoting Hannah More to a generation that preferred Rudyard Kipling. He was out of sympathy with the imperial enthusiasm that gripped the rest of the nation, out of touch with the other leaders of his own party. Gladstone persuaded the Irish members to vote for the prince's annuity, but prominent Liberals on the front bench refused to follow Gladstone and voted against the prince. When Gladstone's former private secretary asked one of the dissident Liberals why, H. H. Asquith replied that Gladstone was underrating feeling against the measure in the constituencies, that the Liberal statesman was 'displaying his old-fashioned Tory ideas – his benightedness was exactly the word'.[73]

Two years later there was a scandal at Tranby Croft, a country house where the Prince of Wales had been staying and gambling at an illegal card game called baccarat.[74] One of the other guests, a close friend of the prince, had been accused by the others of cheating. This man brought a lawsuit to try and clear his name. The Prince of Wales was not charged with any crime, but he was publicly associated with the scandal when he was called to testify in the trial. For several weeks that summer the papers were full of articles critical of the prince's behavior. Knollys asked Gladstone what the prince should do. Gladstone said the prince should make a public statement and give a 'distinct assurance' that the incident would never be repeated nor the prince's influence be connected with gambling ever again. Gladstone knew very well that the prince was as likely to give up gambling as he was to give up cigars. He drily acknowledged that such a distinct assurance would 'involve what is colloquially termed a "large order"'.[75]

Lord Salisbury, on the other hand, thought nothing should be done. He thought a reaction in favor of the prince had begun to spread.[76] Salisbury's unwillingness to intervene and his cold-eyed realism about the prince's behavior differed markedly from Gladstone's interventionist morality. Gladstone preferred to act in setting up the court as a moral standard. This was as true of 1891 as of 1871. Gladstone persisted in idealizing the throne in spite of the queen's hostility to him and in spite of the prince's conspicuous adherence to moral standards less rigid than his own. Salisbury admired and respected the queen; her heir he thought 'trivial'. Salisbury was irritated by the prince's involvement in the Baccarat Case.[77] Mary Ponsonby observed to her husband that Salisbury's 'utter absence of sentimentalism about the Crown is certainly a contrast to Gladstone whose *feeling* was always snubbed'. Even at the worst season of Gladstone's relations with the queen, Mary Ponsonby found in the library at Hawarden:

> on one side his political table, on the other his literary, which he said he greatly preferred, and, rather a touching sight, that terrible picture of the Queen with the bust of Pr[ince] Cons[ort] in the middle of the room, Mrs G.'s writing-table with a small bust of the Queen at the end of the room.[78]

The young man who thought of his ultimate meeting with the Redeemer on his first meeting with the queen preserved his reverence for the position, and worked to defend it, long into his old age.

Early in 1897, when it was announced that a second jubilee would be held, Gladstone's friend, Lord Rendel, wrote in his journal:

> Mr. G. is much exercised in mind over the Diamond Jubilee Celebration. The [1887] Jubilee was well enough. Custom supported such proceedings. To renew them simply on a further decade of reign seemed artificial and unreal. What he seemed not to care for was the gathering of all the Royalties, home and foreign, once more. He appeared to dislike the caste and Imperialistic character of such proceedings.[79]

The sort of celebrations Gladstone admired were those which celebrated and unified the nation, not the empire, those which adhered to custom and precedent, those which, if 'great folks' were at the center, at least showed them in relations of domestic simplicity to one another and humbleness before God. A precedent from the reign of George III supported the 1887 jubilee. The second jubilee he suspected of being cooked up as a show of social hierarchy and imperial slavery.

Gladstone last saw the queen on the French Riviera in March 1897, just before her diamond jubilee. They met in a Cannes hotel room crowded with the queen's relations. As before, he made a long note of their meeting. He and his wife

were shown into a room tolerably but not brilliantly lighted, much of which was populated by a copious supply of Hanoverian Royalties including the Queen of Hanover, the Duke of Cumberland and others. *The* Queen was in the inner part of the room, and behind her stood or sat the Prince of Wales with the Duke of Cambridge . . . I became at once conscious that there was a change in the Queen's appearance, not only as compared with what she used to be during my political life, but as compared with her appearance . . . in the summer of last year.

He thought the queen's manner did 'not show the old and usual vitality' and that she could no longer carry on a proper conversation. He speculated that because her family seemed less afraid of her, she might be senile. Gladstone even thought she ought to consider abdicating in favor of her son, so markedly had her former powers failed.

For her part, the queen also thought the Gladstones were not what they used to be. She wrote in her diary: 'Mr. and Mrs. Gladstone came in for a moment, both looking much aged, and she very shaky and much altered, but she seemed delighted to see me.'[80]

The queen had the last word. When a year later, Gladstone died, she wrote to her eldest daughter:

I cannot say I think he was 'a great Englishman'. He was a clever man, full of talent, but he never tried to keep up the honour and prestige of Gt Britain. He gave away the Transvaal and he abandoned Gordon, he destroyed the Irish Church and tried to separate England from Ireland and he set class against class. The harm he did cannot be easily undone . . . But he was a good and vy religious man.[81]

During the half century between 1861 and 1914 there was no other minister, no clergyman, civil servant or courtier, so intimately involved in every aspect of the staging of a large royal ceremony in London as Gladstone was in the thanksgiving for the recovery of the Prince of Wales. Gladstone helped conceive the plan of the ceremony, persuaded the foremost participant to perform, settled details of the procession and the service inside St Paul's. Further chapters will show how exceptional this level of involvement was.

Large-scale ceremonies like the thanksgiving were, according to Gladstone's scheme of things, exceptional, but also exceptionally important. They were the only occasions on which the religious character of the monarchy and the nation could be brought home and reinforced. Outside of these exceptional occasions he hoped that a high standard of public service and devotion to duty on the part of the royal family would influence the upper classes, that the upper classes would influence the middle classes and so on down the social ladder. The thanksgiving was a rare opportunity to bring all the rungs together in a single act of praise and prayer. His religious views in the second half of the century were composed of diverse elements. Low church emphasis on strictness of personal conduct, high church conservatism on points of doctrine and tradition, both are to be found in his mature written work. It was not at all foreign to him to discuss the Prince Consort's life in terms Hannah More might have found admirable and publish them in a tractarian journal. For Gladstone, royalty questions were invariably questions of religion.

They were also questions that had more to do with Britain and Ireland than with India and the empire. The plan of a royal residence in Ireland addressed Irish nationalist grievances as well as the need for the Prince of Wales to be trained for a model role at the head of society in England. The era of the Prince Consort was one in which England had cultivated her domestic virtues. Imperial self-congratulation was, he thought, characteristic of the new era ushered in by Disraeli. He attacked the policy of the man who had come to power by helping to create imperial enthusiasms and then using them for electoral gain. The diamond jubilee was the last stage he witnessed in what he regarded as the increasingly purposeful identification of the monarchy with the empire. Lord Rendel recorded that in October of the year of the diamond jubilee: 'Mr. G. over his tea spoke with fire about Imperialism. He called it a form of Jingoism, "a vulgar road to popularity and power". He said it was an innovation.'[82]

Ideally the monarchy was sacred, irreproachable, untouchable; in practice it could be used to thwart radicals like Dilke, or in Gladstone's mind, abused to further the electoral interests of the conservative party. This confusion about the monarchy's status, both a symbol to be revered and a tool to be manipulated, is a persistent characteristic of the thinking of men who made the modern British monarchy. In every case this confusion had an impact on their plans for the monarchy's future. In the thanksgiving Gladstone wished to stage a national act of religion and reconciliation, as well as to extirpate republicanism root and branch. This led to a ceremony partly centered on prayers at St Paul's, partly centered on crowds in the streets. The nation saw itself not only in the royal family brought low by a threatened tragedy and a great release, but also in the rough crowds as liable to riot as to cheer for wan princes riding by in semi-state. Anxiety about the prince's health was mixed up with anxiety about mobs rushing down narrow streets and crushing themselves at blind corners. A vague concern about the future of the monarchy became indistinguishable from thoughts about the future of the expanded franchise and reformed constitution. When the thanksgiving came off without a riot, people breathed a sigh of relief not only for the monarchy, they also began to be easier and more accustomed to the idea that an expanded democracy was practicable and safe. This is the snapshot we have of the nation's character in 1872.

The year was decisive for the future of the monarchy. Large-scale royal ceremonies in St Paul's or the Abbey had been comparatively rare until then. After 1872 they came with increasing frequency. Gladstone's ceremony had both reawakened a national memory and helped create a new taste for such ceremonies. There began to be such enormous demand for national acts of prayer and remembrance that Queen Victoria and her advisers felt compelled to answer the demand with expensive, exhausting and precedent-setting ceremonies in 1887 and 1897. The public demand for ceremony was renewed when she died. Once again, the public demand was answered, even though, expert on funerals that she was, she had left detailed instructions that she be buried as quietly as possible.

Gladstone's emphasis on the religious character of state celebration also had a negative impact on the monarchy. He so alienated the queen that it became virtually impossible for them to collaborate. The monarchy might have been a different institution if the two had continued to like one another after the Prince Consort died. The monarchy might have looked more to a domestic, Albertine past than to the vague glories of imperial dominion if Gladstone had had the queen on his side. Gladstone helped re-establish a taste for state ceremonial, but he failed to persuade people about what the substance of those ceremonies should be.

Gladstone's extravagant religiosity also led him to defer to her more than an ordinary politician might have done. He was a silent martyr to her unrelenting hostility. He kept quiet about her Toryism. He swallowed his second thoughts about the civil list and used his personal prestige to quell dissent from within his own party. He endured snubs, censures and double crossings. He confined himself, at the end of his life, to a regret that she had not been more polite to his wife.[83] Thus, Gladstone's reverence for the throne allowed the monarchy to continue to wear the cloak of nonpartisan prestige, especially at dangerous moments when it would have been easy for the century's most popular politician to raise justifiable complaints.[84] Gladstone's fierce and fanatical royalism was a greater and earlier contribution to the stability of the monarchy than Disraeli's offhand and *ad hoc* references to the glory of the queen and empire.

By the 1880s the Albertine monarchy so admired by Gladstone and Bagehot was only a faint recollection in the minds of public men. The wise and tenacious widow queen was the figure these new men chose to lionize. Bagehot and Gladstone did not cease to exert influence. On the contrary, in the 1880s *The English Constitution* was becoming an authoritative text. Dozens of young men who had entered Parliament in the Liberal ranks during Gladstone's prime were now coming into power. One of these men, Reginald Baliol Brett, was already publishing a romanticized account of Gladstone's relations with the queen even before Gladstone's last meeting with her in 1897. Ironically this book and its author would have significant influence in shifting the monarchy's focus away from Gladstone's Albertine ideal. Brett had entered the political world as private secretary to Gladstone's cabinet colleague, Lord Hartington. He would leave it as a consummate courtier, the impresario of the diamond jubilee and the coronation of Edward VII.

3 Lord Esher: Empire Theater

No one in either the Victorian or Edwardian eras had a wider reputation as an expert on ceremony than Reginald Baliol Brett, second Viscount Esher.[1] He sat on the committee that planned Queen Victoria's diamond jubilee in 1897. When she died in 1901, he played a major role in arranging her funeral. In 1902, he was again prominent on the committee that planned the new king's coronation. When Esher himself died in 1930, *The Times* concluded that he was the principal genius behind these three turn of the century spectaculars.[2] He has been regarded as a significant figure in the history of the British monarchy ever since.

In 1911 when he was near the end of his time as a court favorite, Esher wrote a revealing letter to one of his confidantes. He was reflecting on the new regime at Windsor since the accession of George V the previous year.

> Curious vicissitudes we have gone through in the last twenty years under the shadow of this old castle. And how does it all affect or influence the lives of millions of drudges! Not a jot, I imagine, unless dreams and visions and unattainable glories add some colour here and there to the drab of existence . . . Yet they enjoy talking of Kings and Queens.

The 'them' and 'us' here is unmistakable. He appears to have only contempt for the working-class and middle-class 'drudges' who came to see his ceremonies and read his books on the monarchy. But in the next several lines, the snobbery and social distance disappear; 'them' becomes 'us'. 'Is it not strange?' Esher continued, 'That these baubles exist and interest us, when we think at other moments of the solar system and the insoluble problems of life and death.'[3] Although he pretended to disparage royal 'baubles' Esher knew that he was himself as attracted to the monarchy as any drudge.

The secret of Esher's charm and the key to his influence was that he never lost his childlike fascination with the royal family. His politics would swing back and forth from radical to reactionary, but what he was best at communicating to persons of all classes was his own obsession with princes. Queen Victoria coming silently into dinner on the arm of an Indian servant in the 1890s, a frightened Queen Mary in an ugly hat moments after her husband's accession in the spring of 1910 – these were the scenes that moved him. From these he extracted dramatic elements and staged them for a wider audience. As for kings and queens themselves, they could hardly resist Esher's frank compliments or his knack for 'the adroit attack' on people who interested him.[4]

Born in 1852, Esher was Gladstone's junior by more than 40 years. His first significant contact with the court came, not as Gladstone's had through political office, but through a social connection. Esher's friend at Cambridge, Albert Grey, was the son of Queen Victoria's first private secretary. The two young men regularly attended parties in London during the season and were invited to a ball given by the Prince and Princess of Wales. Marlborough House was the center of the fast set in the 1870s. There large sums were spent on entertaining. People danced, played cards, drank and ate late into the night. The Prince of Wales was fat, dignified and genial. The Princess of Wales was an achingly beautiful young woman. She spent most of her time changing clothes and her dresses kept an entire industry going. In 1875 Gladstone began his series of articles on the domestic excellences and clean living of the Albertine monarchy, while a 23 year old Esher led the Princess of Wales on to the dance floor at 3 a.m.[5]

Esher was the son of a distinguished Victorian judge. His father had risen through the ranks of the conservative party to be solicitor general and retired with a viscountcy. Esher's own inclinations as a young man were toward the liberal party. He liked the Whig and aristocratic section of the party best. His first job was as private secretary to the whig leader, Lord Hartington. Although Esher tended to shun the political spotlight, politics were important to him. He had grown up in a political family, attended Eton and Cambridge where young men were trained for power, and absorbed the late Victorian ethic that service to the state was among the most honorable professions open to men of talent and ambition. It was difficult for a man to be a social success without having made some mark in the political world. Esher wanted to do both, it was simply that he took a keener pleasure than did Gladstone in dinner parties, dances and well-dressed women.

Esher's political ideas in the 1870s and 1880s were radical. Among the younger generation of politicians his allies were Sir Charles Dilke and Joseph Chamberlain, both of whom thought the monarchy cost too much money and were in favor of abolishing upper-class political privilege. Esher's chief was milder, but even Hartington thought 'royalties' were a 'damned nuisance'. Esher was a liberal MP during Gladstone's second ministry from 1880 to 1885. He did not speak often in Parliament, but when he stood for re-election in 1885, he made speeches far to the left of center. He wanted to break up large landed estates. He wanted to end ties between church and state.[6] He published an article in which he referred to the monarchy as a burden on the constitution.[7]

Esher's radical ideas brought with them no bitterness about the world as it was. He admired duchesses driving in open landaus down Pall Mall. He loved the tarnished gilding at Devonshire House and the aristocratic accent of Hartington's sister, who kept up the Regency affectation of calling a carriage a chariot, pronounced 'charrot'.[8] When Hartington took office under Gladstone, Esher established cordial relations with the queen's private secretary. One source of Esher's budding influence was his ability to keep up a constant flow of reliable information to people who mattered. Queen Victoria was kept well abreast of what was going on in his chief's department, whether he and Hartington regarded her as a nuisance or not.

Another connection to the court had come in 1879 when Esher married Eleanor van de Weyer. She was the daughter of a Belgian diplomat who knew Queen Victoria through his teacher, Baron Stockmar. Esher and his wife established themselves near Windsor. In the 1890s the couple had four children and their two daughters were taking dancing lessons with some of the queen's grandchildren in the Castle. Esher's daughters were less entranced by the royal family than their father. They remembered Queen Victoria as a terrifying old lady who rapped her cane on the parquet in time with the music.[9]

By the 1890s, Esher was out of Parliament, having been turned out in 1885. Wanting more independence, he had also decided to leave Hartington and was out of a job as well. He was living off a large allowance from his father and writing history. He aimed in part to discuss the imperial ideals he had developed from his friendship with Dilke and Chamberlain. Imperialism is generally thought of today as the bright idea of Disraelian Conservatives. But it was the radical Dilke who fired imperial enthusiasm with his book, *Greater Britain beyond the Seas*, widely read in the 1880s, and 'pushful Joe' Chamberlain, one-time radical mayor of Birmingham, whose tenure of the Colonial Office in the 1890s advanced Britain's political commitment to the empire. Esher's devotion to the empire went back further still to his boyhood at Eton. Esher's grandson wrote of his grandfather's youth:

At Eton his charm, wit and good looks caught the eye of William Johnson (William Cory). This remarkable teacher, who left under a cloud a few years later, implanted in his disciples the two complementary ideals of romantic homosexual love and high-minded service to the Empire. The model was classical Greece, the myth that of Achilles and Patroclus. Floating in a dodger on the silent Thames, then at the height of its elmy beauty, friendships were formed which were to last a political lifetime, and in long tutorials radical imperialism acquired its characteristic stamp.[10]

It is hard to recapture the passion and enthusiasm men like Esher felt for the empire in the 1890s. They thought white, English-speaking men were superior to blacks, women and 'foreigners' in general. They thought the world would benefit from the export of English civilization and English know-how. Indians and Africans would benefit from roads and bridges and dams and eventually, self-government. Englishmen, who were in danger of growing soft from too much wealth and comfort, would benefit from the self-discipline and self-sacrifice necessary to govern colonies and dependencies. Late Victorian imperialists had a vision of improving the lives of those less well-off than themselves, but they were also insular, arrogant and narrow-minded.

Some of the best-known imperialists were homosexuals. Cecil Rhodes, General Gordon and Lord Kitchener of Khartoum were all, like Esher, romantically attached to boys and men. There was a feeling among them that women made life too easy and comfortable. Ruling the empire, like serving in the Army, was for men alone. The idea often appears in Kipling's short stories, where men form close bonds ruling primitive people in harsh climates, sometimes dying in one another's arms.[11] There was also a Victorian convention that young men of good families who felt themselves unsuited for marriage might instead volunteer for service in some post sure to take them to power over some far off preserve of the empire.

Esher's marriage was a happy one. He never volunteered for imperial service. He liked comfort and disliked self-sacrifice. But he did introduce and promote imperial themes in books ostensibly devoted to other subjects. He published two books in the 1890s: *Footprints of Statesmen during the Eighteenth Century in Britain* (1892) and *The Yoke of Empire: Sketches of the Queen's Prime Ministers* (1896). Both books are composed of short biographical essays. Both books concentrate on personalities and are consciously written against what Esher called the 'modern' tendency to look upon 'vast masses of nameless men as the determining factor in great public affairs'.[12] One book drew sketches of eighteenth-century politicians, the other of Queen Victoria's relations with nineteenth-century prime ministers. Both refer to the empire as a harness or yoke for British statesmen. In the book on the eighteenth century, dedicated to a fifteen year old Eton boy, Esher provided two reading lists for younger readers. One was imperial; its theme was 'the enterprise, courage, endurance, and self-sacrifice of Englishmen – qualities ennobling the race, and at the foundation of Empire'. The other was constitutional, based on Bagehot's *The English Constitution*, and painted 'pictures of England at moments while the modern Constitution was making'.[13]

Neither Bagehot nor Gladstone cared very much for the empire. Usually they actively disapproved of it. Esher's innovation was to build a bridge between their devotion to a domestic, Albertine monarchy, the result of indigenous island traditions, and the late-Victorian view of a global empire, which depended on the figure of the sovereign at the center to hold it all together. In *The Yoke of Empire* he praised the Prince Consort in words clearly derived from Gladstone. He also praised the queen whom be showed repeatedly fulfilling the difficult function of a constitutional sovereign and offering up an 'object lesson in democratic monarchy'.[14] Paying homage to the constitutional and moral lessons of the Albertine monarchy, he nevertheless for the first time yoked them both to an imperial idea.

In the 1890s Esher had a good deal of confidence in Britain's imperial future. He had begun to lose his confidence in the ability of a mass electorate to guarantee Britain's safety. He wrote an article asking 'What are the ideals of the masses?' in which he showed his cynicism about the intelligence of the electorate.[15] In another he poured scorn on the 'Nonconformist conscience'.[16] Politics were being ruined, he thought, by the lower-middle-class morality that pervaded the press and voting public. It had driven capable politicians like Dilke and Parnell out of office because of irregular relationships with women that had nothing to do with their abilities as statesmen. He had only contempt for excessively Protestant censoriousness; he preferred the broad-minded aristocratic politics of the eighteenth century. Still, he hazarded a warning in the same article to the Prince of Wales, whose involvement in the Tranby Croft gambling scandal was then a topic of upper-class gossip. There would be no public tolerance for a return to the Prince Regent's days. It is unlikely to suppose, Esher wrote, 'that the monarchy could again stand the strain of fortunes lavished in play, of bankruptcy certificated by Parliament, of mistresses flaunting on the steps of the throne, of usury and buffoonery standing where men have been accustomed to look for culture and decorum'.[17]

Esher's attitude to the monarchy was as complex as his attitude to politics in general. He was critical of the Prince of Wales for endangering the prestige of the Crown, but he was equally critical of provincial Nonconformity. He praised Queen Victoria for doing such a good job as a democratic sovereign, yet his loathing for democracy was rising. He himself wanted some active political role under a political system he was coming to despise. His greatest obstacle was his own private life, which would have hardly borne the inspection of his friends, let alone the public. Since

1889 he had been handling the affairs of Lord Arthur Somerset, a son of the duke of Beaufort, forced by threat of prosecution to live abroad because he had been caught at a homosexual brothel in Cleveland Street. While Esher's emotional attachment to the adolescent Edward Seymour, to whom he had dedicated his book on the eighteenth century, languished in the 1890s, he began another affair, more shocking still, with his younger son Maurice, then a schoolboy at Eton. Perhaps surprisingly Maurice never resented his father's attentions. He later had a happy marriage of his own and remained devoted to his father in old age. Still, it is an understatement to say the relationship posed difficulties for Esher's political ambitions.

In 1895 Esher's friend, Lord Rosebery, appointed him to a civil service post, one that would bring him into increasing contact with the royal family. It was an inside job. Like Esher, Rosebery was an old Etonian, a student of Cory, a Liberal Imperialist, and possibly homosexual as well. Esher's appointment as permanent secretary to the Office of Works in 1895 gave him responsibility for works of decoration, construction and repair in royal palaces, parks and government buildings. Here was a political position, out of the public eye, that suited Esher's talents perfectly.

Among Esher's first tasks were the installation of an elevator at Windsor for the queen and the arrangement of apartments for her daughters at Kensington Palace.[18] The biggest challenge, and one of Esher's greatest successes, was to come in the second year after his appointment.

The press and the public noticed that in September 1896 Queen Victoria would break George III's record and become the longest-reigning sovereign in English history. From all quarters mail poured into the Palace suggesting ceremonies that might suitably commemorate the event. Her private secretaries were overwhelmed, so the queen sent out an official announcement. She wanted no celebrations until she had completed a reign of 60 years in June of 1897.[19] In fact, she would have preferred no celebrations at all. Ten years earlier in June 1887 she had given in to similar public demand and gone to Westminster Abbey to give thanks for completing a reign of 50 years. This was her golden jubilee. Crowned heads from all over Europe had attended and had stayed in London as her guests. The bill had been enormous. She refused to pay for champagne and orchids out of the Privy Purse again.

Lord Salisbury's government wanted to repeat the ceremony of 1887.[20] In an age of strident, pre-war competition, some thought the first jubilee had impressed the European powers with Britain's wealth, strength and national unity. Others thought more modestly that it had reduced English isolation from the continent. However, the queen was firm in her refusal, even when it was hinted to her that this time the government would be willing to foot the bill. She knew there would be a 'powerful public demand for some national demonstration' in June of 1897.[21] She could hardly resist it. The question was how to meet it with less effort and less expense.

As a solution to this question Joseph Chamberlain suggested an idea. By this time Chamberlain had left the Liberals over Irish Home Rule, joined the Unionists and taken office as colonial secretary. Chamberlain pointed out that representatives from the colonies might come to London to celebrate the queen's 60-year anniversary. They would be easier and cheaper to entertain than crowned heads of state. They would also be gratified by the slightest attention from the queen. Once they were in England, riding in royal carriages with liveried footmen, they might also be persuaded to agree to Chamberlain's political plan for imperial federation. He wanted the premiers of Britain's self-governing colonies, softened up by a few royal courtesies, to agree to a system of preferential tariffs within the empire and to contribute financially to a joint plan of imperial defense. At length the queen agreed to Chamberlain's suggestion. As in 1872, the diamond jubilee had nonpartisan origins, but it had been seen by members of the cabinet to present political opportunities and been pressed on the queen as a way of making use of those opportunities.

Early in 1897 the government and the queen approved the naming of a committee, chaired by the Prince of Wales, to plan the ceremony. Esher's *Yoke of Empire*, just published, had sold well in the Christmas rush. Although one of his friends had teased him about the 'courtier-like' tone of the book, the private secretaries of the Prince of Wales and the queen took notice.[22] They decided Esher was sound and asked him to sit on the prince's committee.

As soon as it was appointed the committee ran into difficulties. The queen had agreed to ride in a procession through the City.[23] Lord Salisbury, like Gladstone a deeply religious man, and mindful of the precedents set in 1872 and 1887, suggested that she should stop for at least a few minutes at St Paul's and hear a *Te Deum*.[24] But she was an elderly lady who tired easily and could not get out of her carriage without great effort. This meant an outdoor service at St Paul's. The committee was distressed at the idea of an unconventional, open-air ceremony. What if it rained? What would prevent the queen's horses from emptying their bladders during the *Te Deum*? After consulting ecclesiastics, who were in favor, and after Randall Davidson, bishop of Winchester, pointed out that it would be bad for religion to be altogether omitted on such an important day, the committee reluctantly endorsed the idea of an open-air *Te Deum*.[25] However, there began to be talk of moving the focal point of the ceremony away from

St Paul's, where there was so little space and the service would be so
short. Dignitaries might be seated along the route of the procession, while
the steps of St Paul's could be left to City officials. Esher came forward
and decisively influenced the ceremony by rejecting this idea completely.

Esher knew that the only way to change the mind of the committee was
to change the mind of its chairman. To this end, he wrote an important
letter to Sir Francis Knollys, the Prince of Wales's private secretary. Esher
supported the idea of the outdoor *Te Deum*, but he insisted that the persons
attending at St Paul's had to be seen as an integral feature of the ceremony
itself. On the principal day of the celebration, he argued, there had to be
some dramatic, central scene, which matched the dignity of the occasion
in visual display. The scene in front of St Paul's and the persons seated
there were crucial to the ceremony's success, he told Knollys:

> The whole matter turns upon the use which is to be made of the space
> round the western front of the Cathedral. This will seat about 1,200
> persons – not a large number – but enough to meet the wants of officials
> and others, who should be placed at that spot, if the ceremony is not to
> have *a very meagre appearance.*

There must be 'a marked distinction on the day between Officials and
ordinary spectators'. Special provision had to be made for officials 'who
will be in uniform and . . . they must be located at the central point of the
procession'. Esher ridiculed the idea that undistinguished aldermen and
other City officials who claimed a special connection with St Paul's might
be allowed to witness the queen at prayer, while the prime minister would
be secreted away among a gang of backwoods peers along the route of the
procession. The lord mayor and guild members would be useful if they
had nice uniforms, but they could not displace higher-ranking dignitaries.
Esher's letter to Knollys continued:

> It has been proposed that the whole available space at St Paul's should
> be given up to the Lord Mayor and City Authorities.
>
> This is unnecessary, because the Dean of St Paul's has offered, if re-
> quired, to give up the lower steps of [the] Cathedral to the Lord Mayor
> and City Guilds, where they would mix effectively with the clergy *from
> the scenic point of view* and would be amply provided with space.
>
> Impracticable, because high officers of State, foreign representatives,
> and great officials must be in attendance on the Queen, and cannot be
> said to be in attendance at any other spot than the objective of the whole
> Procession.

Further, to accomplish Chamberlain's goal of impressing the queen's colonial guests, the colonials had to be surrounded by persons with impressive titles.

They cannot be swamped by the friends of the City Aldermen, with no distinguished guests, or officials in their vicinity. Finally, the ceremony itself, *if it is not to be robbed of all dignity*, necessitates the surrounding of the Sovereign at that particular spot with all her Great Officers of State as well as her family.[26]

Esher maintained that there had to be a climax to the procession; the climax had to be at St Paul's; and it had to be an exclusive and visually sensational affair. Otherwise the ceremony would be a failure. The Prince of Wales took notice[27] and the committee accepted Esher's plan for the ceremony.

If it was the colonial representatives who were meant to be impressed at St Paul's, there was another audience, assumed by the Prince of Wales's committee to be equally impressionable, for whom the queen would perform once the *Te Deum* was over. The committee decided that the queen should drive back to the palace via a route south of the river. There she would come into contact with a few of London's working-class and poorer neighborhoods. Everyone from Bagehot in the 1860s to Esher in the 1890s believed that the poor and the working classes were particularly susceptible to radical agitation. The brief success of Dilke's campaign in the industrial north was a similar worry for Gladstone in the 1870s. Equally widespread was the contrary assumption that the working classes could be mollified and placated with royal attention and show. Lord Salisbury in 1897 endorsed the idea of the queen's driving through south London just as in the previous decade he had approved of her visiting depressed districts in London's East End as well as in Birmingham and Liverpool. Of course upper-class ladies had always visited the sick and the poor, but they seldom drove into poor neighborhoods, waved and left without stopping, as the committee planned for Queen Victoria to do in 1897. It was an enduring conceit of those who planned royal ceremonies late in the Victorian era that the vulgar and the uneducated, foreigners and Catholics, colonials and black men were more easily impressed by royal ceremonies than were cultivated members of the British upper classes, who somehow remained impervious and superior to the appeal of such spectacles. Esher shared in this conceit. It was a conceit because he and his colleagues on the Prince of Wales's committee were quite as capable of being moved by the short set piece in St Paul's Churchyard as the colonials or the working classes.

The queen's route on the day of the jubilee was announced two months beforehand. Landlords in south London began evicting low-income tenants with dwellings on the line of the procession to rent them for more money to those who wanted a good view on the day of the jubilee. Esher wanted a peremptory announcement made that the queen's return route south of the river was not fixed and might be changed at the last minute.[28] The last thing Esher and the jubilee committee wanted was for south London to be overrun by daytrippers with money to burn. The queen's drive south of the river was to see the working classes. This was an unprecedented move and one that acknowledged the increased importance of working men and women, both for a democratic parliament elected under an expanded franchise and a democratic monarchy dependent for its survival on working-class loyalty and support. But the class lines were still plain. There was to be an observable difference between the ceremony for dignitaries and colonial premiers in front of St Paul's and the procession for working men down Borough High Street.

One way the dignitaries were to be assured an impressive pageant was through rehearsals beforehand. This had not been common previously. There had been no rehearsals for the thanksgiving in 1872, for example. Now elaborate rehearsals of the scene in front of St Paul's were held. Once again the press heightened public anticipation by printing an account and depictions of the rehearsals. *The Illustrated London News* ran a picture of a rehearsal on its cover.[29] [See plate 4.] There is even evidence that about this time Esher was consulting theatre professionals about the staging of the *Te Deum*. George Edwardes, a well-known theatre manager who produced 'spectacular ballets' at the Empire music hall in Leicester Square, seems to have been called in to give expert advice.[30]

In the last half of the nineteenth century politics, religion and the theatre itself all became more theatrical. Elaborate dramas with hundreds of people on stage and expensive sets were produced on London stages.[31] Henry Irving and Herbert Beerbohm Tree put on 'lavishly spectacular productions of Shakespeare . . . with a magnificence much to the taste of the time'.[32] Gladstone deplored increasing showiness in the theatre. He classified it along with ritualism as part of the materialist tendency of the age to turn away from inward spirituality toward outward display and ostentation.[33] Esher clearly had a liking for such theatre. There were clear resemblances too between Gladstone's own dramatic platform performances late in the century and the art of great actor-producers like Henry Irving.[34]

Esher was an avid theatre-goer all his life. According to his most recent biographer, the stage held him 'in thrall. He was always at the theatre, and with few exceptions preferred the relaxed friendship of actors and actresses to that of politicians.'[35] Esher's daughter, Sylvia, remembered having met many of the best-known actors on the London stage through her parents.[36] Esher's son, Maurice, married an actress. Esher's familiarity with the stage influenced his designs for royal ceremonies. His eye for an event's scenic and spectacular possibilities was well-trained.

When Esher had finished and the curtain went up, the scene in front of St Paul's engraved itself on the memories of those who witnessed it. A photograph preserved in the Royal Archives shows Queen Victoria in her carriage at the brief outdoor service. [See plate 5.] The bishop of London, Mandell Creighton, participated in the service. He wrote the queen a private letter that gives a clear idea of the ceremony's emotional and visual impact on those standing in front of the cathedral.

As the [queen's] carriage drew up before the steps of the Cathedral the bells stopped. There was a moment's silence; then the signal was given and after a brief prelude the choir broke into the strains of the *Te Deum*. It was a new composition, strong, effective and devotional. When it was over the words of the Lords Prayer filled the air. A collect of Thanksgiving was said by the Bishop of London. The Archbishop of Canterbury pronounced the Benediction. Then the choir sang two verses of the Old Hundredth Hymn.

A slight mistake was made at this part of the ceremony. The intention was that during the singing of the hymn, the carriages, which had been waiting in the square, should move on, so that when the hymn was finished the Queen's carriage should be free to proceed. But the other carriages waited; and when the hymn was over there was a pause of intolerable silence. The Archbishop of Canterbury, with splendid audacity and disregard of decorum, interpreted what was in every one's mind, and cried out 'Three cheers for the Queen'. Never were cheers given with such startling unanimity and precision. All the horses threw up their heads at the same moment, and gave a little quiver of surprise. When the cheers were over the band and chorus, by an irresistible impulse, burst into 'God Save the Queen'. All this time the sight of St Paul's Churchyard, with the carriages grouped round it, and the royal princes stationed behind the Queen's carriage, was remarkably picturesque. Seldom was a service held which expressed more truly the wishes of all present; seldom were prayers more sincere. There were few who were not deeply moved.

[. . .] Then she drove on among deafening cheers. No sooner had her carriage turned round the corner than a curious scene took place, not noticed by many. One of the choir boys, unable to restrain himself any longer, dashed from his place, leaped down the steps, and filled his pockets with the gravel on which the wheels of the carriage had rested. The other boys ran down after him, and almost beside themselves with the excitement of the scene, began to ask me all manner of questions. We were recalled presently by the voice of the Archbishop of Canterbury saying laughingly 'Bishop of London, you are spoiling those boys.' Soon the choirmaster came in search of them and recalled them to their places. But the simple naturalness of this little occurrence makes it worth recording. It was really difficult to know how to express one's feelings.

Nothing short of the Colonial troops could have commanded any further attention. But the sturdy appearance, and superb attitude on horseback of the Australian contingent, carried one's mind back again to the greatness of the English Empire. The presence of the Colonial premiers was a significant testimony that our free institutions bind us together into a deeper and more genuine patriotism and a sincerer loyalty than can be attained by more rigorous organisation.

The procession came to an end, and all walked away in silence for some time. There was too much to think about for words to express.[37]

A choirboy's instinct that the gravel under the queen's carriage had become sacred is enough to show the effect of the ceremony on the audience. The diamond jubilee joined the ideas of the monarchy and the empire in a new way for those who witnessed it and read about it. The queen had been Empress of India for 20 years, but the diamond jubilee was a new departure. It symbolized the commitment of the queen to the unity of the empire and, as such, was a new kind of imperial coronation. The monarchy – not Whitehall, not the Army, not P & O steamships or BOAC – has been seen as the first link between Britain and the empire, now commonwealth, ever since. Members of the royal family made repeated visits to outposts of the former empire throughout the twentieth century because of a pledge made by Queen Victoria, and dramatized by Esher, in June of 1897.

The immediate political plan, however, came to nothing. The colonial premiers refused to agree to imperial federation. Chamberlain and Esher were disappointed. The prestige of the monarchy grew so high following the jubilee, however, that they both assumed there would be other opportunities of advancing the political cause of the empire along with it. What they failed to see was that by enhancing the prestige of the monarchy as a ceremonial institution, they were weakening its effectiveness as a political tool. The more splendid and theatrical its ceremonies became, the more difficult it was to regard the Crown as offering a serious way forward for consolidating the power and defense of the empire. If the monarchy were pure theatre, it could hardly be an effective part of imperial administration as well.

Five years later Esher had transformed what was at first only a place on the committee that planned the diamond jubilee into a position of recognized authority on questions of ceremonial. The new king, Edward VII, liked ceremony better than Queen Victoria had. This worried Esher. 'Ceremonial has great charm for him [the king]', he told his son shortly after the accession. 'Not in the Napoleonic manner, as a *setting* for greater issues, but rather, I fear, as an end in itself.'[38] The king's opinion was that the coronation should be streamlined, shortened and freed of all 'tom foolery'.[39] Rumor spread that at the king's coming coronation many of the old customs would be abolished. Many were upset that the king and his staff seemed so 'reckless of precedent'.[40] An article appeared in *The Nineteenth Century* arguing that ceremonies that had fallen into disuse at previous coronations should be revived.[41] Esher used his influence with the king to try and stop him from doing away with ancient precedents. He wrote the king's private secretary:

> I think there is great advantage in following as far as possible, ancient precedents, so long as they are not hopelessly inconsistent with modern conditions. So much of the power and dignity of the Monarchy is derived from its antiquity, and the strict adhesion of our forefathers to 'precedent', that one cannot view, without regret, departure from ancient practices, which, although they would be absurd if allied with modern institutions, appear natural to the subjects of our ancient monarchy, scattered as they are all over the world.[42]

He told his son the same day:

> I have just written to him [the king] a very 'conservative' letter, urging him to adhere to all ancient practices and traditions unless they are 'ridiculous'.
>
> It was the revolt of the young *noblesse* against the old fusty customs which materially helped to bring the fall of the French monarchy.[43]

Fear of the first French Revolution, more than a hundred years later, still preoccupied men like Esher. The same spirit had moved Lord Salisbury to forbid the attendance of the British ambassador at the centenary celebrations of the revolution in France in 1889.[44] The British monarchy represented a link to the past which the French had broken. But Esher's use of the word 'precedent' had social as well as political and historical connotations. To preserve the ancient claims of various peers to perform

services at the coronation was also to preserve the social *precedence* of
the aristocracy.

Arthur Bigge, a bluff former Army officer, lately one of Queen Victoria's
private secretaries, and now serving the new Prince of Wales on a colonial
tour, agreed with Esher. He also told Knollys that

> So long as we have a Monarchy surely to goodness we ought to stick
> to all the *old* customs, observances and ritual ... Perhaps the fact of
> being in these colonies makes one more keenly realize the value of what
> is ancient, of tradition, and of prestige.[45]

Bigge and Esher thought of the empire as new and lacking in tradition.
They wanted to appeal to colonial love of what was old as a way of further
tightening the identification of the empire with the monarchy. Knollys, who
was a firmer Liberal than either of them, had a sense that too much 'showiness' would tip the scale from grave dignity to fancy-dress hilarity. He wrote
back to Bigge saying 'I fear you are a terrible "old Tory" !!' Knollys told
Esher that they could not revive old customs that had last been used at
the coronation of an overweight figure of fun like George IV. Esher, like
any good courtier, recovered his good humor. He began suggesting new
ceremonies to symbolize the link between the king and, in Dilke's phrase,
'Greater Britain beyond the seas'.[46] But he was slightly miffed.

Throughout 1901 Esher gently criticized the new court and the new
king for lacking mystery and dignity, for being too ordinary and 'commonplace'. He missed the aura of 'holy mystery', 'awe' and 'sanctity' that
pervaded Queen Victoria's court.[47] The new court failed to inspire these
semi-religious feelings. Esher told his son in October: 'All this morning I
spent with the King, who was amiable – but he has one great fault for me
– which is his commonplace personality. I cannot find in him any trace of
original thought or feeling.'

Esher was hard-pressed to find the necessary materials from which to
fashion a sensation in the Abbey at the coming coronation. It would be
impossible to recreate the spectacle that had taken place at the coronation
of Queen Victoria in 1838. 'Only young girls or boys should be crowned
monarchs' Esher continued.

> After 20 no one should be allowed to come to the throne! *Then* romance
> would hold her sway. Imagine the sensation of the people when Queen
> Victoria – so small and so young and so fair – walked up the Abbey to
> be crowned. Next June, we can hardly expect a sensation. It will all be
> so very middle aged and unheroic.[48]

Nonetheless, he did what he could. On the model of the diamond jubilee a committee was formed to plan the coronation. Once again Esher sat on this committee. Esher recommended that seating in the Abbey should be significantly reduced from the 10 000 persons who had been seated there in 1887 for the golden jubilee to only 6000 people. He made this recommendation 'on grounds of safety and spectacular effect'.[49] It would also make the ceremony, like the diamond jubilee, more exclusive than formerly. Early in 1902 he told his son that he wanted 'to go and see the young king of Spain crowned on May 17th. Just to get hints. It ought to be magnificent for the splendour of Spanish Palaces is unequalled.'[50] Splendor, exclusivity, magnificence, heroism, romance, these were the scenic effects Esher had in mind. The question of whether these were appropriate to a middle-aged king who lacked his mother's *gravitas* and originality did not deter Esher. Like Bagehot and Gladstone, Esher persisted in praising kingship despite his acute awareness of the ways in which individual kings failed to live up to his ideal.

Esher's talents as an interior decorator did not go unremarked. He had rejected the garish crimson of former coronations in favor of deep blue carpets and hangings. A photograph of the nave from the Royal Archives helps emphasize the relative spareness of the decorations and unusual feeling of space in what had usually been a very crowded and cluttered church during royal ceremonies. [See plate 6.] The reduction in seating he had insisted upon meant that everyone was to have a real seat, not a bench. Social status could be determined not only by where one sat, but by what one sat on: the peers and peeresses had Chippendale chairs.[51] One official, in his final report of the proceedings, said of the interior of the Abbey: 'It was a marvel of care, taste, good arrangement and splendour, all of it owing to the great skill and ability of Lord Esher, who was without a doubt the very genius of the Coronation.'[52]

As the day of the coronation approached rehearsals indicated an impending disaster. Few people knew their lines, nobody knew their places. The heralds gave directions and the grandees ignored them. The king asked Esher to intercede. Esher told his son: 'I was asked by the King today to "stage manage" the ceremonial in the Abbey, and *refused*. Of course very politely, on the ground that the little Duke of Norfolk would be horribly hurt! So I shall help, but nothing more.'[53] Nevertheless, he took a prominent role in the proceedings leading up to the event. When the king fell ill just two days before the ceremony, it was Esher who made the dramatic announcement to an assembly of bishops and peers rehearsing in the Abbey.[54] The king had his appendix removed. The ceremony was abbreviated and the coronation rescheduled for 9 August. At rehearsals for the rescheduled ceremony it was Esher and not the earl marshal, who gave the bishop of Bath and Wells instructions about what to do if the convalescent king felt ill again in the middle of the ceremony.[55] After the event *The Times* gave Esher and the duke equal credit for the arrangements. Esher's friend, W. T. Stead at *The Review of Reviews*, went so far as to call Esher the 'great Master of Ceremonies' and publish his picture.[56]

Esher's ceremonies were less intensely devotional than those imagined by Gladstone, produced for a more select audience than those imagined by Bagehot: they were theatrical set-pieces which resulted from detailed attention to appearance and staging. He attached weight to precedent partly because it added the accuracy of historical detail to the spectacle he wanted to stage, partly because precedent stood for resistance to change, partly because he thought it would appeal to the colonials, most of all because he loved fusty old customs himself. Above all, for someone as highly attuned to fine gradations in social rank as Esher was, 'precedent' also had associations with social precedence. The coronation was a rare occasion on which one spoke explicitly about the social distinctions which were commonplace features of Edwardian society. Homosexual men whose best friends are duchesses, then as now, are learned experts on social precedence. We shall see, however, as we consider some of Esher's published work following the coronation that precedent served also as a basis for reasserting in the twentieth century royal powers that had begun to fall into disuse.

For Esher historical research was less a matter of finding out what happened in the past than a political tool in the present. Esher dismissed the dry scholarship written by the new professional historians.

> For the purposes of statesmanship, the useful historian is not the man of encyclopedic mind, who can array vast masses of fact in proper order and sequence, but he who is able to open a lattice in the closed door of the past and let a ray of light illumine some problem or some character of today.[57]

King Edward VII gave Esher unlimited access to his mother's papers at Windsor. He appointed Esher constable and lieutenant governor of Windsor Castle in 1901. Ten years later King George V appointed Esher the first keeper of the Royal Archives. Esher took these opportunities to be a 'useful historian'. Especially in the Edwardian era, Esher used his influence at court to reassert royal authority. Fearful that the Crown's influence, which had already eroded during Queen Victoria's last years, would be even further diminished, Esher provided the king and his staff with precedents from the correspondence of Queen Victoria's reign, and especially from the early part of the reign when the Prince Consort had grown to exercise considerable influence. The king's private secretary used these precedents to support the king's right to review and inspect important cabinet decisions before they were taken.[58] Edward VII never applied himself to dull business or earned the respect of his ministers as his mother and father had in their best years. Appeal to Esher's precedents only assured that the king continued to see documents; it did not assure that the king's views, when he had them, would have weight with ministers. Still, he might have been passed over altogether if Esher had not interceded. If the sovereign today still possesses the right to be informed, she has Esher to thank as well as Bagehot.

The Yoke of Empire was only the first in a series of Esher's historical works, all of which argued that constitutional monarchy remained valuable to democratic government. The foremost of these was the nine-volume *Letters of Queen Victoria*, which began to appear in 1907 and was finally completed in 1932.[59] Esher laid down the principles on which the whole work was based. He decided that a biography of the queen, which had been the king's original idea, would be unsuitable. The story had already been told. Instead, Esher wanted Queen Victoria to speak in her own words, to be her own biographer. He thought that extracts from the queen's diaries and letters, tacked together with explanations and notes, would be more authentic and arouse greater interest than an authorized biography.[60]

The problem was the great abundance of material. In 1902 Esher had left the Office of Works. He was now devoting his energies to military reform and was too busy to spend months holed up in his rooms at Windsor deciphering Queen Victoria's illegible script. So he asked the writer and Eton schoolmaster, A. C. Benson, to be his co-editor. Benson has left a vivid picture of the slyness with which Esher made him the offer. Benson, summoned to Esher's house, found him

> in the garden in a summer-house, airily dressed, reading, with his son [Maurice] beside him, in a Guards' tie, also reading . . . He made me a statement at once, with a kind of smile, yet holding it back for effect.

Benson resigned his post at Eton and accepted Esher's offer the next day.[61]

For some reason quite a few homosexual men have been responsible for influencing the written records of the court. Longstanding cultural associations divided the masculine from the feminine parts of the constitution even before Bagehot's day. Manly republican virtues associated with the aggressive hustle bustle of the marketplace had long been connected with the democratic House of Commons. While feminine, even feline, qualities were associated with the tact, delicacy and discretion required to succeed at court. Homosexual men have had a knack for capturing the atmosphere of the court. Lord Hervey and Horace Walpole left precise and engaging, if somewhat spiteful, portraits of the early Hanoverian courts. Harold Nicolson and James Pope-Hennessey painted more attractive likenesses of George V and Queen Mary. Benson and Esher did the same for the court of Queen Victoria.

Esher was not an effeminate man. He carried on a series of affairs with schoolboys, but he also got along well with Army officers and Nonconformist newspaper editors, who probably knew little about the other side of his life. In the same era that he was collaborating with Benson, Esher accompanied Major General Douglas Haig on maneuvers, the two sleeping next to each other on the ground under the grandstand at Goodwood.[62] Although Benson was a well-known writer and son of an archbishop, he did not move among royalties, eminent politicians and generals as Esher did. Esher intimidated him. Two days after Esher had asked Benson to join him in editing the queen's letters, Benson had a nightmare about tea with the Prince Consort. It is tempting to see some unconscious confusion in Benson's mind between Esher's superciliousness and the prince's behavior in the dream.

> We were by a tea-table – we two alone. He helped himself liberally to tea, cake, etc.; then turned to me, and said, 'You observe that I offer you no tea, Mr. Benson.' I said, 'Yes, sir.' 'The reason is that I am forbidden by etiquette to do so, and would to God I could alter this!' He was overcome with emotion, but finished his tea, after which a grave man came and served me with some ceremony.[63]

The world Benson was on the verge of entering was forbiddingly, often ridiculously, deferential and archaic. Benson and Esher had before them a daunting task in rendering this world not only attractive, but also comprehensible to the outside world.

As editorial work got under way it proved difficult to select material where there was so much correspondence of historical importance. Midway through the task Esher thought it necessary to clarify the principle of selection for Benson:

> The main object, almost the sole object, is to exhibit the relation between the character of the Queen and the government of her people . . .
>
> It is impossible for us to give full accounts of political and historical episodes and personages.
>
> They come partly as:

a) Illustrations.

b) Scenery and *dramatis personae* . . .

The book must be dramatic or rather possess a dramatic note.[64]

Esher's insistence on the dramatic setting was not an accidental metaphor. The theater was an art form from which he borrowed his ideas not only about ceremonial, but also about the presentation of the queen's letters.

Esher and Benson frankly admitted in the preface to their work that the correspondence between 1837 and 1861 was so extensive that, were it to be published as a whole, it would amount to several hundred volumes.[65] Because they wanted the book to be widely read, they decided that it could not extend beyond three volumes. As with Esher's earlier works, it was not to be a work of massed fact for historians, but a primer on constitutional monarchy for general readers.[66] The editors' emphasis on the queen's character was meant to serve as a permanent shrine to her memory, to show the ways in which she and the Prince Consort had successfully and impartially intervened for the benefit of the nation, to fix an image of her personality on a heroic scale in the minds of the public. They selected nothing that showed the queen in a bad light. There was not much need for deception, as there was plenty that showed her in a rather good light.

Esher returned to the queen's character in a further selection from her journals and correspondence which George V allowed him to publish in 1912 as *The Girlhood of Queen Victoria*. 'It is the character of the Queen', Esher wrote, 'that places her in the small category of rulers who have not only deserved well of their country, but have left an indelible stamp upon the life of their people'.[67] Like Cardinal Newman, Esher believed that people were more influenced by example than by logic. They understood the personalities of great men; they did not follow the complexities of policy. In a lecture he gave in 1909, entitled *Queen Victoria's Journals, Some Unpublished Extracts*, he said that if Newman was right the queen had 'rendered a mighty service'.[68] Esher trusted people to learn lessons from Queen Victoria's character. He distrusted their political instincts. He wrote A. J. Balfour's private secretary an angry letter in 1910 in which he criticized Unionists who supported the idea of a popular referendum on contentious legislative issues.

I am not a 'Democrat' and I hate 'Democracy'. It has always preceded the fall of Empires. 'The People' are fools, and are not fit to govern, and never will be.

Cardinal Newman once said 'Men are influenced by *type* and not by argument' by which he meant that my chauffeur is competent to say whether he will be governed by A. J. B. or by Lloyd George, but *not* competent to say whether he will or will not have any specific Education Bill or Tariff Reform.[69]

Esher's pique in this letter shows him to be an aging man increasingly out of touch with the temper of the times. He was in the awkward position of wanting to persuade an increasingly democratic nation of the value of the monarchy, at the same time as he resented the political changes democracy was bringing about. The changes were not only political. Virginia Woolf believed that at the end of 1910 human character changed. The era of Victorian moralism, romanticism and sentimentality was fading away. With the exhibition of new post-impressionist painters – Gauguin, Van Gogh, Cézanne – at the Grafton Galleries in the autumn of 1910, twentieth-century modernism had come to Britain and with it a turning away from Victorianism. The Victorian models of moderation, paternalism and social hierarchy were giving way to large-scale strikes, militant feminism and impatience with upper-class privilege. World War I 'hastened' all these things but elements of the new age were already present in the Edwardian era.[70]

In 1910 Esher had also begun to lose his sense of proportion about the monarchy. Before he had managed a certain amount of detachment. For example, in the 1890s he was able to poke fun at the monarchy by repeating an account of the death of Queen Caroline, George II's consort. Sir Robert Walpole had asked the archbishop of Canterbury to assist at the queen's deathbed. The queen's daughter resisted and Walpole had replied:

> Pray, Madam, let this farce be played: the Archbishop will act it very well. You may bid him be as short as you will. It will do the Queen no hurt, no more than any good; and it will satisfy all the wise and good fools, who will call us atheists if we don't pretend to be as great fools as they are.[71]

But without a hint of irony in May 1910 at the death of Edward VII Esher made a similar request, noting in his journal:

> I was so anxious that the Archbishop should be in the Palace, that I ventured to ring up his chaplain at Lambeth and suggest his return. Apart from all other reasons, convention to a Monarchy has such powerful meanings.[72]

This was possibly a convention that it would have been better to abandon. The king, unlike his mother, had never been a very religious man. He had ignored Gladstone's advice about giving up gambling and Randall Davidson's advice about giving up his mistresses. Perhaps Esher imagined himself an enlightened cynic bowing to the superstitions of the masses in calling the archbishop to the king's deathbed. But the new era, guided by Lytton Strachey and others, was to be increasingly intolerant of religious hypocrisy. There was a hint of farce in calling the archbishop to be present at the death of King Edward which Esher failed to see. This was an element in Esher's estrangement from the new age and it heralds the loss of his former influence.

In May 1910 the editor of *The Times* asked Esher for an appreciation of the late king and John Murray wanted one for *The Quarterly Review*.[73] Esher's article, 'The Character of King Edward', appeared in *The Quarterly* for June 1910.[74] Again Esher referred to the king's character as that dramatically useful point at which he could be shown to be a mere mortal, with whom everyone could identify, occupying a throne that no one could reach. Although the king had been a charming man, he did not have the shrewd insights decades of uninspired yet constant application to work had produced in his mother. Esher argued that the source of the king's influence was his charm.

> No one ever left the King's presence without a sense of his own increased importance in the worldly scale of things. It was the power of raising a man in his own estimation, which was the mainspring of the King's influence.

It is hard to believe that this charm amounted to a very formidable influence over ministers. Esher claimed that it did. He went a bit too far when he argued that the king's 'personal magnetism' and charm were national assets 'worth more to us in our King than the military genius of Napoleon or the diplomatic gifts of a Metternich'.[75]

Esher wrote this appreciation of the dead king, as he did his other works on constitutional monarchy after the turn of the century, in the light of gathering political controversy about the rights and privileges of the dignified parts of the constitution. Beginning with Lloyd George's 1909 Budget and lasting until the beginning of the war in the summer of 1914, a prolonged crisis disrupted domestic politics in Britain. The Liberal government became engaged in increasingly heated controversy with its Conservative opposition over its legislative proposals. This crisis formed a backdrop to Esher's published work.[76] *The Letters of Queen Victoria* (1907), *Queen Victoria's Journals* (1909), 'The Character of King Edward' (1910), *The Girlhood of Queen Victoria* (1912), all these publications made the case for the sovereign's possessing a wise controlling force in the constitution. Esher frankly admitted that he wanted his research to play a role in prompting contemporary statesmen. At a time when the Liberal government was promising to abolish the veto of the House of Lords, disestablish the Church in Wales and perhaps humiliate the Crown by forcing the sovereign to create an unprecedented number of Liberal peers, Esher's books have to be seen as making a conservative case, if not in fact a Conservative and Unionist case, for the retention of traditional power in the hereditary and non-democratic parts of the constitution.

Esher was not as influential at the court of George V as he had been at the court of Edward VII.[77] However, he was still received and listened to, he was still invited to Balmoral, he still saw the leaders of both political parties and passed on what he learned to the king's private secretaries. Down to 1913, in both his published work and his advice to the king, Esher adhered to Bagehot's view of the sovereign's powers. The king could remonstrate with his ministers in private, but ministers must take responsibility for all the king's public actions. Therefore the king could not intervene and try to resolve increasing political strife between the two parties without the cover of ministerial advice. Esher wished the monarchy's reserve powers and the influence of the sovereign to be respected; but he recognized that George V's options were limited when political animosity between the two parties was running so high.

Even in the autumn of 1913, when civil war seemed to threaten because the Liberals intended to follow through on their promise to grant limited Home Rule to Ireland, while Unionists were resolved to resist it, Esher told the king that he could not intervene in the dispute between the two parties. He had to accept the advice of his Liberal ministers who possessed a majority in Parliament. In a memorandum to the king, Esher again chose a line of Bagehot's to make his point: 'the King would have to sign his own death warrant, if it was presented to him for signature by a Minister commanding a majority in Parliament'.[78]

Then, as the possibility of civil war appeared to grow into a certainty, something snapped. Esher gave up the Bagehotian position and proffered more extreme advice. He told the king's private secretary that the Liberal government should be dismissed by the king and that some neutral statesman, like Lord Rosebery, should be called in to hold the balance between the parties until an election could be held on the issue of Home Rule.[79] Such a dramatic intervention on the part of the king had always been the advice of hard-liners and extremists in the Unionist ranks.[80] Now Esher joined the ranks of the extremists.

The suggestion to call in Rosebery was almost laughable. He had not been a tremendous success when he was prime minister briefly in 1895 and no one believed he could do a good job in such a crisis. Even though the king had militant Tories among his best friends, there is no evidence that he seriously planned to dismiss the Liberal government. In any case, he ignored Esher's advice.

World War I came before the crisis in Ireland could be settled and the problem was shelved. Esher went off to France, acting as an informal liaison between the generals of the British and French armed forces. He continued to espouse his newly extremist views. He was disgusted by politicians' interference in the generals' conduct of the war. In 1916 he put forward the startling proposition that it was better to trust one's fate to kings and emperors one has known since birth than democratic politicians who only happened to possess power for the moment.[81] But kings and emperors annoyed him too. Toward the end of the war he had an interview with Randall Davidson, archbishop of Canterbury. Davidson thought King George and Queen Mary were undoubtedly virtuous, but they failed to grasp changes in the world around them. Esher agreed. Later the same day he called at Buckingham Palace and discovered 'The same routine. A life made up of nothings – yet a busy scene: constant telephone messages about trivialities.'[82]

In 1918 he criticized the court for preventing the Russian royal family from finding a safe refuge in Britain after the revolution. In a letter to Lord Stamfordham of unusual candor he blamed the king and his private secretary for the Tsar's death. He wrote his son Maurice and put the matter more bluntly still: 'There is as much weakness there [Buckingham Palace] as at Tsarskoe Selo.'[83]

Like Gladstone in old age, Esher kept his bitterness about the court largely to himself and a few old friends. For the public who had read his earlier books on the monarchy, he took a more consistent line. In 1918 he published *After the War* and admitted that the war had ended the world he loved.

> War has loosed new and volcanic forces. It has swept away the process – slow, broadening from precedent to precedent – that our fathers found so dignified and becoming. 'Cabinet' government, with its unrecorded mysteries, is no more. Old names survive, but they have lost their meaning. An avalanche of women has been hurled into the political chaos. Institutions as well as ideas will have to be re-sorted.[84]

But he hoped that the monarchy would at least be retained. Like Bagehot he hoped Britain would avoid the 'evils' attendant upon the American style of elective government.

His affinities with Bagehot and Gladstone in other respects are also marked. Like them he had a significant impact on the evolution of constitutional monarchy in Britain. He brought rehearsals, stage management and theatrical professionalism to ceremonial. His ceremonies were visual sensations that heightened the monarchy's prestige. They reinforced ideas about social hierarchy at the same time as they acknowledged the spreading of power down the social scale, for example, by the queen's taking a processional route for the first time south of the river. He adapted the monarchy's ceremonial to the imperial preoccupations of the era and heightened the dignity of the empire as well. Indeed, inadvertently he may have helped the military domination, which some parts of the empire entailed, become more palatable to a country with a strong libertarian tradition. When the empire was yoked to a sovereign whose power was fading away, it was easy to forget how much power over subject peoples the empire involved.

Esher's publications were also influential. He presented the historical evidence in *The Letters of Queen Victoria* that the queen and her husband had made useful contributions to the development of representative government. He was the first to understand how dramatizing the sovereign's character as a kind of august ordinariness could make such a powerful appeal to an expanding democracy. This was especially true at a time when politicians were increasingly framing their proposals as in the interests of ordinary people and opposed to the interests of privileged groups.

Yet his political plans often failed. The colonial premiers were not persuaded by the panoply of the diamond jubilee. Esher loved the landed aristocracy, but the House of Lords lost its power and old family names 'lost their meaning'. Partly by the ingenuity of his opponents, partly by the palace's habit of opting for cautious inaction, partly by chance, the extremist ideas of Esher and men like him before the war were never acted upon. Esher did not see how heightening the monarchy's prestige and restating ideas about hereditary privilege in a ceremonial context gave those ideas antique authority but also rendered them slightly amusing. Like an old black and white newsreel before a modern movie, monarchy and aristocracy came to be seen as historically authentic, yet faintly degraded as varieties of mere entertainment.

Esher always had trouble drawing the line. As a young radical he disapproved of the stranglehold of the hereditary principle on land, but he adored balls at Marlborough House. As an old reactionary, he held the British royal family responsible for the murder of the Tsar, but he asked working men returning from the trenches to retain constitutional monarchy in Britain. One reason he had the success he had may well have been that his confusion was typical. Of course it is risky to draw conclusions about national character from the mind of a single man. It is tempting though to conclude that, because he encapsulated such a characteristic combination of 'reverence and resentment'[85] for the monarchy, it was his vision of the court that proved so compelling. Perhaps the nation as a whole was drawn to the monarchy precisely because a broad cross-section of people was at once attracted and repelled by the social exclusivity it represented.

When Queen Victoria drove away from St Paul's in June of 1897 and crossed to the working-class side of the river, Esher had helped the monarchy enter a new era. It was an era Esher only half understood. Aristocratic equerries, Indian troopers and the queen herself clip-clopped into Kennington, half fearing the people lining the streets and receiving polite applause. Did they know, did even Esher know, that the applause was given because working people respected age and service at the same time that they rejected as impossible, even laughable, a renewal of the politics of privilege and rank?

4 Randall Davidson: Quietness, Compromise, Comprehension

The central part of every important royal ceremony between 1861 and 1914 was a religious service. No clergyman in that half century played a greater role in both planning and officiating at such services than Randall Thomas Davidson. First as chaplain to Archbishop Tait, then as chaplain to Queen Victoria, and ultimately as archbishop himself, Davidson won places of great influence at court and in the Church of England. Under Lord Esher's influence, it was distinctly possible that ceremonial could have been transformed into pure theater. Davidson made sure that the religious acts that lay at the center of royal ceremonies were not forgotten. In shaping the character and quality of those acts, Davidson re-established the relevance of the monarchy to a critical age. His services and his sermons conveyed a rationale for retaining a hereditary monarchy in a democratic and increasingly secular state.

A telling glimpse of Davidson's personality can be had by comparing two memoranda he wrote for himself nine years apart in 1901 and 1910. In January 1901 Queen Victoria lay on her deathbed, her breathing heavy and difficult, surrounded by her family, maids, doctors and chaplains. On one side of the bed knelt her physician, Sir James Reid, occasionally administering oxygen. On the other side, helping to hold the queen up so she could breathe more easily, knelt the German kaiser, her grandson. As the winter evening came on Davidson, then bishop of Winchester, led the crowded room in hymns and prayer. He gave a blessing

> at the very moment that she quietly drew her last breath, the whole Family being present in the room. This was just after 6:30 . . .
>
> We left the Family alone for a few minutes. Then the King came out alone. I was in the passage and was the first to greet him as Sovereign.[1]

He was at home with the queen's family, and they were at home with him. He was a source of good conversation or quiet consolation as the occasion required. Neither preachy nor puritanical, he was broad-minded and could discuss either hunting or the hereafter with equal plausibility and charm. Nine years later Lord Esher asked him to be present once again as Edward VII lay dying in Buckingham Palace. Davidson, by this time archbishop of Canterbury, said

> the Commendatory Prayer, and a few moments afterwards he [the king] simply ceased to breathe. I have seldom or never seen a quieter passing of the river . . . The family remained alone for a few minutes, then the Prince of Wales, now King, came out, and I was the first person to greet him as Sovereign. This was exactly what had happened with his father at the bedroom door at Osborne when Queen Victoria died.[2]

It is a little jarring to find him ready and waiting at the bedroom door, just as he had done at the death of Queen Victoria. Sometimes he was a little too anxious to take his place in history, a little too eager to make his mark. Yet in the course of a long and fruitful career he repeatedly gambled his good favor at court and risked displeasing members of the royal family in order to secure the higher interests of the monarchy. Davidson was a curious mixture of selflessness and ambition. His repeated willingness to surrender position and prestige for the greater good of the monarchy went along with a pure delight in the company of princes and important politicians. He wanted to prevent people from using the monarchy for their own personal gain and so possibly injure the monarchy's nonpartisan reputation. At the same time, he advanced his own career by capitalizing on his connections to the court. Davidson was a sensible and canny archbishop who ended by helping the monarchy and hurting himself.

He was born in 1848 the son of Scottish Presbyterians. His father was a timber merchant who inherited a country estate when his son was nine. Davidson's mother was from a landed family prominent in Berwickshire. Just as Esher's parents were ambitious for their son and Esher was the first of his family to be sent to Eton, so too with Davidson, who was the first of his family to be sent to Harrow. There Davidson was confirmed in the Church of England. This was both natural and useful for a boy whose parents sometimes attended Anglican services and who wanted to fit in with his contemporaries. Even as a schoolboy Davidson took a keen pleasure in mixing with those who seemed to be marked out for success in later life. Originally placed in one of the smaller houses to board, he persuaded his father to move him into a bigger house presided over by the charismatic clergyman, B. F. Westcott, destined as Davidson himself was for higher office in the Church. Davidson wrote his father: 'I have been feeling lately, more than I ever did before, a craving for the society and companionship of other fellows well up in the school, and desire for *intellectual* friends *in the house . . .*' He was no intellectual himself, but early on he was prepared to enter into elaborate and delicate negotiations, setting out for his father all the possible methods of effecting the move to improve his position.[3]

Davidson as a young man was sensible, not particularly holy and a good shot. He and his brothers enjoyed the sport on their father's estate. During the summer holidays of 1866 Davidson and some friends were returning to the house after shooting when an accident happened. One of the guns went off by mistake. The shot hit Davidson in the bottom. His recovery was slow and painful. He felt well enough to go up to Oxford in 1867, but he suffered from a variety of debilitating ailments. He was deeply disappointed when he was only able to obtain a third class degree. Nevertheless, he was well enough to travel. He visited Italy, Egypt and Palestine. He began to study for ordination and mixed his studies with more shooting parties in Scotland. His official biographer is a little mysterious about Davidson's desire to be ordained, saying only that Davidson thought of it as one of his earliest wishes.[4] Afterwards what he remembered best about this period was the guns rather than the theology.

> The fact that we had a great deal of partridge-shooting, and that I became a first-rate shot and was consequently invited to all kinds of rather select shooting-parties, uplifted me at the time, and dented my memory with thoughts which live and breathe for me still.[5]

He later concluded that being a good shot gave him something to talk about, man to man, with politicians who otherwise might have dismissed a bishop as a seer and an eccentric.

After ordination, he went as a curate not to a comfortable rural parsonage, but to bleak Dartford, a poor district not far from London's southeastern sprawl. There he apparently worked hard and earned the respect of the local people. After three years in Dartford his Oxford friendship with Craufurd Tait won him a coveted place in the very center of the Church's affairs. Davidson went in 1877 as chaplain to his friend's father, Archibald Campbell Tait, archbishop of Canterbury.

A family crisis coincided with Davidson's arrival at Lambeth; Craufurd Tait died in 1878. Davidson quickly became a member of the family, an indispensable private secretary and surrogate son to the archbishop, suitor and then husband of the archbishop's daughter, Edith Tait. Davidson loved working in Lambeth Palace. He was delighted with the important people he was getting to know. He told his father that he was enjoying his work 'hugely and making many new friends'. In a postscript he allowed himself to boast that he was just off 'to coach Lord Beaconsfield's secretary in the working of the Public Worship Regulation Act'.[6] Davidson also learned a good deal about ecclesiastical affairs and made reasonable estimates of the

1. King George III at St Paul's in 1789 (*Illustrated London News*, 24 February 1872).

2. 'The Crowd Illuminated' (*Graphic*, 6 March 1872).

3. (*above*) 'The Thanksgiving Day: A Rough Corner' (*Illustrated London News*, 9 March 1872).

4. (*left*) Rehearsal for the Diamond Jubilee in front of St Paul's (*Illustrated London News*, 19 June 1897).

5. (*above*)
Queen Victoria's
Diamond Jubilee
Thanksgiving
Service in front of
St Paul's Cathedra
22 June 1897 (*The
Royal Archives*).

6. (*left*)
The Nave,
Westminster
Abbey, arranged
for the Coronatior
of King Edward V
1902 (*The Royal
Archives*).

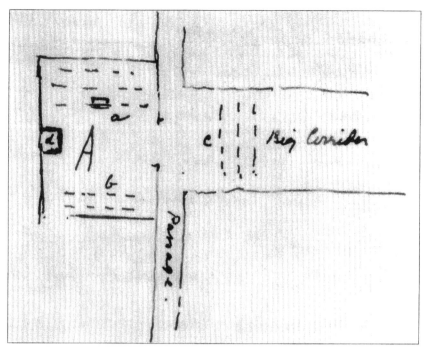

7. Davidson's sketch of Divine Service at Osborne, 1883 (*Lambeth Palace Library*).

8. Queen Victoria's Funeral Procession through London, January 1901 (*The Royal Archives*)

9. 'His Majesty assisting Dr Temple to rise from his knees after paying fealty' (*Illustrated London News*, 16 August 1902).

10. F. Temple, Archbishop of Canterbury, R. Davidson, Bishop of Winchester, and W. Maclagan, Archbishop of York, 1902 (*The Royal Archives*)

11. Procession in Whitehall to the Lying in State of King Edward VII (*Illustrated London News*, 21 May 1910).

12. Lying in State of King Edward VII, Westminster Hall (*Illustrated London News*, 21 May 1910).

13. Lying in State of King Edward VII, Westminster Hall, May 1910 (*The Royal Archives*).

14. 'Bouverie King of Arms'
(*Punch*, 25 June 1902).

15. 'Mr Punch holding a Court
of Overflow Claims'
(*Punch*, 25 June 1902).

men who led the Church. He watched Tait closely and took hints from his inclusive, broad churchmanship, which consisted in steering a middle course between evangelical and ritualist extremes. Davidson himself hoped for power and influence; he aimed to emulate Tait.

A new opportunity came Davidson's way as the aging archbishop entered his final illness. The Victorians were obsessed with deathbed scenes, the legacy of the Romantics' interest in spirituality and transcendence. In this, Queen Victoria was more Victorian than most. She also had a weakness for plain-spoken Scots; she was unusually well-disposed to Tait. Davidson came to the queen's notice by sending an account of Tait's last days alive to one of her ladies in waiting. The queen was touched and wanted to know more. She asked Davidson to come and see her in Windsor. Davidson was then a handsome young man with penetrating eyes and bushy sideburns. He told her about the archbishop uttering her name among his last words and the queen was enthralled. Davidson was a plain-spoken Scot himself and the queen had a little weakness for him the moment he opened his mouth. In her diary she wrote:

> Saw Mr. Davidson, the Archbishop's son-in-law, and was seldom more struck than I have been by his personality ... We went over various topics, and I feel that Mr. Davidson is a man who may be of great use to me, for which I am truly thankful.[7]

Within six months, over Gladstone's objections to Davidson's youth and inexperience, the queen had Davidson appointed dean of Windsor.[8] Edward Hamilton, Gladstone's principal private secretary, wrote in his diary: 'It is somewhat ridiculous to give such a church plum to so young a man.' Davidson was 35.

Davidson's job first and foremost was to serve as spiritual adviser to the queen. She had odd ideas and eccentric practices, but Davidson soon learned that she was a simple, devout woman. As an informal interview for the Windsor post, the queen had asked him to Osborne to stay the night and preach the next morning. On arrival he learned that the queen had asked to see him before dressing for dinner. She received him in a small room the Prince Consort had used as a dressing room. There twenty-two years after his death servants still put out hot water for the prince before the dinner hour. Davidson noticed the hot water steaming in a kettle and towels set out on a washing stand before the queen came in and chatted with disarming frankness about Church politics. She said of the new bishop of Truro 'he is too sacerdotal for me' and complained about how her ladies in waiting had all been scheming to get their own pet candidate appointed to fill a vacant Welsh bishopric.[9]

The next morning Davidson learned what the queen expected of her preachers. For the young Davidson this divine service was something of an 'ordeal'. He told his father:

> Of all the odd ceremonies I ever undertook, it is the oddest. The Queen sometimes goes to Whippingham Church, but not always, and when she does not, there is service in one of the drawing rooms. See the following plan. [See plate 7.] The room A. is a drawing room with folding doors opening at the end of a short corridor. In this room (which is the drawing room we sat in last night) a desk (d) is erected, to be occupied by the officiating Minister.
>
> On his left (a) are the Queen and her family and the ladies and gentlemen of the household. On the right (b) are the upper servants, about a dozen or more. In front, out in the corridor is a big array of liveried footmen and others, about twenty (c). There are no under women-servants present. They go to *Church*.

Rigid class distinction was observed. There was a reduced form of the ordinary service with the queen paying close attention to the text of the officiating minister.

> You may imagine the chilling effect of this sort of service. No music of any sort. A very shortened form of service, and then the sermon. The Queen sitting with a little table in front of her, on which the preacher has placed beforehand his text written out for her use!
>
> I have sometimes found the small chapel service at Addington depressing, but it is enthusiasm itself compared with this Osborne process. And a more chilling audience to whom to wax *eloquent* I cannot imagine. I preached a simple shortish – rather good – written sermon and the whole service which began at *10:45* was over by *11:30*.[10]

Davidson prospered at Windsor. He knew how to cater to the queen's wishes. However, on at least one significant occasion he stood up to her and stopped one of her plans. In 1868 she had published *Leaves from the Journal of Our Life in the Highlands* partly as a way of answering critics who said she did not show herself in public often enough. The book was meant to do the work for her. It was the authentic voice of a widow who remembered better days vacationing in Scotland with an adored husband, far from the responsibilities and routines of London. The book was not a bestseller, but it added to the aura of domestic, even dull ordinariness of her court. It was the forerunner of Richard Cawston's film in 1969 which showed her descendants barbecuing sausages at Balmoral. The film, like the book, was meant to break down barriers and make the monarchy more accessible.

In 1883 when John Brown died, as a way of coping with her sadness, she decided to bring out another selection from the journal, this time covering the years when, after her husband's death, she had grown increasingly attached to her Scottish servant. The publication of *More Leaves from the Journal of a Life in the Highlands* had raised eyebrows, caused titters and revived rumors about her having had a love affair with Brown. One satirical pamphlet made fun of the queen's comments on Brown's physique. Davidson carefully kept the pamphlet, *John Brown's Legs; Or Leaves from a Journal in the Lowlands* among his papers.[11] When the queen began to collect more material, this time for a memoir of Brown she intended to publish, Davidson told her she must stop. His objections were phrased in elaborately deferential, even sycophantic terms, but the queen got the message. She replied that he had given her pain. Davidson stuck to his guns and offered to resign. The queen remained angry with him for a few weeks and then let it drop.[12] Had she been allowed to persist in her plan of keeping the monarchy before the public in a sort of dull travelogue, spiced with familiar references to Brown, who had clearly become more of a companion than a servant, her transformation into a semi-divinity would never have occurred. Davidson took a risk. People who disagreed openly with the queen fell from favor quickly. He had been willing to sacrifice a position he loved in order to save the queen, and the monarchy, from mockery.

The transformation of the queen and the consequent elevation of the monarchy began to occur less by plan, than by hints which people close to the court received of a general desire for giving some public recognition to the length of the queen's reign. A book early in 1886 and a deluge of mail in the autumn persuaded the court that something would have to be done to acknowledge the fiftieth anniversary of the queen's accession.[13] Queen Victoria and Henry Ponsonby decided that a short service at Westminster Abbey, based on the plan of the 1872 thanksgiving, would meet the public demand.[14] Davidson may have been ambitious and a bit of a toadie, but he also helped to channel the public demand for celebration into thoughtful and religious paths. The queen disliked national days of prayer. She liked heartfelt religion, not prayers commanded by the cabinet. But Davidson helped persuade her that a form of service should be approved by her, sanctioned by the Privy Council and distributed for use in parish churches around the country to commemorate the jubilee.[15] If the nation were to come together for the jubilee, it needed a common form of worship, recommended but not commanded by authority, so phrased as to allow for local differences in practice, tradition and doctrine. In the latter part of the eighteenth century these forms of service had been commanded and distributed by the government as a matter of course. Since that time, the practice had been stopped. In 1887 the government was disinclined to command any religious observance and the only means of cheap printing and distribution was through the Society for the Promotion of Christian Knowledge. Nevertheless, after the announcement of the queen's intention of going to Westminster Abbey, requests poured into Lambeth Palace for forms of service – not just from loyalist clergymen, but from laymen and working people as well.[16] Davidson helped the archbishop meet these requests. The emphasis was not on a command to be loyal, but on an appeal to unity, an invitation to consensus.

Davidson proposed a few ideas for the service in the Abbey to the queen's private secretary. One of his ideas was to insert Handel's 'Hallelujah Chorus' in the musical arrangements. Ponsonby rejected this as 'unnecessary and hackneyed'.[17] The exchange points up a contrast between aristocratic whigs, like the Greys and the Ponsonbys, who dominated Queen Victoria's court in the early years after the Prince Consort's death, and the younger men like Davidson, Esher and Arthur Bigge, who rose to influence in the later 1880s and 1890s. The older generation, like Queen Victoria herself, disliked triumphalism, state and showiness. Mary Ponsonby, who was related to the Greys, wrote her husband in the 1870s that 'glitter' annoyed the older aristocracy and real intellectuals, but that most other people loved it.[18] Both Ponsonbys were surprised that Lord Salisbury had allowed the Indian Viceroy to put on such a showy durbar in 1877 to mark the queen's becoming empress of India. The younger men, on the other hand, had a taste for magnificence. As she got older Queen Victoria let go a little and gave in to this newer taste. Gladstone criticized the jubilee in 1897 as political advertising for the tory party, even though he himself had given the movement its start by reviving the large-scale state ceremony of 1872. In 1887 although there was a grand service in the Abbey, Ponsonby held the line against the Hallelujah Chorus. He and the queen opted for the simpler setting of the Prince Consort's *Te Deum* instead.

Even though there was a gap between the generations in their attitudes to royal ceremonial, there were also distinct continuities in the way they judged the success of large royal events in the capital. A few days after the service in the Abbey, Davidson wrote a letter to the queen. 'Congratulation not merely on the great event which has evoked this outburst of loyalty, but also on the *manner* in which the people of England and Scotland, and indeed of the Empire, have given expression to their enthusiasm and loyal love.'[19] Gladstone and the queen had heaved a similar sigh of relief about the behavior of the crowds in 1872. It was as if they all expected an outbreak of football hooliganism every time the working classes had a holiday in London. Large royal spectacles had a way of bringing the nation together, but also keeping the lines of social demarcation plain. While they allayed upper-class fears about the future of the monarchy and the safety of democracy, they also remained potentially disorderly shows of working-class strength. The crowds in the streets were reassuring and threatening at the same time.

Queen Victoria loved Davidson dearly. She could sit quietly with him and have little talks about life after death. She had delicious ideas about all the friends and relations she would meet in heaven and Davidson was loathe to disappoint her. Thus, it came as something of a surprise when, two years after the 1887 jubilee, she began to hear hints that Davidson might like to leave her and be named to a bishopric. Wounded, she began to have her first doubts about him, wondering in December of 1889 whether he was 'an ambitious man'.[20] He certainly was ambitious, but even Gladstone, who was a good judge of clerical aptitude, had concluded early on that Davidson had merit and was sure 'to go up'.[21] She decided she was prepared to let him go as long as he stayed somewhere close to Windsor. She intrigued to get him the see of Winchester, but Lord Salisbury put his foot down and refused to give so high a place to such a young man. After a tantrum, the queen gave in and permitted his being given Rochester instead.[22] She warned Davidson not to get overly inflated-notions of his dignity in the new position. She confessed that she found bishops seldom remained 'what they were before'. For one thing, she told him, they were worse preachers: 'The whole atmosphere of a cathedral and its surroundings, the very dignity itself which accompanies a bishopric, seems to hamper their freedom of speech.'[23] She understood rather precisely that her own appeal lay in a sort of dignified simplicity. She rued the fact that promotion in the Church sometimes made decent young clergymen into pompous old men.

Although Davidson was anxious to be promoted, he maintained, at least with the queen, the plainness she so much liked in him. Soon he was translated to Winchester. If the queen had had her way, he would even have had Canterbury as early as 1896. But once again Lord Salisbury refused to hear of it.[24] Davidson managed to keep in touch with the court and was on the spot as preparations for the queen's diamond jubilee began to go forward. As with the celebrations ten years earlier, Davidson made sure that the ceremony had religious themes and not just simply secular and patriotic ones. As soon as the queen agreed, rather reluctantly, that some sort of public ceremony was going to have to be held to meet the renewed demand for celebration, there had been talk of an outdoor religious service at St Paul's. Lord Salisbury's original idea was to have a brief service so that religion would not be overlooked in the celebration. His private secretary, Schomberg McDonnell, and Arthur Bigge had expanded on the original idea, making more elaborate and baroque additions to Salisbury's suggestion. They even considered taking the queen's carriage inside and up the nave of the cathedral.[25] As talks went on, A. J. Balfour and the Prince of Wales raised serious objections. As usual the queen wanted a short service, very short. There was no question of the hour-long service Gladstone had insisted on as a minimum in 1872. They doubted whether so brief a service would match the magnificence of the day. The general feeling was that the focal point of national religion should be on the Sunday before the jubilee, when the queen would give thanks unmolested and away from the London crowds in Windsor.[26] On the jubilee day itself, a Tuesday, the queen might confine her activities to a purely secular carriage drive through London.

Just as Esher rejected the idea that the focal point of the celebration could be anywhere else but at St Paul's, Davidson knocked on the head the idea that religion might be omitted altogether from the jubilee day. He urged his point of view on one of the queen's private secretaries.[27] When he had to be absent from one of the committee meetings called to discuss the form of celebration, he wrote a sharp note to the new archbishop, Frederick Temple, telling him that it was 'imperative' that the religious service 'be *short* (very short!) *in all*, both because the Queen would I know desire it so, and because of the possibility of bad weather'.[28] He worked out a compromise announcement with Arthur Bigge that the service at St Paul's would be given out not as the 'objective' of the queen's drive through London – for which a 20-minute service he agreed would be inadequate – but as an 'incident' on the day. In the end he got his point accepted that it was essential 'to mark the religious recognition of the national demonstration'.[29]

Mounted soldiers with breastplates had to stop on their march, colonial premiers had to get down from their dress landaus. Together they took part in a form of service that suggested pride will be humbled and that there was a dominion next to which the British empire looked small. The service was a counterpoint to the stridency of the patriotism prevalent in late-Victorian Britain. It called for calm and reflection in the midst of all the shouting.

Queen Victoria's cousin, the grand duchess of Mecklenburg-Strelitz was not convinced. In a letter to the future Queen Mary she wrote: 'No! that out of door Service before St Pauls! . . . has one ever heard of such a thing! after 60 years Reign, to thank God in the Street!!!'[30] And Davidson himself had some second thoughts about the monarchy in the queen's diamond jubilee year. He veered back and forth between sycophancy and deciding that the aging queen had lost her senses. She had a new favorite in her Indian servant, Abdul Karim. She made him a few gifts, gave him a little cash and allowed him to live in tied cottages on her estates. This was enough to outrage her Household, who thought Karim was a scoundrel. Davidson told the queen's doctor, Sir James Reid, that she was 'off her head' about Karim.[31] This did not stop Davidson from writing the queen one of his oilier letters in May that same year. He told her that the jubilee year would 'inspire and stir, most deeply of all, the hearts of those of us whose high privilege it has been to be allowed a nearer access and a closer relationship of personal service to the Sovereign . . .'[32] By overcoming objections to the open-air *Te Deum* Davidson helped make national religion and the monarchy more accessible to a wider audience; even if the space in front of St Paul's was restricted, there was something undeniably democratic in taking the religious service out of the choir and holding it in plain view under a blue sky. At the same time as he served the future interests of the Church and the Crown, broadening their popular appeal, there was something demoralizing in the role he was forced to play, and admittedly enjoyed playing, as courtier clergyman.

In the autumn after her diamond jubilee Queen Victoria began to think more definitely about death. She dictated instructions to the Prince of Wales and Princess Beatrice saying: 'I wish not to be laid out in State and my Funeral to be simple and with as little pomp as possible.'[33] She had three years to wait and kept up her strength well into the autumn of 1900. After she died in January 1901, Davidson comforted and annoyed members of the royal family. He held three religious services in the room where the queen had died. Her body lay there surrounded by flowers and draped with her wedding veil as Davidson said prayers. In the last service, he administered the Sacrament to the new king and the German kaiser who knelt together side by side. This was not enough to temper a burst of anger from the volatile German emperor. Meaning to be helpful but uninvited, Davidson had accompanied the kaiser, the new queen and Reid to interview the undertaker's assistant, who had forgotten to bring the queen's coffin with him from London. The kaiser blew up at the undertaker's man. According to Davidson the kaiser 'frightened the poor fellow into helpless obedience'.[34] After this was over and Davidson had left the room, the kaiser turned his wrath on the bishop of Winchester. He told Reid 'If I were dead and my pastor came in the room like that he would be hauled out by the neck and shot in the courtyard!'[35]

The British royal family was milder and less authoritarian than their

German cousins. However, it was impossible for them to keep the queen's funeral as calm and quiet as she had wished. Lord Esher saw that, once again, the demand for a public demonstration in London would be inescapable.[36] Requests for some officially-sanctioned religious service once again arrived in bundles at Lambeth Palace. Davidson helped meet this demand and facilitate the archbishop's request for official approval from the new king.[37] There was a military procession through London, dressed not in black, but in purple as she had requested, but bigger and grander than she would have liked, as her coffin was transferred from the railway station where it arrived from the Isle of Wight, to Paddington for the trip to Windsor. A photograph of the queen's funeral procession through London conveys some of the interest and eeriness of the day. The crowds on both sides of the street are deep and the bare winter trees are full of overcoated onlookers who have climbed into the branches for a better view. [See plate 8.] In Windsor there was a service at St George's, which she had specifically ruled against, in order to accommodate all the royalties and personages who wished to be present. At last, she had her quiet interment next to the Prince Consort in the Mausoleum at Frogmore. She lay there undisturbed until 1991, when vandals broke into the Mausoleum. They tried – unsuccessfully – to open the heavy granite sarcophagus, damaging it slightly, and fled into the Home Park.

Davidson made his most important contributions to the establishment of the modern monarchy in 1902, 1910 and 1911. With Esher he was one of the principal architects of the coronation of Edward VII in August 1902. He suggested and spoke at King Edward's lying in state eight years later in 1910. He crowned King George V and Queen Mary in June of 1911. The common thread that runs though all three is Davidson's insistence that pride and celebration be tempered with quietness and contemplation.

In January 1902 *The Times* reprinted Davidson's New Year's letter to his diocese in which he referred to the coming coronation. He said:

> It would be calamitous if the splendour and dignity of the pageant were to divert people's minds from its essential and inherent character as a solemn religious act, the expression of an Empire's corporate loyalty to the King of Kings and Lord of Lords.[38]

The coronation represented a recognition that the government of the nation was a sacred responsibility. This sacred responsibility was the burden not only of the king but of even the smallest town or parish official:

> The people of a Christian empire deliberately set themselves, at such an hour, to acclaim the sacredness of a civil ruler's responsibility, and in so doing to declare how, in its measure and place, the trust of every public

office, political, judicial, magisterial, municipal, parochial, is a profoundly sacred thing.[39]

Davidson took the opportunity of a preaching engagement at Cambridge University to speak on the same topic. The coronation was a national act in which the nation declared its 'fealty to Christ'. In his emphasis on religious nationalism Davidson echoed Gladstone's conception of the thanksgiving in 1872. In his imperialism, however, Davidson was very unlike Gladstone. In the same sermon, he reflected on the late queen's jubilees. He noted that they had impressed the idea of the empire on the people at large more effectively than 'those who devised the pageants had dared to expect'.[40] This is the less pleasant side of Davidson, the side of him that saw the jubilees as a useful spur to imperial enlistment in the Boer War. *The Times* put the point even more crudely.

Sentiment which overrides reason is amongst the most dangerous forces in modern politics, but the masses of men will never suffer or die, as Englishmen have suffered and died in the struggle we are still waging, for a cause or an ideal which does not stir their blood.[41]

Although Davidson was not untainted by the militaristic imperialism widespread among the Edwardian upper classes, he also had a few saving graces. He wanted the people at large to think about the coming coronation, but he also wanted those in the narrower political world to consider it as well. There were three political problems involved in staging an ancient coronation ceremony under modern conditions. Only careful advance preparation would provide the solutions. First, there was the anomaly of Indian representatives, 'aliens in race and faith', who would stand with Christian officials in Westminster Abbey in June. How was this anomaly to be resolved? His impulse was to reach out and embrace them. The empire was only worth having so long as, like a broad church, it was based on a respect for differences in culture and creed.

Second, among the regal ornaments presented to the king at his coronation would be a jewelled sword symbolizing warfare and justice. How was justice to be done as the Boer War drew to a close in South Africa, where Christian rule had to be administered over Britons, Boers, and black South Africans alike? If the empire were based only on armed troops in dusty colonial outposts, the whole thing would collapse. The coronation was a useful reminder that fundamentally the empire was based on a will to keep the peace and be fair.

Third, the domestic problem of popular education was then being debated because of the Unionists' education legislation. Here, there could be no compromise: every child in the kingdom had to have a Christian upbringing.[42] This was a more partisan solution than he had proposed for the other two problems. He certainly sympathized with the Unionists' support for the established Church in the education debates. Here too, though, Davidson was only arguing that children's education should have ethical and moral components. The Church, he claimed, was as well-suited to that task as the coronation was fitted to keep ethical and moral questions, framed on a broad non-doctrinal basis, before the public.

Davidson had help preparing the coronation service from a liturgical scholar and canon of Westminster Abbey, John Armitage Robinson. The two men delved deep into ecclesiastical records with the idea of returning to an older, simpler form of service. The king rejected their first draft, just as his mother would have, as 'too long'.[43] Once they had reduced the service and satisfied the king, they made a point of trying to make their arcane scholarship accessible to a broader public. Armitage Robinson spoke on Easter Sunday in Westminster Abbey about the ceremony planned for June. The coronation service, he said, represented the continuity of English history. It had been in use for more than a thousand years. The changes which he and the bishop of Winchester had made amounted to a return in places 'to the older, briefer language and a reduction of the verbose expansions of the end of the seventeenth century'. He noted that 'every change' had been 'justified by some earlier precedent'. He emphasized that the coronation service was a consecration of the sovereign consciously modelled on the consecration service for a bishop. The king was in early English history spoken of as a *persona mixta*, part clerical and part lay. In the modern age the 'mixed person' of the sovereign would help to remind everyone of the king's unique position in relation to the Church. The monarchy combined sacred and secular functions. The coronation service was not a mere spectacle of this world, but a call to contemplate the higher claims of a world beyond.[44] Armitage Robinson's points were in line with those Davidson had made earlier in the year. It was all part of the same attempt to meet anticipated public interest in the coming ceremony with informative, comprehensible statements about its significance.

The coronation was scheduled for 26 June 1902. Two days beforehand the king developed appendicitis. Feverish and resisting to the last any delay in the ceremony, he was laid out on a billiard table at Buckingham Palace, arms flailing, as the doctors administered anesthetic.[45] They removed his appendix and ordered him to be quiet. The king's staff asked Davidson to help reschedule and further abbreviate the coronation service. They also invited him to stay for a few days with the king while he recuperated on his yacht.

Davidson feared for the future of the Victorian monarchy in King Edward's hands. Power had dwindled away from the throne and detailed attention to personal behavior now counted for so much in the monarchy's popularity, indeed in its reason for existing, that he doubted very much whether a gambler and adulterer king could command much respect. He risked offending the king by having a few talks with him about responsibility and conduct. There they both were on the yacht anchored in the Solent: the adept bishop delicately hinting to the king about how much the English people expected from him. The one longed to have a worthy example of self-sacrifice in a conspicuous place; the other wondered whether he might possibly have a little restorative champagne. The king did not resent Davidson's interference. Others had tried and failed to reform him after his illness in 1871. He had settled the matter in his mind years ago and did not intend to change now. Perhaps he had a better sense than his advisers of the popular appeal in a little honest self-indulgence. But Davidson deserves some credit for once more telling the sovereign straight that the best-loved princes were those who perversely resisted a few of the temptations inevitably offered up to them.[46]

The coronation itself, held only seven weeks after the king's surgery, was quiet, pared down, watched by fewer people in the streets, pervaded by a chastened mood. Once more at a critical moment for the monarchy, King Edward had nearly died. The event made the monarchy a renewed focus of seriousness. While Davidson tried to teach the king to look for possible long-term lessons of the illness, others took similar messages to their pulpits. The bishop of London argued that the coronation before the king's illness would have been 'too much a great show' and 'too little a great national Sacrament'. The bishop of Southampton said 'that we had been too much absorbed in thoughts of Imperial greatness and earthly prosperity'.[47] Like Davidson they wanted humbleness and humility on state occasions to accompany the inevitable brass bands.

The postponed ceremony was filled with minor mishaps. George Kennion, bishop of Bath and Wells, had to tell the king several times to slow down as they walked in procession up the nave toward the choir.[48] The boys of Westminster School, who were meant to greet the king's arrival in the choir with '*Vivat Rex Edwardus!*' shouted their *Vivats* early and had to repeat them.[49] When the king reached the altar, the archbishop of Canterbury took charge. The octogenarian archbishop was feeble and in poor health. He kept his place in the ceremony by reading from scrolls, held up by Davidson, on which the order of the service had been printed in large type.[50] Davidson hoped that reading from the scrolls would be taken as a practice 'of remote antiquity', but in fact, to Sir Almeric Fitzroy, a member of the coronation committee, it looked 'ridiculous'.[51] The archbishop

complained that Davidson shook the scrolls and made him stumble over
the text.

In the most important part of the service the king gave the coronation
oath, in which he promised to govern according to law enacted by Parliament, to execute justice and to defend the Church of England. As waves
of Handel's massive setting of the anthem 'Zadok the Priest' rolled in
from the choir, the archbishop touched the king with oil and then handed
him a series of jewelled ornaments, the regalia, in return for the promises
he had given in his oath. Finally, the archbishop placed the crown on the
king's head. The bishop of Bath and Wells observed:

> though I suppose it ought not to get out, the Archbishop who could
> not see very well, put on the Crown the wrong way to the front, and,
> endeavouring to alter it, made it worse, and I had to take hold of it
> with one hand . . . and help to put it straight on his head. Someone else
> assisted in this, I think it must have been the Bishop of Winchester. I
> was in mortal terror lest the whole thing should give way, for on the
> previous day I had been carefully instructed by the Keeper of the Regalia,
> how to hold it in both hands, but at the critical moment only one hand
> was available.
>
> The King in rather a low voice, as though to excuse the Archbishop,
> said to me 'It is very difficult to put it on rightly.'

As soon as the king was crowned, in a new twentieth-century touch, the
electric lighting was turned on. The peers put on their coronets, there were
shouts of 'God save the king!' and trumpets sounded. 'This was fortu-
nate', noted the bishop of Bath and Wells, 'for it was during the noise that
we were busy putting the Crown straight'.

> The acclamation ending, the archbishop said: God crown you with a
> crown of glory and righteousness, that having a right faith and mani-
> fold fruit of good works, you may obtain the crown of an everlasting
> kingdom by the gift of him whose kingdom endureth for ever.

Was it wrong to wish for a crown of glory and righteousness upon the
head of an unremarkable, middle-aged man, who ate too much, loved
his wife too little and saved most of his concentration for card games?
It may have been precisely that combination of high hopes and level-
headed expectations that produced such an emotional response in those
who watched the ceremony. Here were lovely words that called for blessings on the head not of an impossibly saintly man, but of an ordinary
one, marked as everyone else was by failures, weaknesses and regrets. It
was the contrast between divinity and imperfection that moved those who

watched and read about the ceremony. Even the archbishop, who had been through dozens of rehearsals for the service and knew what to expect, was overcome. When he knelt down before the king to do homage, his eyes filled with tears. He departed from the formal order of the service saying: 'God bless you, Sir. God be with you, God be with you, Sir.'[52]

A little light comedy followed the archbishop's soliloquy. When he tried to get up, he lost his balance and nearly fell over. The king gave the archbishop his hand. Davidson tried to help too but he nearly pushed the old man over again. An illustration from *The Illustrated London News* shows the king offering the archbishop his hand while Davidson hovers in the background. [See plate 9.] After a few minutes, when the archbishop had regained his feet and wobbled away, Davidson went over to see whether he was all right. The archbishop snapped at him in a ringing voice audible to everyone near the throne 'Go away!'[53]

When it was all over the bishop of Bath and Wells decided what had impressed him most. What persisted was 'a sense . . . of colour', 'exquisite sounds', and 'a mysterious religious awe'. The 'solemnity of the occasion' had 'exceeded all expectations'.[54] Everyone agreed that the success of the service was due to Davidson.[55] A picture preserved in the Royal Archives of Davidson standing behind the archbishops of Canterbury and York, all three in the copes worn at the coronation, hints at his unusual involvement in planning the event. [See plate 10.] His success was in his ability to adapt and compromise: he adapted an old service to the needs of theologians who demanded fidelity to historical detail as well as to those of press men who wanted a short and simple explanation for immediate publication. He preached an unpleasant sermon to the recuperating king in his deckchair overlooking the Solent and he coached the proud archbishop who was jealous of interference. The ceremony that emerged asked everyone not only to celebrate but also to contemplate faith, responsibility, service to the nation and a solemn promise to do better.

Frederick Temple died a few months after the coronation. The prime minister, Arthur Balfour, wrote Davidson to say that his name would be recommended to the king as Temple's successor. Davidson, sitting up in bed recovering from flu, protested his inadequacy and accepted immediately.[56] He had felt cruelly separated from high politics during Temple's primacy. Now he would return to the center of the Church's affairs, just a short carriage ride across the river from Whitehall and Westminster. A. C. Benson saw this when he confided waspishly to his diary:

Randall is *not* a great man: but he is a splendid combination of good sense, good feeling and dutifulness. He is avid of affairs, interesting, stimulating – he is not a mystic or a poet – has no idea that a dreamer of dreams is anything but a fool – and that *he* should be the chief exponent of the religion of Jesus of Nazareth is strange. Randall would have listened to Christ politely, but without interest, and then would have gone back to the Sadducees and arranged a little matter of legislation.[57]

Davidson's love of politics and negotiation went along with a certain partisan blindness to the shifting balance of political forces at Westminster. This blindness led to political defeats that would deeply alienate him from politics and politicians. At the same time he retained a penetrating vision about how the monarchy needed to embrace democracy. As with Bagehot, Gladstone, and Esher, political defeat and alienation went along with marked success in transforming and adapting the monarchy to new, democratic conditions.

Davidson as archbishop consciously cultivated a reputation for evenhandedness and nonpartisanship. At the same time, he had deep conservative instincts. As an old Harrovian, an Oxford man and a prince of the Church, it may have been impossible for him to be otherwise. But he worked hard to acquire a reputation for impartiality. This position had its severest test in the period of political controversy from 1909 to 1914. He repeatedly offered to mediate between the two parties; he ended by offending them both.

In the fall of 1909 a Unionist majority in the House of Lords rejected Lloyd George's 'People's Budget'. As a result the Liberals resolved to reform the upper house and abolish its veto. Davidson abstained from the highly-controversial vote on the budget and most of the bishops followed his lead. In declaring his intention before the vote, he told one of his fellow bishops that half a century before the bishops had 'constantly intervened in partisan political debate'. But, Davidson pointed out, 'It has been less common recently, and I have myself endeavoured to keep clear of that sort of controversy, where no moral question seems to be directly and obviously involved.'[58] Once the vote had been taken, the archbishop defended the ecclesiastical abstention. By adhering to 'an independent standpoint' and by 'sitting loose to party ties' bishops increased their power of intervening on moral, religious, education and social questions.[59]

In January 1910 Davidson offered himself to Knollys as a mediator should the king be placed in a difficult position by the extreme animosity between the two parties aroused by the proposed reform of the upper house.[60] Lord Esher approved. Esher told his son:

The Archbishop was here [Windsor] all day and preached a political sermon in the private chapel. He wrote a very sensible letter to Francis

Knollys offering, should it become necessary, to act as mediator between the two parties. No one would be more suitable.

Esher leaked the idea to the leader of the opposition. He told Balfour that Davidson 'who is no partisan' would be a good mediator; Davidson was 'not brilliant' but had 'plenty of common sense'.[61]

Certainly there were other experienced politicians who thought Davidson was nonpartisan.[62] However, Davidson made statements quite early in the crisis that betrayed his conservative and Unionist inclinations. He had already failed once as a mediator by showing his prejudice in favor of the Unionist opposition to the Liberals' Education Bill in 1906.[63] He was hostile to the Liberals' announced intention of disestablishing the Church in Wales. One who loved the House of Lords as much as Davidson did could only be suspicious, no matter how much he claimed to be impartial, of the Liberals' determination to curb the powers of that house.[64] In January 1910, the same month in which he offered himself as mediator to Knollys, he preached a sermon at Canterbury Cathedral on the election which had just returned the Liberals to power. His message was a conservative message. He praised the continuity of the English constitutional system and implicitly condemned the Liberal threat to swamp the House of Lords with a mass creation of Liberal peers. Such a creation would be an irreparable break with historical continuity. The difference between England and other European nations came down to this, he declared from the pulpit of Canterbury Cathedral:

We have had a continuity of system, and rule, and constitution, and usage, secular and sacred, which has in the main survived for many centuries unimpaired through all sorts of changes in the conditions of the world's life . . . Abundant modifications in details, but the structure, after all, one and the same. No building in England or in Europe offers a more telling object-lesson on those facts than this our own Cathedral.[65]

Davidson used this image of the cathedral as the embodiment of continuous, monumental and sacred English history over and over again in his sermons. When asked to speak on the thirteen-hundredth anniversary of Rochester Cathedral, Davidson did so in a style resonant of Bagehot's description of the dignified parts of the constitution. 'Walk in the gloaming round the aisles and transepts of a great cathedral', Davidson said

and you will see shadows that you cannot explain and dark bits that you do not penetrate – yes, and beauties too of arch and buttress and moulding which owe their glamour and their suggestiveness in no small degree to the fact that they are not standing out in the glare of daylight, or as isolated things, however beautiful, but are parts of a larger and more mysterious whole, whereof it is impossible for us just then to understand aright either the proportion, or the harmonies, or the origin, or the meaning. As with the stone of the building, so in the living history, there are usages and phrases and forms which have become endeared by association and hallowed by sacred memories, and which refuse to limit themselves to the prosaic bounds of common parlance and etymology. But not for that reason have they lost their power.[66]

Admirers of Burke had been using the analogy of the 'ancient building ... an image of endless renewal without loss of identity, of repairs and even additions and improvements entirely compatible with the essential integrity and continuity of the structure' throughout the nineteenth century.[67] Bagehot himself had used it in criticizing Disraeli's Public Worship Regulation Bill in 1874.[68] Both Bagehot and Davidson were making a conservative and romantic plea for preserving unaltered what was old, despite the impossibility of fitting it into a perfectly rational scheme of Church or parliamentary administration. When Davidson commented on the first election of 1910 and hoped that politicians would remain committed to preserving the continuity of the English constitution, he was in fact declaring his hostility to the Liberal program.

In April of 1910 the House of Commons adopted resolutions calling for limits on the power of the upper house. There were rumors of an immediate dissolution, and of ministers extracting an early promise from the king to create the hundreds of peers necessary to push the resolutions, drafted into a bill, though a hostile House of Lords. Davidson began writing letters with dramatic proposals. If Liberal ministers asked for such a promise from the king before dissolving, or if they asked for the creation of peers immediately, Davidson wanted the king to take an unprecedented measure of independent initiative. The king should speak to the public over the heads of the politicians. He should say that he naturally wanted to give effect to their wishes, but that the importance of the contemplated change, the doubling in size of the House of Lords, required that their wishes be clearly expressed. Davidson defended this proposal in an April memorandum which he sent to the king's private secretary:

> If it be said, and said with perfect truth, that for the King to make public some statement of his own position at so critical a moment is unconstitutional and unprecedented, the explanation is obvious, that no such occasion has ever before arisen. If the King is asked, by creating 400 peers to take a wholly unconstitutional step, he must be allowed to speak also in an unprecedented statement.[69]

A truly impartial observer might have noted that the House of Lords had made a habit of wrecking important Liberal legislation ever since the rejection of Gladstone's second Home Rule Bill in 1894 and that the Liberals had been driven to extreme measures under extreme provocation from the Unionist majority in the upper house. Moreover, it was the Conservatives who routinely looked to the sovereign for some dramatic intervention to save them from what they regarded as a tyrannical Liberal majority in the Commons. Indeed, when Davidson's idea was presented in somewhat modified form to the leader of the conservative party, Balfour agreed and said he thought that it would 'add much lustre to the position of sovereign'.[70]

Shortly after Davidson had made his proposal, the king died. Political controversy was set aside. The archbishop turned his attention to consoling the royal family. The new king noted in his diary that all the family gathered 'in darling Papa's room, with him lying in our midst and received the Holy Sacrament, it was very affecting'. Again two days later: 'May and I with the three eldest children went to BP at 7.0 and the Archbishop of Canterbury read a short service, in darling Papa's room, we the family knelt round his bed. We kissed him for the last time.'[71]

Davidson was affected by the royal family's grief, but he also thought of ways to use anticipated public sympathy for the long-term benefit of the monarchy. First he suggested a departure from the tradition of burying dead sovereigns at Windsor. Edward VII should be buried in Westminster Abbey. Davidson argued: 'if it be decided that our beloved King – perhaps the most "popular", in the true sense, of all England's sovereigns – should be laid to rest in the Abbey, it would obviously accord far better with popular sentiment than an interment at Windsor'.[72] Edward VII had mixed with different classes more widely than any recent sovereigns. It may be difficult to imagine this in an age when the sovereign mixes with crowds of bystanders on regular occasions; but through horse-racing, regular outings in London to the theatre and in continental spas Edward VII had had more opportunities of meeting a wider range of persons than his mother ever had. He had developed a 'hail fellow well met' quality. Davidson thought the late king's reputation for geniality and amiability should be turned to account for the monarchy in a service at the Abbey. Such a service would have more impact on the monarchy's sacred and democratic associations than a quiet burial away from the crowds in Windsor.

Davidson's second initiative affected the designation of Queen Alexandra in the Prayer Book and in other official statements. He wanted her referred to not as 'queen dowager', but as 'queen mother'. 'The whole country would welcome the title', Davidson told Francis Knollys, 'and it marks a

relationship which everybody prizes'.[73] Davidson wanted the parallel between the royal family and millions of other families made clear. He also
had in mind the reverence that still surrounded Queen Victoria's maternal
image. The new title would emphasize the maternity of the widowed Queen
Alexandra.

Davidson's larger objective was to invest the royal family with an aura
of democratic domesticity. He preached at Westminster Abbey on the
evening of May 8th, two days after the king's death. He said that, beginning roughly at the time of the queen's first jubilee in 1887, a series of
national events, centering in every case but one on a royal ceremony, had
connected the domestic life of the royal family with the domestic lives
of the widest possible range of the people at large. 'Wide experience',
Davidson said, 'has taught us how it is through the central home and
household of a nation's life – the representative home in which everybody
claims a share – that a trumpet call to the people at large can ring out in
clearest note'. He gave as examples the 'call to thanksgiving' in 1887 and
1897, 'to stern conflict' at the beginning of the Boer War, 'to high enterprise
and hope' at the coronation of Edward VII, and now at his death 'to the
quiet facing of sudden bereavement and loss'.[74] His careful emphasis on
the royal household as a 'representative home' shows his desire to portray
the monarchy as a democratic institution. It was as if voluntary public
loyalty to the throne demonstrated on each of these occasions served as the
equivalent of an election to a seat in Parliament. In short, the royal family
held its place in popular esteem, according to Davidson, because it represented the people. Its reason for continuing to exist was that people
continued to cheer its processions or, without being compelled, they came
to Church when any of its prominent members died.

'Queen mother' was eventually adopted as the designation for Queen
Alexandra, but the royal family declined to have the king buried in the
Abbey. Instead the new king suggested a different departure from precedent, one that would go some way toward recognizing the connection
between the dead king and his people that Davidson had wanted. George
V's idea was for his father to lie in state at St Stephen's Hall in the Palace
of Westminster, just as Gladstone had after his death in 1898. Anybody
who wished might be allowed to file by for several days to look at his
coffin before the official funeral at Windsor.

It was not extraordinary for a dead sovereign to lie in state. In the past
lyings in state had generally taken place in Windsor and had been attended
by the same narrow and exclusive political world that was welcome at
court entertainments when the king was living.[75] Queen Victoria had decided
in advance that she did not want to lie in state after she died. None of her

Hanoverian predecessors had ruled against the ceremony before their deaths. The real departure in 1910 was for the king's lying in state to be in London at Westminster Hall, where no king had ever lain in state before, and for the ceremony to aim at allowing large numbers of the general public to attend. Up until the early decades of the nineteenth century there had been an increasing trend to move away from great public and heraldic displays in London at the deaths of kings toward relatively private and subdued affairs at Windsor.[76] Thus, the decision to stage a public lying in state in London after the death of Edward VII represented a significant departure. It was a return to public spectacle more characteristic of the sixteenth and seventeenth centuries.

When Lord Esher heard of the new king's proposal,[77] he opposed it. He pointed out to Schomberg McDonnell, his successor at the Office of Works, that Gladstone's lying in state in 1898 had honored 'a great *subject* and a great *commoner*. The only association of Westminster Hall with a Sovereign is a very unhappy one.' He meant the trial of Charles I. 'Besides', Esher continued, 'a King's Lying in State should have some ecclesiastical significance – and Westminster Abbey or St Paul's are equally convenient, and *far more suitable*'.[78] It is some measure of Esher's declining influence at court with the beginning of the new reign that the objections of Edward VII's master of ceremonies were overridden by the new king.

One part of Esher's advice was noted, however. Davidson observed in his memorandum of the planning of the ceremony that after a discussion with George V: 'I was impressed . . . by his anxiety that the Lying in State should be so managed as to prevent its being a mere show. "Let it have some sacred character."'[79] They discussed how this could be done, first considering handing out cards with several prayers or texts to the crowd lined up to enter the Hall. The police, however, warned them that 'other purveyors of cards or information e.g. suffragettes' might follow suit. In those rowdy pre-war days the whole ceremony might turn into a slanging match and a scuffle with mourners and suffragettes being mixed up and indiscriminately dragged away by the police. Eventually 'at the King's direct request' it was decided that the archbishop would say a few words when the two houses of Parliament were assembled in the Hall at the opening of the lying in state 'with the certainty that these words would then be everywhere published and would strike the sort of key note that was wanted'.[80]

It was the working classes and the poor who had aroused such anxiety as the audience for Dilke's anti-monarchical oratory in 1871. It was the working classes and the poor whom the planners of the diamond jubilee had hoped to please by having the queen drive south of the river in 1897.

Once again in 1910 they were expected to be the chief mourners at the lying in state. Schomberg McDonnell made two submissions for the king's approval which show what the organizers of the ceremony had in mind. First he submitted that the Hall should be open from six in the morning on the two full days it would be open to the public. This would enable 'many workmen to pay their last tribute of respect and it also gives an opportunity of doing so to thousands of the same class who will travel to London by night for the purpose'.[81] This was approved. Second he reluctantly suggested that permission be granted to photographers who wanted to take pictures of the processions to Westminster Hall and from the Hall on the day of the funeral. He noted that the Office of Works was

> being inundated with applications to take photographs of the Procession to Westminster Hall on Tuesday next and also when the Funeral takes place on Friday. Personally I loathe photography, so that it is most repugnant to me to have to submit such a proposal; but it must be remembered that photography in the case of great Ceremonials of public mourning is an extremely popular institution. I use the word popular advisedly and in the best sense. What I want to convey is that it enables poor people who live at a distance and cannot afford to come to London to see in the illustrated papers photographs of what has taken place and that it would be a great deprivation not to have the opportunity.[82]

A privileged photograph of the coffin in procession down Whitehall gives an idea of what, though unremarkable to late twentieth-century eyes, was regarded by McDonnell and others as an important new departure. [See plate 11.]

Davidson did not ignore the fact that there was to be a select, official audience for his sermon at the opening of the lying in state. They too were meant to learn lessons from the ceremony. The text of his sermon, delivered to the two Houses of Parliament in Westminster Hall on Tuesday 17 May 1910, afterward published in the newspapers, indicates that he wanted to use the occasion to recall the thoughts of both official and non-official alike, to the moral and ethical foundations on which human lives should be built.

> Brothers, the Sovereign whom his Empire and the World delighted to honour is suddenly taken from our head, and perhaps we find it difficult to fix in our thoughts the significance of these memorable days, the lesson of this scene for us and for the multitudes who will throng to look upon it. Here in the great Hall of English history we stand in the presence of Death. But Death is, to us Christians, swallowed up in a

larger Life. Our common sorrow reminds us of our common hope. Rise from sorrow to thanksgiving and prayer. We give thanks. We thank God for a Ruler devoted to the service of his people; we thank God for the peace and prosperity which have marked King Edward's reign; we thank God for teaching us still to see His hand in the story of our Nation's well-being. And we pray: we pray God that as we are united by this great sorrow we may be united for the tasks which lie before us, for the fight against all that is unworthy of our calling – as the Christian inheritors of a great Empire – the fight against selfishness and impurity and greed, the fight against the spirit that is callous or profane. Let us pledge ourselves afresh from this solemn hour to a deliberate and unswerving effort, as Christian folk, to set forward what is true and just, what is lovely and of good report, in the daily life, both public and private, of a people to whom much is given and of whom much will be required.[83]

Before him in the audience were royal mourners, peers and MPs; outside a line was already forming of those who would walk through after the service. All these were intended to hear or read Davidson's words and reflect. Reflection was meant to produce high-minded statesmanship as well as loyal citizenship.

The elements of 'them' and 'us', of the gap between the upper classes and the working classes, are unmistakable in the planning for the lying in state. Critics too have sometimes argued that the family imagery which surrounded the monarchy in these years was being consciously concocted by people who wanted to coopt and control working people. The eloquence of Davidson's sermon at the lying in state suggests that more was at stake than social control. The participants in the ceremony were sure that they shared their grief with the nation and that the family feeling of the ceremony was not false. Queen Mary, writing to her Aunt Augusta, compared the lying in state to the formal funeral several days later.

Tuesday's ceremony of taking dear Papa to Westminster Hall was perhaps the most touching day, as it was quieter and more a family affair. Words fail me to give a description of the solemnity and dignity of the sight in that beautiful old hall, with the coffin in the centre, the guards, all too upsetting . . .[84]

More than fifty thousand people passed through Westminster Hall on the first evening the Hall was open. House of Commons officials estimated that more than half a million came through during the 38 hours the coffin was on view. Many of these were working people, but to judge by the number of requests for tickets from peeresses and other people writing on heavy stationery, the aristocracy and middle classes were just as interested in coming to see the catafalque.[85] The ceremony's success lay in its ability to make a non-partisan appeal that was felt as much by Queen Mary as it was by those who came and stood in line at six in the morning.

An illustration from *The Illustrated London News* captures precisely the democratic character of the ceremony that Davidson and others hoped to convey. Captioned 'The People's Lying in State', it shows persons of all classes viewing the coffin: a Chelsea pensioner, a middle-class mother and daughter, a clerk with a cloth cap. [See plate 12.] A photograph from the Royal Archives gives another view of what all the spectators actually saw inside Westminster Hall. [See plate 13.]

Did all the crepe, the dirges and the archbishop's intoning affect the struggle between the Liberals and the Tories? There was at least one sustained attempt at compromise. A conference between the two parties met all summer, but failed to resolve their differences. The second general election of 1910, fought this time not on the budget but on the Liberals' stated intention of curbing the power of the upper house, once again returned the Liberals to power. Davidson was deeply disappointed.

He need not have been so sad. The months during which the political parties had tried to reach agreement were testimony in part to the enhanced prestige of the monarchy. If there had been no feeling for the old king, no desire to save the new king from fresh political controversy, there could hardly have been as serious an attempt at compromise. There were also political benefits to be had from compromise, but the impulse toward the meetings had come from the death of King Edward and the themes of reconciliation and renewal Davidson had spoken of at the lying in state.

Preparations for the coronation of King George V began almost as soon as his father's funeral was over. Most of the ceremony had only to be recovered from the pre-illness plans for King Edward's coronation nine years earlier. One new controversy arose that is instructive about the way Davidson was helping to change the monarchy's character in the years before the First World War. For the first time ever the coronation committee considered allowing photography at the ceremony. Approached by Sir Benjamin Stone, known for his camera portraits of parliamentary personalities, the committee decided to let him be the official photographer of the occasion.[86] The committee rejected as 'neither fitting nor feasible' the proposal to allow a cinematograph operator inside the Abbey to take moving pictures of the ceremony. The duke of Norfolk, chair of the committee, consulted Davidson for more specific instructions to pass on to the official photographer and received this reply:

I regard it as essential that there should be no photography at the moment of the most solemn parts of the Service – e.g. the celebration of Holy Communion, or I think the actual Coronation or Anointing of the King ... The subject is one upon which wide criticism is certain to be excited whatever is done, and it is most important that no mistake should be made.[87]

But another committee member, Schomberg McDonnell, disagreed with what Davidson intended to allow. McDonnell had assumed that Stone would *not* be allowed inside the Abbey during the service itself. He had interceded on behalf of the photographers at the procession to the lying in state the year before. Now, however, he sent a hot letter of protest to the archbishop. He asked the archbishop to make the king understand

that it would be a great shock to the feelings of Churchmen and of those who value the maintenance of reverence in Church if pictures appeared of him and The Queen in Illustrated Papers from snapshots by Sir Benjamin Stone, taken of Their Majesties at the most serious moment of their lives. [88]

Davidson and the king had already given their permission. Although they both retreated a little, forbidding Stone to take pictures once prayers had begun, they would not withdraw their permission altogether.[89] Davidson was less hot-blooded on the question of photography than McDonnell, certainly less rigid than some of his fellow churchmen would have been in the same situation. No doubt his conservative instincts made him cautious about admitting Stone to the Abbey, but the idea of providing some photographic record of the ceremony was also consistent with his intention to make historical and arcane ceremonies accessible to as wide an audience as possible. The Crown and the Church together had an interest in making the religious services at royal ceremonies comprehensive and inclusive. In approving Stone's admission to the Abbey, Davidson departed from the tradition that only a few privileged spectators were allowed to witness the king's coronation. Henceforth, hundreds of thousands of readers of the illustrated press would see what took place. As long as people were interested in what occurred, as long as they accepted the argument that ancient and formerly exclusive institutions still had worthwhile messages about duty, self-sacrifice and state service for a democratic age, then the institutions Davidson cared about would still be of use.

Some have said that the coronation and its attendant festivities hardened the resolve among Unionists to resist the Liberals' Parliament Bill at all costs. In the months following the coronation the bill, having passed through the Commons, was headed for a final confrontation between the two parties in the House of Lords. Davidson worked hard to reach a compromise, but his sympathies were with the Unionists, and this disqualified him as a mediator.

The Liberals in any case refused to compromise. The Unionists split into a moderate wing, which disliked the bill but preferred for it to pass without a large creation of Liberal peers, and a reactionary wing, which meant to fight to the bitter end whether this meant a large creation or not. Davidson and the king were horrified by the prospect of creating hundreds of peers at once. They hoped the moderate wing of the party would prevail. But Davidson wanted something more. He also hoped that the Unionists of the future would be free to undo the damage the Liberals would inevitably do with their Parliament Bill. To this end, he discouraged one peer who proposed an amendment Davidson believed would hinder Unionist politicians in the future:

> I do not scruple to say that to my mind the passage of the Bill, even as it stands, would be preferable to the creation of 300 peers and the consequent *farcical* ending of our old constitution. But if the House *has* to pass it, or acquiesce in it, let it be with as few attempts as possible to impose disabilities upon the Unionists of the future.[90]

The moment of truth came on the night of 11 August 1911. Davidson, fearing that the extreme Unionists had mustered enough votes to defeat the bill and bring on the creation of peers, reluctantly decided to vote *with* the government, rather than abstain, which had been his original intention and that of the Unionist leadership. Most of the other bishops voted with him. The crisis was averted and the Parliament Bill passed into law. But in voting for the bill, Davidson alienated the extreme right wing of the Unionist party without allaying the suspicions of Liberals. He swallowed his own conservative inclinations to save the king from the humiliation of having to create hundreds of peers at a stroke. After the vote Davidson received bundles of abusive letters from Unionists.[91] He had clearly sacrificed the natural prestige of his position among some politicians whose opinion he respected. Nor did his stock rise among Liberals. When his name came to be mentioned three years later as a possible mediator in the dispute between the parties over Ireland, Asquith dismissed him as 'the inevitable shifty Archbishop'.[92]

Part of Davidson's problem was that he tried to establish himself as a mediator before he had adequately established his credentials as a wise man of the Church. Part of his problem too was that he saw clearly how the monarchy had to be adapted for survival in a democratic age, but failed to see how similar institutions, like the Church and the House of Lords, might be required to give up some of their former authority and power if they too were to survive. The result was that he became disillusioned in the years before the beginning of the war. Lying sick in bed at Easter in 1913 he decided to review the first ten years of his primacy. Feeling old and gloomy he reflected that those ten years since 1903 constituted a radical break with the old order.

> We are passing through a time of revolution – the revolution is of a peaceful sort, perhaps surprisingly so considering how complete is the sweep of change from old-fashioned ideas into a thoroughly democratic age, instinctively hostile to the old notions of feudalism and its outcomes, and rather suspicious of what we have been accustomed to regard as loyalty and patriotism and a proper historical pride . . . Phases or aspects of it are what people call Socialism, as the practical outcome of vehement democratic views or 'Lloyd-Georgism', as the anti-feudal swing of the pendulum, or Parliament Act Government, instead of the old constitutional theories . . . It is not evil-intentioned, perhaps it is not pernicious.[93]

Even before the war began, Davidson felt thoroughly out of touch with the predominant trend in political life. He who saw that the monarchy and the Church needed to appeal to as wide a constituency as possible if they were to survive in the twentieth century failed to sympathize with the increasingly democratic tone of twentieth-century Britain. Only a decade into a primacy of twenty-five years, he dwelt on his powerlessness and ignored his achievements.

If he had loved the House of Lords less, if he had held himself a little more aloof from the company of politicians, if he had been less eager to provide his services during the political crises that began in 1909, perhaps he would have been more sought after as a mediator, his advocacy of compromise more valued by both political parties. His connections with Windsor, along with several of his public pronouncements, made the Liberals suspicious of him, even though he himself felt he had sacrificed his convictions to advance their Parliament Bill. Nor was he ever militant enough to satisfy the extreme Unionists who increasingly dominated the party councils in the years before the war. With the coming of the First World War, he retreated a little from the company of big men at Westminster and devoted himself more to the problems of the Church.

Still, his failure to gain his political objects or slow the course of change in those years should not overshadow what he managed to achieve. Davidson's honest striving for impartiality, even when his conservative instincts got the better of him, preserved a modicum of respect for the Church. Above all the monarchy profited from the early efforts of Davidson's career. Royal ceremonies under his hand were opportunities for contemplation, dwelling on responsibilities, duties and problems, as well as for pride and patriotism. Service to the state, whether as king, under secretary or clerk, these ceremonies claimed, was something higher and worthier than merely working for a salary. By heightening the prestige of the Crown, Davidson's ceremonies indirectly increased the prestige of government service.

Davidson tried to make royal ceremonies as inclusive as possible, whether by reaching out to Nonconformists or by making it possible for readers of the illustrated press to take part. He interpreted and explained arcane, historical rites, while providing spiritual advice and comfort to the sometimes eccentric family that was at the center of all the stately fuss. All this added to the Crown's stability and its ability to survive in changed political circumstances.

During Davidson's primacy Britain became a less religious nation and attendance at Anglican services declined. Nevertheless, religious services on state occasions were retained. The Church had an increasingly tenuous influence on the formation of public policy, while its services remained central to days of national celebration. This is evidence of a certain schizophrenia in British national identity.[94] The dual personality emerges from a ritual that declares the Church and the Crown to be absolutely central to national life. The ritual appears in a political and social context that says, on the contrary, that no two institutions could be more peripheral to the exercise of power. Modern royal ceremonies have always verged on becoming theatres of the absurd. On the personal level this deeply divided attitude toward the monarchy is abundantly clear in the minds of men like Davidson. Obsequious and sycophantic at one moment, he could be critical and dismissive the next. In the autumn of 1911, after he had voted with the Liberals on the Parliament Bill and saved the king from a massive creation of peers, Davidson felt no particular pride. In fact he blamed and resented George V for forcing the unpleasant vote upon him. This happened only two months after he had placed the crown on the king's head saying reverently, as Temple had to Edward VII, 'God crown you with a crown of glory and righteousness.' He betrayed the distinctive combination of respect and bitterness that often marked the others.

The final instance we need to consider of a man who was influential in making the modern monarchy was also a religious man. He was a Roman Catholic, indeed, the foremost Roman Catholic layman in Britain. We shall next have to ask how the duke of Norfolk, who built cathedrals of a faith that many in Britain still regarded with prejudice and hostility, saw his role as a hereditary and high dignitary in a newly-democratized form of ceremonial.

5 The Duke of Norfolk: Authenticity, Eccentricity, Absurdity

The train from London to Arundel, after it leaves Croydon's sprawl and scarlet 747s drawn up at Gatwick Airport, eventually passes into the hills of West Sussex. In the last several miles before Arundel, the green is so calm, the fields so even, that it is as if the train has entered another country, crossed some frontier into an imaginary England that surely never was. Then the grey stone towers of Arundel Castle loom up on the right-hand side of the train and confirm the impression that one is about to arrive in a strange land. The castle and the town and the fields on either side of the railway all belong to the duke of Norfolk. His servants and retired servants and the dowager duchess's servants live in consecutively numbered houses in the town. The duke has an estate agent who drives around in a brisk Ford indistinguishable from dozens of small cars parked at the station. He also has a librarian, an urbane expert on architectural history, who comes down by train two days a week from London. The duke's wife paints pictures that are sold for charitable purposes at parties featured in *The Tatler*.

In a trip by train less than two hours from London it is possible to take in a number of the paired opposites that make up modern England: ugly suburbs and rural idylls, antiquated railway carriages and brightly-colored 747s, late Victorian castles made to look early medieval, amateur dukes and duchesses assisted by cultivated experts. The monarchy still sits on top this heap of strange combinations because a late-Victorian duke of Norfolk helped to reinforce its position and renew its appeal. The modern monarchy and the castle in Arundel are the fifteenth duke's twin monuments; both are testimony to his energies and convictions. His rebuilding of Arundel Castle at the turn of the century runs parallel to his contribution to the transformation of the monarchy. The duke made himself an expert on gothic architecture and insisted on the fidelity of royal ceremonies to late medieval conventions. Just as Arundel was a massive expression of family pride, so too was the late Victorian monarchy an immodest celebration of the extent of imperial dominion and power. In the duke's mind Arundel Castle stood for bravery, faith, service and self-sacrifice. These were the same values that late Victorian officials hoped would inspire a new generation of Englishmen, who were without the duke's aristocratic connections, but who were invested with a new electoral power both to guide and to serve the state.

The duke's values were already beginning to seem old-fashioned and out-of-date in the late Victorian period. The fifteenth duke of Norfolk rejuvenated the out-of-date and rendered it appealing by also highlighting the patent absurdity, and hence considerable entertainment value, of adhering to some old customs under modern conditions. He held a hereditary title, earl marshal of England, which he used to reassert his family's claim to arrange the two royal funerals and the two coronations held between 1901 and 1914. His inexperience repeatedly threatened to turn solemn ceremonies into farces. As a result disputes broke out between the duke and officials who had grown accustomed to managing royal ceremonies during the latter part of Queen Victoria's reign.

These disputes had a curious impact on the argument for retaining the monarchy in the modern era. Under the duke's influence, democratic royalism came to be an argument that anything that was legitimately of great age deserved to be retained along side of newer institutions. This was so not only because longevity implied durability and worth, but because great age was charming and new institutions were, by definition, lacking in the charm and attractiveness that age could confer. Part of the evidence for the age of the monarchy was the eccentricity and perversity by which a Roman Catholic duke was allowed to superintend Anglican ceremonies. This had a certain quirky appeal to the national mind that was more powerful than any logically-developed position about the political utility of the Crown.

The appeal had its limits. The ceremonial and political controversies in which the duke became embroiled before the First World War proved that there had to be bureaucratic and democratic controls on the power and influence of ancient institutions. In nineteenth-century Britain, unlike in France, Germany, Austria or Russia, royalism was only really attractive when combined with its political opposite.

Henry Fitzalan-Howard was born in 1847. Before he was four years old, his father and grandfather had a quarrel that would seriously affect his later attitude to his religion and his family. During the eighteenth century the dukes of Norfolk had been quiet whigs in politics, and with one exception, part of a tradition of aristocratic and unassertive Catholicism in religion.[1] During the nineteenth century all this changed. The removal of Roman Catholic disabilities in 1829, the pope's reinstitution of the English ecclesiastical hierarchy in 1850, the revival of Catholicism fostered by powerful converts like Newman and Manning, the resurgence of anti-Catholic prejudice along with waves of Irish immigration – all these brought the dukes of Norfolk, as premier dukes and prominent Catholic laymen, back into the limelight. In 1850 the thirteenth duke, whose loyalty to Catholicism was weakening and who disliked foreigners, was outraged at the pope's reinstitution of the English hierarchy of the Roman Church. In response the duke publicly took communion in the Church of England at Arundel. He supported Lord John Russell's bill forbidding the new Catholic titles. The duke's son, whose faith had been nourished during travel in France by the stained glass and passionate sermons in Notre Dame, was a much more committed Catholic. He rushed back to England from the continent in order to vote against the titles bill in the House of Commons. His father was so angry that his doctors thought, if his son arrived in Westminster in time to vote, it might give the old man a stroke.[2] The bill passed, but was never enforced. Father and son patched up their quarrel, but more than half a century later, the thirteenth duke's public communion in the Anglican Church still rankled and was regarded as a betrayal by the fifteenth duke's family.

The fifteenth duke made it his life's work to demonstrate in as public a way possible that Englishness and Catholicism were not contradictions in terms, but a legitimate and authentic product of the nation's history.[3] He was prickly, quirky and always on the defensive. He made it his business to increase the public status of English Catholics and to deny their disloyalty to the Crown; at the same time he distrusted Irish Catholics and was happier to see them crushed by the imperial forces of law and order than to stand up for their liberties. He was a modest man, carelessly dressed who could be easily mistaken for a railway porter; yet he was perpetually asserting the rights of his dukedom. He was a charming eccentric with all the appeal of his bizarre, antique titles; yet he was extremely rich, well-placed and capable of insisting not only on a dignified role, which was expected of him, but also an efficient one, which was not. Like the monarchy itself at the turn of the century, the duke's attractiveness was a certain ancient silliness that overlay a deadly serious reserve capacity to interfere at the highest levels of the state. That combination of silliness and serious-ness was the duke's most characteristic and most significant contribution to democratic royalism.

Henry Fitzalan-Howard succeeded his father, the fourteenth duke, at the early age of 13 in 1860, the same year his mother sent him away to the Oratory School in a suburb of Birmingham. To make things worse, as a mark of his eminence, he was set apart from the other boys in a private room.[4] Under these monastic conditions he came under the spell of one of the century's great lights, John Henry Newman. Newman made an enormous impression on Norfolk. A man of great charm and many susceptibilities, a fierce controversialist as well as a shy priest, he did more than anyone else to make no-nonsense Victorians appreciate the possibility of an immense unseen world beyond the narrow, visible world in which they lived. Newman enhanced the religious reputation of the mysterious and the supernatural. You did not need to be a Roman Catholic to accept Newman's point that religion is a way of penetrating a world we do not and cannot ever fully know. An organ thundering in a minor key, dark cathedrals, guttering candles, all these could only hint at the incomprehensible vastness of what was there beyond our ordinary daily routines. This was certainly what most impressed Bagehot about Newman.[5] Gladstone and Esher were also sincere admirers. At Newman's knees Norfolk learned to appreciate the value of the emotional and romantic elements in religious faith. Father Bernard Vaughan said of the duke that 'He was steeped in the supernatural, heavy with it, like a sponge soaked in water. It was natural to him to be supernatural.'[6]

In later life the duke felt so much respect for his old teacher and was so anxious that there should be some official recognition of Newman's efforts to raise the reputation of the Catholic Church in England that he persuaded the pope to make Newman a cardinal. The duke's close friend, Wilfrid Ward, who had married one of the duke's nieces and who was himself the son of one of Newman's followers in the Oxford Movement, helped in the effort of establishing Newman's reputation. Ward wrote the authorized biography of Newman in 1912.

Ward's biography helped to render legitimate, or at least acceptable, an image of Newman that was sly and effeminate without being derisive. Here was the powerful intellect and eminent theologian as remembered by Ward's father and published in Ward's biography.

His keen humour, his winning sweetness, his occasional wilfulness, his resentments and anger, all showed him intensely alive, and his friends loved his very faults as one may love those of a fascinating woman; at the same time many of them revered him almost as a prophet. Only a year before his death, after nearly twenty years of misunderstandings and estrangement, W. G. Ward told the present biographer of a dream he had had – how he found himself at a dinner party next to a veiled lady, who charmed him more and more as they talked. At last he exclaimed, 'I have never felt such charm in any conversation since I used to talk with John Henry Newman, at Oxford.' 'I am John Henry Newman', the lady replied, and raising her veil showed the well-known face.'[7]

The cultural connections in Victorian England between femininity, spirituality and religion were strong. With the rise of Newman's reputation, his defeat of Kingsley and muscular Christianity with the crushing *Apologia Pro Vita Sua*, so also did a certain clerical effeminacy, an intuitive cultivation of the mysteries of God and the early Church become less suspicious, more worthy of respect. If it were all right for Newman's official biographer to transcribe his father's dream that Newman was actually a lady, then surely the shocking quality of Newman's insistence on the Catholic element in the nation's history must also have been diminished. Rehabilitation of Newman went along with a larger degree of acceptance of the religious mysteries hinted at by royal ceremonies and celebrating the nation's past. Newman and, as we shall see, the fifteenth duke of Norfolk, both reinforced the suggestion that the nation's history was Catholic, medieval and monarchical as well as Protestant, parliamentary and Anglican.

After leaving the Oratory School, Norfolk travelled on the continent. Because of his religion, neither of the ancient universities was open to him, but this was less of an injury to Norfolk than it was to Bagehot. Society was automatically open to the duke and it was a mark of his elevation that he usually disdained it. Nevertheless, his first marriage in 1877 to Lady Flora Hastings was an enormous affair attended by Disraeli and one of the queen's daughters.[8] The leaders of both political parties paid court to Norfolk as if he were a minor prince. Gladstone offered him the garter in 1870, which Norfolk politely declined saying he was more inclined to side with the conservative party.[9] Disraeli paid court in his own way; he turned up ostentatiously late to Norfolk's wedding. From Disraeli's description of the ceremony in a letter to Lady Bradford, it is clear that the wedding was as great a state affair as the wedding of any potentate and attracted as big a throng as a carnival.

> There was a great crowd from Hyde Park Corner to Brompton as on Lord Mayor's Day. When I arrived, it was supposed to be the bride, and the whole church, very long and very full, rose, and were sadly disappointed when it was only I, in a fur coat and your rustic stick . . .
>
> My speech [proposing the bride's health] was not too long, as, tho' the repast was most elaborate, it was necessary for the bride and bridegroom to arrive at Arundel in full daylight, as there was an immense reception prepared for them.[10]

The duke had a curious attitude toward social showiness. Like many other members of old aristocratic families, he disliked it; but as he increasingly identified himself with Disraelian Conservatives he also saw it as a part of his job. Not a very tall man, he wore ill-fitting suits. On holidays in Arundel he was mistaken for a daytripper.[11] He preferred entertaining schoolchildren in Sheffield to shooting parties at Arundel.[12] Disraeli ushered in a period in late Victorian England when social life became more showy. Plutocratic ostentation replaced aristocratic dowdiness as the dominant tone in social life. Even the queen, who had a true Presbyterian horror of vanity or display, was persuaded by Disraeli to wear more of her jewels. Just as in *Love in a Cold Climate* Canadian Cedric gets Lady Montdore to abandon her tweeds, pluck her eyebrows and wax her legs, Disraeli got old peers to act their parts with more visibility and style.[13] He got them to see that his vision of social life was, if a bit middleclass, certainly more amusing and imaginative than theirs. The duke of Somerset once asked Disraeli 'what he considered the most desirable life'. He replied: 'A continued grand procession from manhood to the tomb.'[14] The duke of Norfolk, a short man in a scruffy suit, was willing to join the parade.

Much of the duke's income came from urban property in Sheffield. He gave substantially to schools, public parks and charities there. In the 1890s he accepted the town's invitation to serve as its first lord mayor and its university's first lord chancellor. In return he brought attention and publicity to Sheffield by persuading Queen Victoria to come and open the new town hall in May 1897.

Likewise, Norfolk accepted the garter and minor political office from Lord Salisbury, not because he merited these rewards, but because he knew his name and rank lent a certain prestige to the party and the government. When Salisbury wrote to Norfolk asking him to be postmaster general in 1895, he teased him by saying, 'You will have plenty of work, and you will have no one over you; on the other hand the office is as nondemocratic as you could possibly desire.'[15] The irony of such a comment passing between two heirs to great landed estates would not have been lost on either sender or recipient. Neither of them liked democracy particularly, but both of them understood the appeal of crusty marquises and shy dukes to a large, middle-class electorate.

Norfolk also wanted the association with the tory party to increase the respectability of English Catholicism. Public attachment to the Conservatives helped distance Norfolk and other English Catholics from their Irish nationalist co-religionists, whom they frankly abhorred. By assuring Salisbury of Catholic support, Norfolk hoped Salisbury would in return restrain the anti-popery of some of his Protestant followers and give the Catholics support on the education issues that were important to them. Salisbury, though grateful for public signs of attachment from Norfolk, was more likely simply to use Norfolk for what he was worth in the party than to enter into any genuine reciprocal agreements.[16]

The founding of the Primrose League in the 1880s made clear how openly the Conservatives intended to use ancient associations in their efforts to win electoral support. The organization was meant to honor Disraeli and drum up popular support for the conservative party. Imperialism quickly replaced social reform as the League's central concern, but its most striking feature was the use of medieval-sounding terms for its activities. Dues were 'tribute', members were 'knights' and 'dames', local chapters were 'habitations'. There were badges, pageants, clasps and ribbons, all intended quite frankly as a way of winning over the middle and working classes to the idea of maintaining institutions controlled by the upper classes. The prime minister's wife, Lady Salisbury, replied to a protest in 1890 that a planned Primrose League function was 'vulgar' by saying 'Vulgar? Of course, it is vulgar! But that is why we have got on so well.'[17]

The duke of Norfolk headed the Primrose League for some years just after the turn of the century. It would be a mistake to see all the ersatz pageantry as only a cynical ploy to capture the masses for the conservative party. Despite his personal modesty the duke of Norfolk was a determined and inflexible believer in social hierarchy and *noblesse oblige*. The pseudo-medieval titles of the league were a means of preserving what he considered to be the genuinely medieval descent of his family's faith, estates and obligations.

The same is true of the duke's spectacular and expensive rebuilding of Arundel Castle, begun in the 1870s and finally completed in 1902. Personal diffidence went hand in hand with militant family pride. John Martin Robinson has described what the duke and his architect were trying to do at Arundel.

> They were creating an appropriate seat for the hereditary Earl Marshal of England and an expression in stone of the family history with all its associations, religious as well as baronial; statues of Our Lady stand in canopied niches alongside displays of the almost infinite quarterings of the ducal heraldry. The genuinely medieval parts of the castle and the Fitzalan Chapel were restored with painstaking archaeological accuracy while the unfinished patchwork of late eighteenth- and nineteenth-century Gothic which formed the residential part of the castle was sweepingly reconstructed to form an evocation of what a medieval castle should look like.[18]

Almeric Fitzroy, clerk of the Privy Council, visited the duke at Arundel in 1902 when they were working together on the coronation committee.

Fitzroy described the castle as a place 'where the traditions of a stately and reverent life still survive'.[19] He also admired the humbleness and piety of the duke's character, which Fitzroy thought was as irreproachable as that of a medieval saint.[20] Fitzroy was an arch-reactionary, but his comment is valuable because it captures the fact that he saw no necessary contradiction between the duke's grandiose building of an immensely showy castle and his personal modesty and quietness. Nor did the duke: it was the family and the estate and the heritage that were important, he was just a temporary placeholder.

When in 1899 the Boer War began, Norfolk gave up his place in the government in order to go and fight. The pope had made anti-English, pro-Boer remarks, and no matter how ridiculous it looked, the duke felt he needed to defend the loyalty of English Catholics by going out to South Africa. Turned down once, he persisted. Finally the War Office gave up and let him go out, aged 53, with the Sussex Imperial Yeomanry. He had no experience. When he got to South Africa he fell off his horse and was sent home immediately. He was the first to make fun of his performance. At a banquet called to honor the efforts of the auxiliary and volunteer forces, the duke spoke about why he had gone out in the first place. Someone had 'suggested that family pride called me out. I wish I had thought of that before.'[21]

At a different dinner he spoke about his service in the auxiliary forces using a gently self-mocking tone, but with an underlying vein of utter seriousness. 'I represent', he said,

the primeval instincts of those who panted behind the chariots of Boadicea, those who passed the wine-cup at the Round Table of King Arthur, those who tracked the cattle-lifter to his lair across the border into Scotland, those who were called together by feudal chiefs without any notion of scientific fighting, and those who had formed the second line behind the trained archers at Cressy.[22]

He believed that hard-drinking, cock-fighting Merrie England was a real place. He thought it was necessary to nurture the native, war-like spirit that went with that vision of the past if the nation and the empire were to be defended. The government appointed him as head of one of the commissions to evaluate the Army's performance in the Boer War. His commission's conclusions indicate just how serious he was about cultivating a military spirit in the people. Long before the First World War, the Norfolk Commission recommended universal compulsory training for home defense in either the militia or volunteers.[23] The Conservative government rejected the Norfolk Commission's recommendations as politically impossible. Once again, though, it shows how the duke mixed a capacity for charming self-deprecation with rigid commitment to traditionally aristocratic views about the importance of fighting.

In short his attitude toward what was required of being a descendant of a medieval duke late in the nineteenth century was a version of democratic royalism writ small. The argument for preserving a modern aristocracy rested on a mixture of modesty, showiness and inflexible pride; it relied on persuading a larger and more critical segment of the population that noblemen knew something about service and self-sacrifice, but were in the main content to take a ceremonial role in public affairs.[24] The argument had to be phrased in such a way that the humbleness and shyness were as real as the readiness to dragoon working men drinking in pubs into the fighting forces. As we shall see, however, though the duke tried very hard to support the argument, he was always in jeopardy of upsetting it as well. In a variety of different contexts he wanted to 'translate essentially ceremonial duties into positions of substantial authority'.[25] This led to trouble.

Being a duke was only half Henry Fitzalan-Howard's identity in the years before the First World War. Being a Catholic was the other half. It was also the context in which he was best known to the late Victorian and Edwardian public. Issues that affected his religion were those on which he was most willing to take a prominent, and often controversial, stand. In 1874 when Gladstone published his pamphlet attacking the dual loyalty – to both pope and queen – of English Catholics, Norfolk asked Newman to reply. Newman dragged the reluctant duke into the controversy by entitling his pamphlet, *Letter to the Duke of Norfolk*.[26]

As he got older the duke was a more confident controversialist; but he often took an independent and unexpected line. The Conservatives repeatedly made use of him as an anti-Home Rule speaker on political platforms. This was to show that their policy was not motivated by prejudice against Ireland's Catholic majority. The duke's second wife admitted that his presence at Orange meetings was 'a nightmare to many onlookers', who expected the duke's sympathies to be with his fellow Catholics rather than with Protestant Ulster. The duke was careful about explaining his seemingly perverse position – in Ireland he thought religious grievances were secondary to the problems of order – but to many he must have seemed a little eccentric.[27] By the late 1890s the duke was known as 'one of the hardest workers' against Gladstone's Irish policy. The irony of his taking a leading role in arranging Gladstone's state funeral was not lost on *The Illustrated London News*.[28] Then again the duke never did quite what was expected of him and there was a sort of fitting crotchetiness about his being charged with the funeral of the century's most famous Anglican statesman.

For late Victorians the questions of education and religion were joined together, so Norfolk also spoke out in the House of Lords on education. He opposed his own party's willingness to interfere in the management of denominational schools in 1902.[29] But he also disliked the Liberal education legislation of 1906 quite as much, arguing not only that the bill was unfair to Roman Catholics, but endangered religion as a whole.[30]

The duke wrestled publicly with deeply-rooted, unreasoning, anti-Catholic prejudice when he spoke out after the turn of the century against the royal accession declaration. This oath required the sovereign, on coming to the throne, to declare not only that he or she was not a Catholic, but that sacraments of the Roman Catholic Church were 'idolatrous'. The duke objected that this was needlessly insulting, but neither Conservative nor Liberal governments were in a hurry to remove the insult.[31] After much delay the oath was finally amended in 1910 so that George V was not required to offend his Catholic subjects as his father had. Once again the duke's obstinate persistence was one of the reasons why.

The duke was also prominent in dealings with the Vatican. He led an official deputation, the first in centuries, to give Queen Victoria's congratulations to the pope on the fiftieth anniversary of his ordination as a priest, celebrated coincidentally in the same year, 1887, she celebrated the fiftieth anniversary of her coronation. Salisbury hoped to fob off the duke with this minor ceremonial duty, but the duke was intent on converting the trip to a more serious purpose. He eventually persuaded the pope to condemn publicly the Irish nationalists among the Catholic hierarchy in Ireland for inspiring lawlessness among the general population.[32] To look into his correspondence with Wilfrid Ward is to find a rat's nest of complicated religious controversies. On a variety of issues he tried repeatedly to use his influence either to circumvent, resist, or deflect actions of men prominent in the Roman Catholic hierarchy in order to protect the reputation of the Catholic Church in England.[33]

Only in his church building did he have unhampered scope for asserting his religious views. He was the largest contributor to two large churches that changed the landscape of London, Westminster Cathedral and the Brompton Oratory. He built another cathedral in Arundel and an immense church in Norwich hoping that it too would one day be the seat of a bishop. Arundel was already under his thumb. Norwich was more difficult: it was the urban center of his territorial title, but he had little property there and the town was less amenable to his influence. Once the building of St John the Baptist was well under way, the town council argued with him about the boundaries of his property; but, he eventually got his way and the church – a gloomy and lugubrious recreation of early gothic architecture – rose up on a hill dominating the city.

Thus, he came to be seen as a very rich, rather prickly Roman Catholic. The touchiness and independence of his views rendered him a little less suspicious in the public eye than he would have been had he taken a more consistently pro-Vatican line. In fact, to successive generations between the French Revolution and the First World War who were obsessed with the feudal past, who built railway stations, law courts and country houses all to resemble medieval fortresses, who thought even of modern liberty as a gothic bequest, the appeal of a duke who could trace his lineage back into the middle ages must have been irresistible.[34] His eccentricity and seeming perversity were grotesque evidence, like a gargoyle's strange grin, of his historical authenticity.

When Queen Victoria died in 1901, the Lord Chamberlain's Office, assisted by the Office of Works, began plans for her funeral. The duke of Norfolk saw the king within 24 hours of the queen's death and protested. He told the king that it was his hereditary right as earl marshal to manage the sovereign's funeral. A 'heated discussion' took place. As in the Boer War, the duke had little experience and court officials had to protest as politely as possible that they were sure he would make a mess of things. The king reluctantly decided in the duke's favor. 'But', Almeric Fitzroy observed,

> in the next ten days he may have cause to repent having so strenuously preferred his claim, as without any regular organisation he will have to arrange all the details of a notable pageant – I am afraid with no great help from the Lord Chamberlain's officials.[35]

The Lord Chamberlain's Office and the Office of Works were certainly displeased. They recorded their displeasure in a series of unending complaints about the duke. Alfred Akers-Douglas, first commissioner of Works, grumbled: 'The Earl Marshal has no office or staff for such work & it has ended in our having to do the whole thing for him. He getting all the kudos and half pence & Esher the work and the kicks.'[36] For Akers-Douglas and Esher a stately and decent funeral was of the utmost importance. For Norfolk, medieval precedent and family honor were at stake. Neither side was willing to give ground. The dispute shows how not only royal ceremonies, but also the right to organize them, rested upon a complicated set of precedents and traditional practices.

Norfolk rested his claim to superintend the sovereign's funeral on history.

The Howard family had been dukes of Norfolk and earls marshal since the end of the fifteenth century.[37] In the same year King Richard III gave the Howards their peerage, 1483, he granted a royal charter as a mark of official sanction to the College of Arms, which was under the jurisdiction of the earl marshal. The College was a corporation of genealogists and antiquaries who investigated and registered orders of knighthood, hereditary rank and pedigree. It was composed of 13 members, or heralds, who had fantastic titles: they called each other Norroy, Lancaster, Portcullis and Rouge Dragon.[38] Originally the earl marshal was a martial or military figure. The heralds granted and certified coats of arms used for identification and display in battle.[39] Between the fifteenth and seventeenth centuries the earl marshal and heralds organized large royal ceremonies, primarily coronations and funerals, where it was necessary to acknowledge, differentiate and adjust the various grades of nobility, status and precedence of those who surrounded the king. The earl marshal and heralds were all members of the Royal Household. Officers of the College of Arms were appointed by the Crown on the recommendation of the duke of Norfolk as earl marshal.[40]

By the end of the seventeenth century, however, the planning of funerals and certain other royal ceremonies was increasingly being taken away from the earl marshal. They were then carried out mainly under the direction of another official of the Royal Household, the lord chamberlain. A succession of sovereigns felt that public, heraldic display was no longer appropriate to such occasions, which they thought should still be dignified, though they should now be more private and domestic affairs.[41] Between the eighteenth and nineteenth centuries the earl marshal and College of Arms continued to be involved in planning coronations and the state-funded funerals of a few statesmen and national heroes; but the lord chamberlain traditionally regarded the earl marshal as incompetent and directed most royal funerals himself. In the latter half of the nineteenth century the only two large ceremonies which the earl marshal and College of Arms directed were the state funerals of the duke of Wellington (1852) and Gladstone (1898). The thanksgiving for the recovery of the Prince of Wales in 1872 and the two jubilees were all designated 'semi-state' occasions, where the earl marshal's duties were performed by the lord chamberlain. Although the earl marshal remained nominally affiliated with the Royal Household in the Victorian era and the heralds continued to receive small salaries from the civil list, the queen never wanted them or had any use for them. Henry Ponsonby thought the heralds were only paid by the queen because no one else would pay them. The heralds made a living by collecting fees when new peerages were created and by doing genealogical research privately for clients who were curious about their family history. But even that was not very much. The police caught one herald, Bluemantle, trying to hawk his free ticket to the golden jubilee for 15 guineas.[42]

As the earl marshal's functions had atrophied, other offices of the Royal Household had grown. In the nineteenth century these other offices had been reorganized to resemble government departments. There were three principal offices organized along these lines. The Lord Steward's Office catered royal banquets and arranged lodging for guests; it dealt with all 'below stairs' matters such as catering, heating, lighting and laundry. The Master of the Horse's Office arranged transportation. The Lord Chamberlain's Office arranged routine domestic ceremonies, such as levees and drawing rooms, as well as ceremonies called for on special occasions; in general it dealt with 'above stairs' matters, such as supervising pages, doctors, chaplains and librarians. Each of these offices was headed by a political peer who had usually performed useful services for his party in the House of Lords. Each of these peers drew salaries from the sovereign's civil list. During Queen Victoria's long retirement the work was not hard and the court appointment was regarded as a political honor and reward. The lord steward, the master of the horse and the lord chamberlain all changed with the government of the day, though none of them sat in the cabinet. They were each assisted in their offices by permanent officials who resembled nonpolitical heads of the Civil Service.

When Queen Victoria died the lord chamberlain pointed to sixty years' experience of managing royal funerals and other domestic ceremonies during the late queen's reign. The duke of Norfolk as earl marshal pointed to precedents that dated from the later fifteenth century. In 1901 the sovereign still had a good deal of power to arrange his own ceremonial. In this case Edward VII recognized the rights of an ancient, hereditary office over those of a relatively modern, bureaucratic one.

On the day of the funeral the queen's coffin had to be moved from Osborne to London, and from London to Windsor. The king asked Frederick Ponsonby, the son of the queen's long-time private secretary, to prepare the Windsor part of the ceremony. Ponsonby called on the Earl Marshal's Office, temporarily set up in Norfolk House, where he found

> absolute chaos. The Heralds, who claimed the right to manage the funeral under the direction of the Earl Marshal, had little precedent to work on since there had been no Sovereign's funeral for sixty-four years, and being accustomed to work out coats of arms and genealogical tables at their leisure, were swept off their feet with the urgent arrangements for the funeral.[43]

Ponsonby asked to see the duke of Norfolk: 'and here I found a thoroughly businesslike and capable man . . . quite unconscious that the work he was delegating to his subordinates was not being done'. Ponsonby drew up an outline for the Windsor portion of the ceremony and submitted it to Norfolk, who made some corrections. The duke told Ponsonby:

> some of the Heralds had complained of my rudeness and had resented some remarks on their inefficiency which I had made. I at once apologized to him, but I pointed out that had I not come to London no arrangements of any sort . . . would have been issued.[44]

Further, what the heralds did manage to issue was not correct. They commanded Lady Cadogan to come to St George's Chapel wearing trousers.[45] The funeral service referred to Queen Victoria as 'he'.[46] On the day of the funeral itself, no one had assigned seats in the choir at St George's. So the comptroller of the Lord Chamberlain's Office, who was old, feeble and nearly blind, tried to make up for the duke's mistake by searching at random for suitably prominent persons in the nave, and moving them up to the choir even as the queen's coffin was being brought in by the west door of the chapel.[47]

Lord Esher wanted to prevent something similar from happening at the coronation. He told the king's private secretary, Sir Francis Knollys, that if it were impossible to stop the duke from taking charge of the coronation, he should be a 'nominal figurehead' presiding over a committee composed of representatives from the more regular departments of the Royal Household and the government. 'If the Heralds have anything to do with it, failure (or less) is inevitable. The Duke is all right, not at all a bad man of business. His *Heralds* are *anathema maranatha!*'[48] Arthur Ellis, comptroller of the Lord Chamberlain's Office in the new reign, called the heralds all 'ghastly cads, not a gent among them and Cath[olic] hangers-on of the D. of Norfolk'.[49] Esher's idea was for the duke to serve as ceremonial chairman of a coronation committee just as the Prince of Wales had done for the committee that planned the diamond jubilee. In short, he wanted the management of the coronation itself divided into dignified and efficient parts. The duke was to act in a dignified capacity. Permanent officials of the Civil Service and from the departments of the Royal Household organized along Whitehall lines were to do the real work.[50]

The government appointed a formal committee of the Privy Council as usual to consider preparations for Edward VII's coronation. What they did for the first time in 1901, on the precedent of the diamond jubilee, was to place the earl marshal at the head of a second committee, the Coronation (Executive) Committee, and charge this body with responsibility for the ceremony. This was designed to placate the duke of Norfolk while at the same time ensuring that the ceremony would have the attention not of inexperienced heralds but of qualified civil servants.[51] Esher and Knollys had succeeded in surrounding the duke with permanent officials so that his hereditary claim was hedged in and limited by bureaucratic expertise.[52]

The committee met three times in July 1901. Its meetings were long and tedious, there were too many members and the duke of Norfolk had trouble getting them to make decisions.[53] Moreover, it soon became clear that the duke refused to give up his right to be involved personally in issuing invitations, ordering the ceremonies and arranging the rehearsals. Edward Hamilton, former private secretary to W. E. Gladstone, now joint permanent secretary of the Treasury and a member of Norfolk's committee, saw trouble. The plan had been for the duke 'to sink his Earl Marshalship in the Chairmanship of the Committee'.[54] Without an experienced staff, he would bungle the ceremonial arrangements again. As joint permanent head of the Treasury, Hamilton was also joint permanent head of the Civil Service. He worried that the committee, composed mainly of civil servants, might be blamed for the duke's mistakes. When later that year the duke called on Hamilton at the Treasury, Hamilton recorded this impression:

> He is a curious mixture of 'unpushfulness' with tenacity for his heredi-
> tary rights. He is the most unassuming Duke; but quite a self-asserting
> Earl Marshal. He was appointed Chairman of the Executive Committee;
> but I see he wants to do everything himself as Earl Marshal. The
> Committee won't like to be ciphers and merely an advisory Board. So
> there may be some risk of a rumpus. I have written to warn Francis
> Knollys. We must try & keep the peace if possible. It will never do to
> quarrel with him. But it is the Committee that will be held responsible
> for any break-down in the arrangements.[55]

Knollys told Hamilton that he too liked the duke, but found him 'a very obstinate little man'. If Norfolk were forced to accept the lord chamberlain's advice, he might resign altogether, creating a public scandal that would raise protests among Roman Catholics. Knollys, Hamilton, Esher and Schomberg McDonnell, the prime minister's private secretary, conferred about the situation that autumn. They could do nothing but ask for frequent meetings of the committee and try to diminish the duke's power of doing harm by breaking into sub-committees. Ultimately they failed in their plan to take power away from the duke and place it in the committee. Esher complained of the duke's power and the committee's impotence telling his son: 'the body is effete!'[56]

These disputes about control of the coronation went on behind the scenes.

What the public saw of the coronation preparations was a different sort of farce. According to precedent, the duke of Norfolk called together a Court of Claims, duly announced in the newspapers. The court was a strange body attended by hereditary officials, like the earl marshal, political officials, like the lord chancellor, and senior judges. These men heard 'all kinds of ancient claims entitling persons to render certain services to the Monarch at his Coronation'.[57] One peer claimed to carry the king's spur, another his glove, a third his cap. Claimants paid lawyers and collected documents to buttress their cases. The court considered utterly trivial matters with the greatest gravity; *Punch* sent it all up in its coronation number.[58] Mr. *Punch* appeared first as a comic member of the Heralds College, 'Bouverie King of Arms', so called because *Punch's* offices were in Bouverie Street. [See plate 14.] Next he appeared with a slightly reddened nose at a table covered with empty wine bottles, holding 'a Court of Overflow Claims'. [See plate 15.] There followed a list of prominent public figures who, *Punch* said, had made outrageous claims before the Court of Overflow Claims. *Punch* not only made fun of the Court of Claims,[59] but also of the increase of ceremonies surrounding the actual coronation. The plans called for there to be two days of celebration rather than one. One day was to feature the crowning in the Abbey; the other a long procession, or 'progress' through the streets of London. *Punch* joined in by proposing a 'Procession of Emblematic Motor Cars' and a 'River Pageant' with a political regatta before the terrace of the House of Commons. The procession of motor cars was to be 'a glorified Lord Mayor's Show . . . to cover ground, if any, not included in the Royal Progress . . .'[60] The Lord Mayor's Show, then as now, was a byword for absurd but entertaining fluff.

All this was a departure for *Punch*, which had treated most of the other large royal occasions in the last half century using the same serious and sentimental tones to be found in the rest of the press.[61] Here was the ridicule that Knollys had worried about when Bigge and Esher kept insisting on expanding the size of the coronation by reviving old ceremonies. *Punch* now appeared to be saying that the expansion of ceremonial was a little foreign, certainly funny, perhaps more Catholic than Protestant. London itself, *Punch* suggested, was being transformed for the coronation, like Rome, into a city of seven hills.[62]

Of course all the big ceremonies at the end of the century risked turning into open-air carnivals. Knollys rejected one suggestion for the queen's diamond jubilee that there should be a procession through the streets of London representing the principal events of the reign. He told Bigge: 'this would be like a Lord Mayor's Show and would inevitably bring ridicule down on the whole business'.[63] What Knollys failed to see, and *Punch* had captured by fixing on the Court of Claims, was that the absurdity of it all was part of its appeal. The conservative messages about hereditary privilege were not acceptable because the nation was fundamentally Tory, but because the ceremonies that celebrated them were, at distinct moments, laughable. The survival of hereditary privilege could only be tolerated in a democratic society if it could also on occasion be lampooned.

Life, however, was sometimes funnier than fiction. It was the duke's good luck that the coronation scheduled for June never took place. Hamilton attended one mismanaged rehearsal shortly before the ceremony and watched a scene of total disarray. The heralds were incapable of marshalling the processions and nobody was in control.[64] The king's sudden and unexpected illness announced two days before the coronation saved the earl marshal. The duke obtained an additional six weeks to rehearse the performance. As Fitzroy observed, 'only a miracle in June could have averted a fiasco'.[65] The duke scheduled six additional rehearsals after the announcement of the delayed coronation.[66] When the coronation was finally held on 9 August, the endless drill beforehand resulted in everyone finally knowing his or her role. Only the unsteadiness of the archbishop gave rise for anxiety and this was beyond the duke's control.

After the coronation was over the duke was unrepentant. A report prepared by his secretary pointed out that though the Coronation (Executive) Committee had sometimes given valuable advice, it had not exercised any executive functions. All these were carried out by the earl marshal in his own office.[67] The dispute between the earl marshal and the civil servants was shelved. Score one for the duke of Norfolk. What the people in the streets thought about royal ceremonies was sometimes of less importance to the planners of ceremony than competing claims among themselves about the right to stage the event. To martial the sovereign's state appearances was itself a mark of status to be jealously contested. Those who could claim to stage a ceremony with efficiency and precision in this case reluctantly deferred to the claims of revived hereditary right.

Edward VII died in May 1910. Courtiers soon began to have clear memories of the earl marshal's incompetence. The duke took charge of the funeral arrangements, just as he had done in 1901. He had so successfully re-asserted his claim nine years earlier that this time there were no objections. Brian Godfrey-Faussett, an equerry to the new king who was charged with supervising a portion of the ceremony, called at Norfolk House. There he found the scenario of 1901 being repeated all over again.

The offices in the Earl Marshal's house appeared to be in some confusion, the staff there consisting of Heralds, Red Dragons and Whatnots were working on the funeral arrangements, no light task, and they [were] all perspiring and pissing like mad . . .[68]

Kenneth Rose confirms Godfrey-Faussett's impression of the funeral arrangements:

> On the very day before the service, the ceremonial published by the Earl Marshal proved to be full of mistakes; a senior courtier and four clerks shut themselves up for several hours rewriting it correctly. 'I love the Duke', King George told Schomberg McDonnell, 'he is a charming, honourable, straight-forward little gentleman, no better in the world. But as a man of business he is absolutely impossible. I ask you, Pom, is it not hard on me?'[69]

On the day of the funeral the printed service prepared by the heralds still had in it two anthems that were not sung and never intended to be sung.[70] Margot Asquith sat in St George's Chapel and was impressed by the disorganization of the seating arrangements, which she called 'a mosaic of indecision and confusion'.[71]

Once the funeral was over McDonnell, who had succeeded Esher as permanent secretary to the Office of Works in 1902, asked the earl marshal for a plan of seating inside St George's, probably with the idea that the plan should never be used again. Norfolk's response offers a key to his perspective. 'My object', Norfolk wrote McDonnell,

> has been as much as possible to avoid any record of the actual seat occupied by any person and to prevent any notion of precedence or of one person being better placed than another. To make it simpler for myself I made out an allocation of blocks but I was careful not to make this a rigid arrangement.[72]

The right to be present at the sovereign's funeral or coronation could be regarded as a mark of status. The College of Arms had for centuries confirmed and established individual claims of rank, precedence, pedigree, and status. A seat at one function established a precedent or claim for seating at the next. Norfolk wished to avoid a seating plan at St George's that could be regarded as an official pronouncement, an authoritative endorsement of rank, which might be used hereafter to limit his or a future earl marshal's freedom.

The Office of Works kept elaborate records of precedents on ceremonial occasions so as to stage orderly ceremonies when occasion arose. The earl marshal was less concerned with the staging of the ceremony than he was with the precedence of those who were invited to attend. Once again the duke opposed the difficulties of deciding on precedence to the Office of

Works's insistence on orderliness and efficiency. And once again the Office of Works gave in.

Because the Earl Marshal's Office only came into being as occasion arose, the duke was not even very good at establishing questions of rank. Jack Sandars, Balfour's private secretary, complained to Esher that even he knew more about status than the earl marshal 'and his myrmidons':

> The trouble is that he [Norfolk] has no adequate or instructed staff: that I could see as I was referred to by him on an elementary matter of the status of the Army Council and politico-militaries respectively.
>
> There is an officer mentioned in Mme. LaFayette's memoirs who much resembles our E. Marshal *'Qui exerçait extrément bien sa charge quand il n'avait rien à faire'*.[73]

In fact Norfolk wanted to uphold his family's honor by asserting the rights of the earl marshal, but he personally disliked ceremony and was a little contemptuous of those who insisted on recognizing rank. His second wife says the earl marshalship was a duty rather than a pleasure: 'State functions, because they were in the first place alien to his homeliness, became a part of his self-discipline.'[74] This was partly a native English distaste for the very idea of ceremonial. 'Ceremony' had been used in a pejorative or disparaging fashion to indicate a practice that was empty, idle, a mere formality, since the sixteenth century.[75] The duke's wife, for example, used this metaphor to describe her husband's mission to the Vatican in 1887 on his official mission from the queen: 'All the formalities, to the uttermost farthing of them, were observed.'[76] She quoted approvingly from *The Times's* assessment of her husband which referred to him as the host of formal entertainments at Norfolk House:

> there was a John Bull element in his nature that made the details of entertaining foreigners somewhat of an effort to him. He did not care to give bow for bow or compliment for compliment in the grand Italian manner.[77]

Ceremonies and formal entertainments, *The Times* was saying, were fundamentally not English: they were more characteristic of quick-spirited Frenchmen or credulous Italians, and in his dislike of such shows the duke as a Roman Catholic was at odds with himself as an Englishman. But in fact an earl marshal who was amateur, casual and *ad hoc*, as the fifteenth duke was, preserved the authentic historical office and traditional duties at the same time as he showed a peculiarly English and aristocratic insouciance for the business of the office.

After the mishaps at the funeral of Edward VII, the Office of Works and

George V's private staff were determined to disestablish the earl marshal and the heralds before they could start on the coronation. The first commissioner of Works, Lewis Harcourt, wrote the prime minister a memorandum on the subject.[78] Sir Arthur Bigge, George V's private secretary, wrote a draft letter for the prime minister's signature to send to the duke of Norfolk. Bigge's draft, referring to planning of the coming coronation, pointed out that: 'His Majesty wishes to preserve unbroken the titular authority and the historic tradition by which this work is entrusted to the Earl Marshal', but because the earl marshal did not have an adequate clerical staff, he should preside over a staff drawn from the Civil Service and the Royal Household.[79] McDonnell told Bigge that it was essential for the officers of Arms to understand that they 'are not in future to take any part whatever in the organisation of any Ceremony, but are merely to occupy an ornamental position in the Processions and Services'.[80] The first meeting of the coronation committee was even changed from Whitehall to St James's Palace as a way of asserting the king's control over the ceremony and pre-empting the earl marshal.[81]

The duke of Norfolk refused to give ground without a struggle.[82] The first meeting of the committee resulted in a deadlock: the earl marshal insisting on hiring his own staff, the rest of the committee against him. The comptroller of the Lord Chamberlain's Office, Sir Douglas Dawson, said: 'The situation was comical had it not been too serious' – comical because it involved a short duke with medieval pretensions, but serious enough for the prime minister to have been called in to help restrain him.[83] With the intervention of the prime minister, it began to appear inevitable that the duke would have to reduce his control over the coronation. Even so, Alfred Scott-Gatty, who as garter king of arms was the principal officer of the College of Arms, pressed the duke to claim his hereditary right in connection with the organization of other ceremonies. The newspapers announced in September 1910 that the new heir to the throne would be formally invested as Prince of Wales in July 1911 at a ceremony in Carnarvon Castle. Scott-Gatty told the duke that this struck him as a party maneuver on the part of the Welsh chancellor of the Exchequer, David Lloyd George:

> as this 'smacks' very much of *a political move*; the question arises, *and should be answered at once*, whether the King intends allowing the Welsh Members of Parliament to run their own show or whether he wishes the ceremony to be carried out according to precedent.

Scott-Gatty told Norfolk that he should try and influence the king 'in favour of a dignified State Ceremony rather than a political one'.[84]

In the first months of the reign of George V, a variety of different persons were vying for the control of royal ceremonial. The earl marshal had revived his claim to be involved actively in the planning of state occasions, but he was resisted by a loose alliance of civil servants and officials of the Royal Household. When David Lloyd George and the bishop of St Asaph, A. G. Edwards, proposed holding an investiture of the Prince of Wales at Carnarvon, a third alliance asserted its right to stage royal ceremonies. This testifies to a good deal of official interest in royal ceremonial and a variety of motives. Lloyd George's motives were no doubt political.[85] He certainly liked irritating old Tories and appealing to Welshmen, but he probably also wanted to assure possible allies who distrusted his radicalism that he was loyal to the Crown. Civil servants and members of the Royal Household who had been displaced by the earl marshal's revived claim wanted to assure order, predictability and regularity in royal proceedings. They also wanted back the powers that, in their view, had been wrongly taken away from them. They could hardly assure the prestige of the Crown, and the government along with it, if royal ceremonies continued to be filled with farcical mistakes. Norfolk and Scott-Gatty wanted to make sure that precedent was observed and respected; they were afraid of the earl marshalship and the College of Arms being reduced to nothing.

The new king, George V, also wanted to place his stamp on royal ceremonial. He told the cabinet that he wanted to go to India and be crowned king-emperor at a durbar in Delhi soon after his coronation. Over some opposition, the king won his point and his trip to India, planned for late in 1911 was announced in the fall of 1910. The announcement, like that of the investiture, took Scott-Gatty by surprise, but he was not slow to respond. He wrote off busily to the duke Norfolk, no doubt imagining himself sailing out to India in the ducal suite: 'I am sure it would very much accentuate your Imperial jurisdiction and help your Department to keep upon its feet if we could attend – i.e. you and me.'[86]

The earl marshal and garter did not go to India with the king, nor is there any evidence that they were allowed any large role in the planning of the durbar. The king's private staff and the civil servants involved did allow the earl marshal a token role in the investiture of the Prince of Wales, but kept him out of the planning until arrangements were well advanced.[87] As for the coronation of George V, the duke was still allowed to hire his own staff to issue invitations, but the king told him the heralds had to be kept out of it.[88] Almeric Fitzroy observed in January 1911 of the fourth meeting of the coronation committee: 'The Duke of Norfolk, having accepted the Committee as a curtailment of his authority, is so studiously deferential as to take next to nothing on himself and McDonnell almost assumes direction.'[89]

In the midst of all this ceremonial activity at the beginning of the reign, a compromise was achieved. The politicians had the final say. Asquith forced Norfolk to sit in a more purely dignified capacity at the head of the coronation committee. It was Asquith and the cabinet whose approval was sought and reluctantly given to George V for his trip to India. Lloyd George had his way about the investiture in Wales, but was not allowed an active role in its arrangement. The committee that organized the investiture was composed of permanent officials from the Civil Service and the departments of the Royal Household organized along Whitehall lines. These were the same persons who now organized George V's coronation under the deferential chairmanship of the duke of Norfolk as earl marshal.

Thus, the management of ceremonial after 1911 was, like the English constitution itself, divided into dignified and efficient parts. The duke and heralds added color to the proceedings; permanent officials and politicians organized pageants behind the scenes. Royal ceremonies were conceived to be a regular part of the business of the state and were deemed significant enough to merit their own bureaucratic organization. This organization was already largely in place when the duke reasserted his hereditary right at the funeral of Queen Victoria in 1901. It continued in modified form afterwards, but the duke had succeeded in entering an element of doubt in the proceedings.

Courtiers and civil servants had a few uncomfortable moments until the duke was finally forced to give up personal direction of state ceremonies in 1911. It was virtually impossible for the king, the lord chamberlain and the Office of Works to deny the duke's hereditary right when the ceremonies in question celebrated hereditary right, precedent and tradition. Despite everyone's reasonable fears about the duke's incompetence, the logic of traditional ceremonial gave him direct control of three large ceremonies between 1901 and 1910, which repeatedly threatened to become nightmares. Even if that logic was eventually circumvented, it did re-establish the duke of Norfolk and his heirs in a prominent place, if not as executive directors, then as chairmen of the board supervising all state ceremonies. Since that time it has always been possible for particularly forceful earls marshal to take ceremonial business back into their own hands.

It is significant that people like Esher, Bigge and McDonnell, who were all suspicious of democracy, should have been brought face to face with the downright inconvenience of their own attachment to hereditary privilege. They all liked the idea of powerful dukes, but here was a duke whose incompetence and hereditary claims positively enraged them. If the duke's participation in staging royal ceremony suggested to the public that the monarchy was in fact old, eccentric and bound up in queer precedents, what it taught courtiers was to reconsider the value of what was modern, efficient and meritocratic.

The duke himself was also a little stung in wrangling with the court over the second coronation. The townspeople of Arundel and Sheffield were happier for him to play the role of hereditary magnate than were people in the Lord Chamberlain's Office and on the king's private staff. He showed unusual pique in arguing with them.[90] He must have reflected afterwards that a return to the feudal past, which required him to submit loyally to the wishes of the king, his lord, was perhaps not as desirable as he imagined.

Even those who were most deeply committed to retaining a world where power remained in the hands of a few rather than many, where old institutions retained just respect, had second thoughts about their ideal. They occasionally resented kings and dukes. They sometimes stumbled as if by surprise on the discovery that democracy was a much more desirable part of the equation than they had thought.

Few people knew about the dispute over the earl marshal's authority. At the same time a different fight broke out into plain view. The two are distinctly related. Here the duke's insistence on hereditary privilege, and his refusal to accept the sort of quiet compromise worked out over the coronation, nearly brought everything to an end. For here there was no quaint earl marshal, insisting on his rights, but a militant duke seeking not only to refurbish the political power of the hereditary principle, but also to thwart the duly-elected government with armed force.

The duke's modesty made him dislike the rough and tumble of political contest and, unless it affected the position of Catholics, he usually shunned even the dignified debate of the House of Lords. But in the controversy over the budget of 1909 he spoke out in favor of rejection in the Lords. He said he thought the electorate ought to approve of the Lords' rejection of Lloyd George's controversial budget.

> I believe if the reason, common-sense and intelligence of the people of this country were allowed to prevail, they would clearly see that in giving them the opportunity of expressing their opinion on this measure the House of Lords is doing a democratic act and an act which ought to merit their regard.[91]

Norfolk argued that the House of Lords was able to exist and flourish in the twentieth century not because it successfully resisted democratic politics, but because it enabled the people to express their opinions more readily than the Liberal majority in the lower house was willing to allow. It was here, when the House of Lords tried to claim that it was more democratic than the Commons that it, and Norfolk along with it, came to grief.

The confrontation between the two houses of Parliament made many search for precedents to see how they should act. Many looked back to the confrontation between Lords and Commons over Gladstone's Irish Church Bill in 1869.[92] Bagehot had advised the House of Lords in 1869 that they would reject Gladstone's bill at their peril. In an article entitled 'Quiet Reasons for Quiet Peers' he argued that such a rejection would give the advantage to violent and articulate radicals who would offer voters persuasive reasons for doing away with the House of Lords. The aristocracy's authority rested on inarticulate deference; it could not withstand argument and discussion.

> The merits of it [an aristocracy] are so hidden, and the objections so very strong and plain, that the mass-vote of mankind must always be against it. An hereditary legislature exists because it exists and is accepted; but it will perish if the common mass of men are set to inquire into it, to discuss it, and vote on it as they themselves wish.[93]

In 1869 the House of Lords followed Bagehot's advice and passed the Irish Church Bill. In 1909 peers took the opposite course and threw out Lloyd George's budget. The duke of Norfolk made a rare series of platform appearances during the election that followed. He spoke in favor of the Conservative candidate at Littlehampton in terms Bagehot would have recognized. He said that if the House of Lords had wished to remain in possession of their hereditary powers and members of a legislative chamber, they would not have acted as they did, but stayed as quiet as possible.[94] Instead, their rejection of the budget showed they welcomed reform and looked forward to taking a more active part in the legislature.[95] It would have been better to heed Bagehot's advice. When hereditary peers tried to intervene decisively in politics, their message was blocked by a rising feeling of class resentment and antagonism.

The duke took similar messages to election platforms in Taunton and Bognor.[96] But when he tried to make the same speech in Brixton, he was brought up short. There his audience jeered; there was no deferential pulling on forelocks. Although the duke engaged in good-natured raillery with his hecklers and sang along with a song asking him to sit down, the audience prevented him from speaking. The electors of Brixton refused to hear his argument about the House of Lords welcoming reform.[97]

By rejecting the budget, the House of Lords had given the advantage, just as Bagehot had predicted, to radicals who could portray the election contest as peers versus people. The election returned the Liberals to power, although it substantially reduced their majority and forced them into an uneasy alliance with the Irish Nationalists. Two months after the election, Lloyd George gave the duke ironic congratulations for his performance in Brixton, calling out to him from some distance down the table at a dinner in Buckingham Palace to do so. After dinner, Lloyd George came up to the duke and told him: 'Ah, you dukes, you get the better of me!'[98] The election showed the opposite: Lloyd George had gotten the better of the dukes.

Norfolk and some among the most vehement of his fellow peers stubbornly refused to admit defeat. During 1910 the House of Lords considered various methods of reforming itself. The duke got up and told the Lords that they should by no means abandon the hereditary principle in their schemes of reform.[99] He was as immovable in his insistence on the hereditary right of the House of Lords as he had been on the rights of the earl marshal and the College of Arms. Even a year later, after a second election had endorsed the Liberal intention of curbing the Lords' veto and the government had revealed the king's promise to create hundreds of peers, if necessary, to insure the passage of its Parliament Bill through the Lords, the duke refused to move. Norfolk allied himself with the most impetuous, diehard wing of his party, led by Lord Halsbury.[100] The Conservative leadership in the Lords, finally paying heed to Bagehot, advised quiet abstention from the final vote on the legislation. At the last minute the duke of Norfolk spoke in favor of the diehard position and changed the votes of a number of peers who had originally planned to abstain.[101] However, in the final vote, Halsbury's party lost and the government bill became law.

Some peers, and indeed prominent Conservatives outside the House of Lords, refused to accept even this check to their insistence on their rights. Conservative extra-parliamentary resistance to the Liberal program remained a potent force in the years between the passage of the Parliament Bill and the beginning of World War I. A rash alliance of Ulster Protestants, English peers and Conservative politicians determined to resist the Liberal intention of granting Home Rule to Ireland. They supported raising armed resistance to the duly-constituted government in Westminster. The duke of Norfolk gave public support to this rash alliance. He appeared on the platform at a Unionist rally in July 1912 at Blenheim Palace, where Edward Carson was presented with a sword and said he could imagine no lengths to which he and his party would not go to resist Home Rule.[102] He was also seriously involved with the organizers of the British Covenant, who had publicly resolved in March 1914 to prevent the British armed forces from enforcing Home Rule in Protestant Ulster. He may well have given them financial support.[103] The duke's extremism and that of the British covenanters might have produced a good deal of violence, if not civil war, had the beginning of hostilities on the continent not forced the dispute aside in the summer of 1914. World War I would severely reduce the influence of hereditary nobilities in Germany, Austria and Russia; it would bring about the fall of their monarchies. The extremism of men like the duke jeopardized those institutions in Britain. Eventual victory in the war allowed traditional institutions in Britain to escape the ruthless scrutiny that resulted either in their abolition or their humiliation on the continent.

Chance played a certain role in preserving monarchy, aristocracy and established Church in Britain. All these were endangered by the potential civil war in Ireland on the eve of the bigger war in Europe. Norfolk contributed perversely to democratic royalism by losing related disputes over the 1909 Budget, the House of Lords and Home Rule and then at last being persuaded to drop the issue altogether by the continental war. He was a defeated reactionary and this was as important to the survival of hereditary institutions in Britain as his deferential but defeated chairmanship of the coronation committee: a great deal of color, a few hints of power, utter secrecy about how far he might have been willing to take his battle to preserve hereditary privilege had the war not arrived. This was the compelling combination that made hereditary institutions still acceptable, but really rather vulnerable, in a critical, democratic age.

If royal ceremonies heightened the prestige of the monarchy by highlighting its legitimate historical associations, they also rendered the monarchy in a demonstrable way politically harmless and non-threatening. A return to feudalism was made not more but less possible by a ceremony with a Roman Catholic duke and crazy costumes. The Tory reactionaries who thought they were furthering their plans of making the masses loyal were also making the ideas connected with medievalism a little absurd. Royal ceremonies did foster loyalty, but they also made people laugh.

Of course the king, a handful of very rich peers and bishops sitting in the House of Lords were not quite as powerless or as laughable as royal ceremonies sometimes made them out to be. But their power rested on its being exercised with subtlety, modesty and charm. The events of the period between 1909 and 1914 showed that a significant number of political conservatives had not yet learned how much indirection and circumspection was necessary if they were to retain a modicum of influence under modern political conditions. The duke of Norfolk had to be taught the lesson twice: once when he was compelled to contract his power as earl marshal; a second time when he finally gave in over the House of Lords and Home Rule. Probably he only dimly understood the lesson even then. The Great War was the lesson that there was no mistaking and the duke died before it was over. His heir came to the dukedom, as he had done, a mere boy. But this boy grew up in completely changed circumstances. Bloomsbury mocked Victorian morality and imperial extravagance. The war poets wove bitter ironies around the old ideals of heroism, service and chivalry. In 1919 landed families sold off and broke up their estates on a larger scale than in the sixteenth-century dissolution of the monasteries. Church congregations dwindled and diminished in size. Aristocratic humbleness, clerical modesty and royal quietness became, even more than before, the order of the day. Esher, who survived the war, wrote to Bigge, now Lord Stamfordham, and told him that any return by the court to the old Edwardian show would be a dreadful mistake.[104]

There was a sense, though, in which democratic royalism had enhanced the prestige of the monarchy beyond the ability of the First World War to harm it. The monarchy, through the perpetual reminder of royal ceremonies before the war, had become one of the most authentically antique parts of the state. The connection of a Roman Catholic duke with the principal state appearances of the sovereign was a small reminder of the nation's religious history and an eccentric guarantee that the monarchy's pedigree had not been invented.

Concern with authentic descent has remained a fascination for British people late into the twentieth century. It appears not only when a Spencer marries into and then tries to leave the royal family, but also in dogs, racehorses and the general titillation when a descendant of the first duke of Marlborough turns out to be a drug dealer. Nor is it solely an upper-class concern. It appears in deserted Norfolk churches where prominently-displayed maps with six different colors show the different centuries in which different parts of the church were built, or in carefully-preserved Victorian slag heaps in windswept suburbs of Manchester. The same interest underlies and explains the enduring popularity of a book which dates the birth of the modern working class not from the nineteenth-century factory system, but from much older seventeenth-century ideas about free-born Englishmen.[105] Today when you hear a Victorian gothic church derided, you will find that it is not the attachment to the historical past that is criticized, but the destruction of seventeenth- and eighteenth-century fragments that is decried. The assumption is that somewhere in the past there is an older and hence a better example. Even a modern Englishman who criticizes Arundel Castle as ersatz gothic is actually implying that had the fifteenth duke retained the elements of eighteenth-century and regency gothic, he would have left a better record of the house's legitimate history. Alongside a wide variety of attempts to mock the royal family in the latter half of the century as hopelessly out of date runs a genuine and equally wide attachment to Morris dancing, top hats at horse races, historical re-enactments of battles from the Civil War and textile reconstruction of tartans worn by Charles Edward Stuart. All of these, like the fifteenth duke of Norfolk, combine a silly charm with a persistent relevance to the lives of Englishmen in the later twentieth century.

Conclusion

In the decades before the First World War British politicians anchored a new and more thorough-going democracy in old, seemingly-antithetical, royalist traditions. They purchased stability, consensus and a sense of historical place by retaining the monarchy alongside a more powerful and a more representative House of Commons. This was the measure of their achievement by the end of the Victorian era: no British institution epitomized national identity more forcefully than the monarchy. No other institution inspired such a universal feeling of loyalty and attachment. The Crown had reached this position in the half century after 1861 by gradually, sometimes unwillingly, giving up its residual prerogatives and concentrating its efforts on ceremony. Through these ceremonies the monarchy ceased to be a vestige of the old regime; it was transformed into a powerfully symbolic institution capable of providing a strong sense of continuity in an era of rapid political change.

The men examined here developed a new rationale for maintaining the monarchy in the modern democratic era. Their attitude to the monarchy and their rationale for retaining it can best be characterized as a sort of strategic compromise between two opposed themes in English constitutional history. All were strongly attached both to parliamentary and monarchical traditions, hence their argument can best be described as democratic royalism. They set out the reasons why the monarchy still remained of use, even though Queen Victoria had few formal powers and the House of Commons had ceased to look for political leadership from the throne. They argued that the monarchy gave an elevated moral and ethical tone to national life, that it provided a religious sanction for the state, that it served as a valuable reminder of the nation's past, and that it provided a sense of unity that was capable of transcending class divisions.

They did not believe that the monarchy possessed any automatic claim on the nation's loyalty. Just as public men would have to present themselves for approval to an expanded electorate, kings and queens in the democratic era would have to win the confidence of the people and show themselves worthy of the nation's respect. This would improve the moral character of the monarchy; and the monarchy would in turn help keep the nation's mind focused on the moral, historical and ethical ideas necessary for successful democratic government.

These men's rationale for the monarchy also had irrational elements. They thought that mystery was an attractive and necessary part of the monarchy's appeal. They were convinced that the monarchy occupied a unique place in the constitution because it inspired an emotional devotion that other governmental institutions lacked. They felt a kind of wordless wonder in witnessing the central acts of state occasions and hoped that spectators would, sharing these sentiments, rededicate themselves to a higher standard of duty and service to the state. Royal ceremonies were also colorful and entertaining; they were sometimes, whether intentionally or not, absurd and amusing to watch. In short, democratic royalism was a logical argument, a diverting spectacle and an emotional appeal for the continuing existence of the monarchy. The result of these men's elaboration of democratic royalism – in royal ceremonies, in essays on the constitution, in sermons and in biographies of kings and queens – was that the monarchy not only survived into the twentieth century, but was given new life and strength. The massive popular attendance at royal ceremonies and the continuing demand for more was an emphatic affirmative to their implied question, 'Is the monarchy still worthwhile?' Those who think it is easy to cook up a little loyalty by staging a big royal show have missed the element of calculated risk in calling for these ceremonies. A thin crowd and extra tickets in the Lord Chamberlain's Office, or a large crowd full of angry faces would have been a difficult-to-hide 'no' to the implied question and a rejection of the rationale. A royal family that repeatedly experienced such hostility, or, even worse, apathy, would as surely have gone into eclipse as any defeated politician, no matter how much courtiers and clergymen wanted to keep it in place as the centerpiece of national loyalty.

These men created a renewed ceremonial style for the monarchy. Their ceremonies were designed to please crowds of people in the streets. Royal processions grew longer than before. They passed through different, often poorer, neighborhoods. Contingents of troops from the empire escorted royal carriages. Yet ceremonies were not so infinitely manipulable that they could be staged solely for the masses of people in the streets, those masses that stood for the new democratic electorate in the minds of the men planning state occasions. Royal ceremonies were traditional rites for which meticulous precedents had been kept. Constantly consulted, these precedents specified attendance at St Paul's or Westminster Abbey. In the new style of ceremonial, even with its increased sensitivity to feeling out of doors, it was not forgotten that indoors men and women, kings and queens, needed to acknowledge their humbleness and sinfulness before God in both praise and prayer. The new style of ceremonial, like the old, was as much about ethics, codes of conduct and high-minded behavior, it was as much about human weakness, failing and resolving to do better, as it was about the orderliness of people in the streets.

Democratic royalism has had an impact on the nation's strangely con-
tradictory sense of itself. Today the oldest of European monarchies lives
cheek by jowl with the mother of parliaments. The arrangement is an
artifact of persuasive arguments and successful ceremonial appeals crys-
tallized in democratic royalism during the era before the First World War.
People standing on street corners, packed together high up in the arches
of cathedrals, or at home in their armchairs were riveted by a new vision
of national identity that was part moral crusade, part self-congratulation
and part plain snobbery. Despite these flaws, it was a vision of national
identity that assured a relatively peaceful passage from narrow, plutocratic
oligarchy to relatively successful, twentieth-century democracy.

The absence of the sovereigns who were at the center of these ceremonies
from a contributing role in the development of democratic royalism may
well be questioned. Queen Victoria, King Edward VII and King George
V all had their own notions about ceremonial. All of them believed that
the monarchy had a useful role to play in the constitution. Yet, their
contributions to the rationale which underpinned the monarchy's successful
transformation were more equivocal than those of any of the five men
examined here.

The 1887 jubilee would not have been held without Queen Victoria's
decision to meet the public demand for some commemoration of the length
of her reign. However, she considered Bagehot a 'radical' and in a well-
known letter refused to be queen of a democracy. Edward VII had a liking
for ceremonial, which Esher and others remarked upon. Yet, Esher also
had to restrain him when he would have abolished wholesale large tracts
of the coronation ceremony. Equally, George V extended Esher's ideas by
taking royal ceremonial to India, though he too was frequently in danger
of mistaking the temper of the times. At the end of the First World War,
both Esher and Davidson agreed that George V's court had not yet registered the vast impact of the war on English society. By the nature of the
position, the sovereign is insulated from the outside world, surrounded by
people who are afraid to be critical and frequently applauded for having
done nothing very much. Sovereigns at the turn of the century were not
well placed to take the nation's pulse and decide how best to respond to
it. They needed honest experts who were prepared to take risks, potentially
annoying their employers, to meet public demands and to shape public
tastes.

There have been others who followed in the footsteps of these five
and contributed to adapting the rationale after World War I. There was
much that happened in the war that called for a re-examination of the late
Victorian settlement. The involvement of women in the domestic workforce

during the war and their enfranchisement after the war blurred the old clear distinctions between home and work, spirituality and warfare, dignity and efficiency. This required a readjustment of the old feminized monarchy handed down from Queen Victoria's reign. Similarly, the next war brought the empire to an end and challenged Britain's status as a world power. Key individuals helped the monarchy to meet some of these changes. For example, from within the royal family, Queen Elizabeth, the Queen Mother, Lord Mountbatten and Lord Snowdon, and outside it, Harold Nicolson, Cecil Beaton and Elizabeth Longford have all been influential. The sixteenth duke of Norfolk, who came as a boy to the earl marshalship and served in that office for nearly six decades, was able to recapture some of his father's influence and place his personal imprint on royal ceremonies. His daughters wrote out the invitations to the 1937 coronation by hand.

There was a sense in the late twentieth century, however, that all this was a little too quaint, that the monarchy was responding too slowly, or not at all, to important changes in the society it still claimed to represent. Perhaps the monarchy clung too long to the secrecy Bagehot had enjoined, to the imperial theatrics which were Esher's legacy. Clearly there needs to be a new rationale if the English public is to be persuaded of the monarchy's continuing relevance to a nation on the verge of a new century.

Humanity in the midst of what appears to be exalted, hard work and service, as well as a persuasive embracing of modesty, simplicity and plain speaking have repeatedly won popularity in the modern era for British sovereigns. Anyone who would be king or queen in the twenty-first century could hardly do worse that to try to emulate these values. The resolve to reform the weaker self, to contemplate and encourage the better self as well as one's small ability to do good, this is what has taken place in the still moments at the center of every royal ceremony in the modern era. It took place in the candlelight of the eighteenth century. Revitalized and modified, it took place in the gaslight of the nineteenth century. If it can continue to take place under the television lights today, if this humbleness can be sustained with sincerity and honesty in the future, it may still be cause for quiet celebration.

Notes

Introduction

1. 'Elizabeth R', BBC (1992).
2. D. Cannadine, 'The Context, Performance and Meaning of Ritual: The British Monarchy and the "Invention of Tradition", *c.* 1820–1977', in *The Invention of Tradition*, E. Hobsbawm and T. Ranger (eds) (Cambridge, 1983) 101–64. Also see his 'Introduction: divine rights of kings', in *Rituals of Royalty*, Cannadine and S. Price (eds) (Cambridge, 1987) 1–19.
3. 'Tradition, Continuity, Stability, Soap Opera', *The Economist*, 22 Oct. 1994, 32.
4. E. Hobsbawm, 'Mass Producing Traditions: Europe, 1870–1914', *Invention of Tradition*, 263–307.
5. Ibid., 282.
6. 'The Not So Ancient Traditions of Monarchy', *New Society*, 2 Jun. 1977, 438. This was a preliminary version of the essay that appeared in the Hobsbawm collection.
7. 'British Monarchy and the "Invention of Tradition"', *Invention of Tradition*, 122.
8. Ibid., 124.
9. Cannadine quoting Lady Longford, ibid., 141.
10. Ibid., 161.
11. D. Cannadine, *The Pleasures of the Past* (London, 1989) 30.
12. Ibid.
13. Ibid., 259.
14. L. Colley, *Britons, Forging the Nation 1707–1837* (New Haven and London, 1992) ch. 5; idem, 'The Apotheosis of George III: Loyalty, Royalty and the British Nation 1760–1820', *Past and Present*, no. 102 (Feb. 1984) 94–129. See also M. A. Morris, 'Monarchy as an Issue in English Political Argument during the French Revolutionary Era', PhD thesis, University of London, 1988, esp. ch. 7, 'Royalist Ritual and the Support of the State'.
15. L. Colley, 'Whose Nation? Class and National Consciousness in Britain 1750–1830', *Past and Present*, no. 113 (November 1986) 117.
16. Colley, *Britons*, 230.
17. J. C. D. Clark also casts doubt on the notion of invented tradition in *English Society, 1688–1832* (Cambridge, 1985); the cover illustration is taken from the thanksgiving for the recovery of George III at St Paul's in 1789.
18. P. R. Williams, 'Public Discussion of the British Monarchy, 1837–1887', PhD thesis, Cambridge University, 1988, 255, 192–3.
19. D. Cannadine, 'The Last Hanoverian Sovereign?: The Victorian Monarchy in Historical Perspective, 1688–1988', in *The First Modern Society: Essays in English History in Honour of Lawrence Stone*, A. L. Beier, Cannadine and J. M. Rosenheim (eds) (Cambridge, 1989) 127–65. For another perspective on how late Victorian ceremonies were continuous with earlier traditions see W. L. Arnstein, 'Queen Victoria Opens Parliament: The

Disinvention of Tradition', *Historical Research*, 63, 151 (Jun. 1990) 178–94.

20. C. Geertz, *Negara: The Theatre State in Nineteenth-Century Bali* (Princeton, 1980) 122.

21. D. Sinclair, *Two Georges: The Making of the Modern Monarchy* (London, 1988) 4.

22. T. Nairn, *The Enchanted Glass: Britain and its Monarchy* (London, 1988) 282–3.

23. C. Hitchens, *The Monarchy* (London, 1990) 42; E. Wilson, *The Myth of British Monarchy* (London, 1989) is in the same vein.

24. F. Hardie, *The Political Influence of Queen Victoria, 1861–1901* (London, 1935); idem, *The Political Influence of the British Monarchy, 1868–1952* (London, 1952).

25. See his Prothero Lecture, 'The Survival of the British Monarchy', *Transactions of the Royal Historical Society*, 5th ser., no. 36 (1986) 143–64; his Stenton Lecture, *The Modern British Monarchy: A Study in Adaptation* (Reading, 1987); idem, and R. Griffiths, *The Oxford Illustrated History of the British Monarchy* (Oxford, 1988) vii.

26. For example, Sir S. Lee, *King Edward VII: A Biography* (New York, 1925–7); E. Longford, *Victoria, R. I.* (London, 1964); idem, *Elizabeth R.: A Biography* [of Elizabeth II] (London, 1983); H. Nicolson, *King George the Fifth: His Life and Reign* (London, 1952).

27. H. Fast, *The Selected Works of Tom Paine and Citizen Tom Paine* (New York, 1946) 122–3, 166.

28. L. Colley, 'Introduction', *Crown Pictorial, Art and the British Monarchy* (New Haven, 1990) 4.

29. Cannadine, *Pleasures of the Past*, 268.

30. Arnstein, 'Queen Victoria Opens Parliament', *Historical Research*, 178–94.

31. J. Grigg, *Lloyd George: The People's Champion* (London, 1978) 303. A. G. Edwards, archbishop of Wales, *Memories* (London, 1927) 242, 260.

32. I. V. Hull, 'Prussian Dynastic Ritual and the End of the Monarchy', in *German Nationalism and the European Response, 1890–1945*, Hull, C. Fink and M. Knox (eds) (Norman, 1985) 13–41. Also relevant are Hull's *The Entourage of Kaiser Wilhelm II, 1888–1918* (Cambridge, 1982); and several of the contributions to *Kaiser Wilhelm II, New Interpretations: The Corfu Papers*, J. C. G. Röhl and N. Sombart (eds) (Cambridge, 1982). For Austria, see J. Shedell, 'Emperor, Church, and People: Religion and Dynastic Loyalty during the Golden Jubilee of Franz Joseph', *Catholic Historical Review*, 76, 1 (Jan. 1990) 71–92. On Russian royal ceremonial, R. Wortman takes a more sophisticated view, arguing that royal ritual was mainly for elite consumption, in *Scenarios of Power, Myth and Ceremony in Russian Monarchy* (Princeton, 1995).

33. Cannadine, 'The British Monarchy and the "Invention of Tradition"', 111.

34. Ibid., 129.

35. H. C. G. Matthew, 'Introduction', *The Gladstone Diaries*, idem (ed.) 10 vols (Oxford, 1968–94) [hereafter *GD*] X clxii.

36. Even Disraeli's biographer, Lord Blake, in his centenary Romanes Lecture, *Gladstone, Disraeli and Queen Victoria* (Oxford, 1993) comes very near to endorsing this position.

37. The anthropologist, Ilse Hayden, arrived at a similar view of how the monarchy appears able to combine seemingly opposite political philosophies in her study of the later twentieth-century ritual: *Symbol and Privilege: The Ritual Context of British Royalty* (Tucson, 1987).

38. B. S. Cohn, 'History and Anthropology: The State of Play', *Comparative Studies in Society and History*, 22 (Apr. 1980) 198–221.

39. E. Shils and M. Young, 'The Meaning of the Coronation', *The Sociological Review*, n.s., 1 (1953) 80.

1 Walter Bagehot: Male Efficiency and Female Dignity

1. A. V. Dicey, *Lectures Introductory to the Study of the Law of the Constitution*, 2nd edn (London, 1886) 7. Dicey's tributes to *The English Constitution* are reprinted in Walter Bagehot, *The Collected Works of Walter Bagehot*, N. St John-Stevas (ed.) 15 vols (London, 1965–86) [hereafter *Works*] XV 78–81.

2. R. H. Hutton, 'Walter Bagehot', *Dictionary of National Biography*, 1967 edn, I 865. S. Collini, 'A Place in the Syllabus: Political Science at Cambridge', in S. Collini, D. Winch and J. Burrow, *That Noble Science of Politics* (Cambridge, 1983) 351–52.

3. A March 1872 article on the civil list from *The Economist*, over which Bagehot had direct editorial control, appeared in 'Notes on the Civil List, 1897', Welby Papers, PRO, T250/2, part I, fol. 549, p. 100, prepared at the Treasury during Lord Salisbury's second administration; *The English Constitution* is quoted from as among 'the chief constitutional authorities' in a cabinet memorandum on the House of Lords, 8 Mar. 1910, Asquith Papers, Bodleian Library, Asquith MS 103, fols. 37–40.

4. N. St John-Stevas, 'Bagehot and the Monarchy', *Works*, XV 305.

5. T. Nairn, *The Enchanted Glass* (London, 1988) 360–61; J. Cannon, 'The Survival of the British Monarchy', *Transactions of the Royal Historical Society*, 5th ser., no. 36 (1986) 151. Cannon later argued that Bagehot was not only the starting place for discussion, but also had a decisive impact on the monarchy's evolution; see his Stenton Lecture, *The Modern British Monarchy: A Study in Adaptation* (Reading, 1987) 17.

6. The best brief look at Bagehot's life is N. St John-Stevas, 'Walter Bagehot, A Short Biography', *Works*, I 29–83.

7. Quoted in ibid., 38.

8. 'Mr Macaulay' (1856), *Works*, I 408.

9. Bagehot to his mother, 8 May 1851 [apparently misdated: the actual opening day of the exhibition was May 1st], *Works*, XII 317–19.

10. Bagehot's ambivalence is also explored in D. Spring, 'Walter Bagehot and Deference', *The American Historical Review*, 81 (Jun. 1976) 524–531.

11. Spring, 'Bagehot and Deference', 525.

12. *Works*, V 203 [hereafter all references to *The English Constitution* unless noted otherwise].

13. J. Burrow, 'Sense and Circumstances: Bagehot and the Nature of Political Understanding', in Collini, Winch and Burrow, *Noble Science of Politics*, 163; N. St John-Stevas, 'The Political Genius of Walter Bagehot', *Works*, V 75.

For a complete bibliography of commentaries on *The English Constitution* see *Works*, XV 426–42.

14. *Works*, V 204.
15. Ibid., 206 [Bagehot's emphasis].
16. Ibid., 241.
17. Ibid., chapter 7, 'Its Supposed Checks and Balances', 344–66.
18. Ibid., 226.
19. Ibid.
20. Ibid., 229.
21. Ibid., 208.
22. Ibid.
23. Ibid., 386.
24. *Physics and Politics* (1872), *Works*, VII 104–5.
25. *Works*, V 230.
26. Ibid., 209.
27. Ibid., 243.
28. 'The Cost of Public Dignity' (1867), *Works*, V 411–13; 'Sir Charles Dilke on the Cost of the Crown' (1874), *Works*, V 414–17. The civil list was an annual sum granted to the queen by parliament to defray the costs of running the royal household, to pay the salaries of household officers and servants, and to provide her with funds for her own personal use.
29. 'The New Title of the Queen' (1876), *Works*, V 447–9.
30. 'Quiet Reasons for Quiet Peers' (1869), *Works*, VI 20–1 [Bagehot's emphasis]; see also *Lombard Street* (1873), *Works*, IX 81.
31. 'The Position of the Lords at this Juncture' (1869), *Works*, VI 29 [Bagehot's emphasis].
32. *Works*, V 234, 239.
33. 'Mr Bright on Republicanism' (1873), *Works*, V 427–30.
34. *Works*, V 239.
35. Ibid., 240.
36. Ibid.
37. Ibid., 369.
38. Ibid., 259.
39. Ibid., 280.
40. John Burrow has placed Bagehot in a tradition of skeptical Whigs who defended the established order. Hume, Paley, Burke and Macaulay were cynical about the crowd's reverence for tradition, yet reverential themselves. See his *Whigs and Liberals: Continuity and Change in English Political Thought* (Oxford, 1988), ch. 3, especially 68–9; idem, *A Liberal Descent* (Cambridge, 1981) 53–4, 293–4; idem, 'Sense and Circumstances . . .' in Collini, Winch and Burrow, *Noble Science of Politics*, 175.
41. *Works*, V 263 [Bagehot's emphasis].
42. 'Aristocratic and Unaristocratic Statesmen' (1855), *Works*, XIV 206–11.
43. 'Béranger' (1857), *Works*, II 32. Partly quoted in N. St John-Stevas, *Walter Bagehot* (London, 1959) 23.
44. 'Edward Gibbon' (1856), *Works*, I 380.
45. *Works*, V 263.
46. Ibid., 178.
47. Ibid.

48. 'On the Emotion of Conviction' (1871), *Works*, XIV 46–51. Also: St John-Stevas, 'The Political Genius of Walter Bagehot', *Works*, V 51.
49. *Lombard Street* (1873), *Works*, IX 67.
50. *Works*, V 210, 209.
51. 'The First Edinburgh Reviewers' (1855), *Works*, I 315.
52. Quoted in N. St John-Stevas, 'Bagehot's Religious Views', *Works*, XV 252–3. My point about Bagehot's vacillating attitude toward the mystical ele-- ments of religion owes a good deal to St John-Stevas's reading of Bagehot.
53. Burrow speaks of the necessity of considering religion in evaluating the skeptical Whig tradition, to which he argues Bagehot belongs, in *Whigs and Liberals*, 57.
54. 'The Public Worship Regulation Bill' (1874), *Works*, VII 312; St John-Stevas, 'Bagehot's Religious Views', *Works*, XV 287.
55. 'The Public Worship Regulation Bill', *Works*, VII 317; 'The Proposed Ecclesiastical Legislation' (1874), *Works*, VII 322.
56. Quoted in St John-Stevas, 'Bagehot's Religious Views', *Works*, XV 277.
57. R. H. Hutton, 'Walter Bagehot' (1877), *Works*, XV 114.
58. *My Dear Duchess, Social and Political Letters to the Duchess of Manchester 1858–1869*, A. L. Kennedy (ed.) (London, 1956) 181, 183–4.
59. *Works*, V 226.
60. [Lord R. Cecil], 'The Queen', *The Saturday Review*, 26 Mar. 1864, 367; noted in M. Pinto-Duschinsky, *The Political Thought of Lord Salisbury* (London, 1967) 182.
61. [Cecil], 'The Queen', 26 Mar. 1864, 367.
62. [Cecil], 'The Queen', *The Saturday Review*, 9 Dec. 1865; noted in Pinto-Duschinsky, *Political Thought of Lord Salisbury*, 188.
63. *Disraeli, Derby and the Conservative Party, Journals and Memoirs of Edward Henry, Lord Stanley 1849–1869*, J. Vincent (ed.) (New York, 1978) xv.
64. Ibid., 214.
65. *Works*, V 207, 209.
66. 'The Monarchy and the People', *Works*, V 431–2.
67. M. Poovey, *Uneven Developments: The Ideological Work of Gender in Mid-Victorian England* (London, 1989) 6–10.
68. *Works*, V 234.
69. L. Colley, *Britons, Forging the Nation 1707–1837* (New Haven and London, 1992) 271–3.
70. *Works*, V 236.
71. *Works*, V 244.
72. *Works*, V 253.
73. 'The Constitutional Relations of the Lords and the Commons' (1871), *Works*, VI 35.
74. 'Mr Macaulay', *Works*, I 406.
75. 27 Feb. 1872, 'Diary of Eliza Wilson Bagehot' [microfilm], Yale University Library, Manuscripts and Archives Department.

2 William Ewart Gladstone: National Acts of Religion

1. 2 Jan. 1896, *The Prime Ministers' Papers: William Ewart Gladstone*, J. Brooke and M. Sorensen (eds) (London, 1971–81) I 168–9. I am grateful to Peter Stansky, who pointed me in the direction of the dream.

2. Quoted in N. St John-Stevas, 'Bagehot as a Writer and Literary Critic', *Works*, XV 224.

3. See 28 June 1838, *GD*, II 381, n. 7; D. Hudson, *Martin Tupper* (London, 1949) 25.

4. J. C. D. Clark, *English Society 1688-1832* (Cambridge, 1985) 418; 6 Jul. 1838, *GD*, II 382.

5. *The State in its Relations with the Church*, rev. edn (1838; London, 1841) II 5-6, 8.

6. Ibid., I 158-9.

7. Quoted in Clark, *English Society 1688-1832*, 413.

8. See 29 Aug. 1840, *GD*, III 56. I am grateful to Dr. Matthew for this reference.

9. 10 Apr. 1842, *GD*, III 192-3.

10. J. Morley, *The Life of William Ewart Gladstone* (London, 1903) II 428; and P. Guedalla, *The Queen and Mr Gladstone*, reprint (1934; London, 1969) [hereafter *Q & G*] ch. 4.

11. On the 'royalty question' and plans to associate the royal family with Ireland see Gladstone to Granville, 3 Dec. 1870, *The Political Correspondence of Mr Gladstone and Lord Granville 1868-76*, A. Ramm (ed.), Camden Third Series, vols 81-2 (London, 1952) [hereafter *G & G*] I 170-2; also the commentary in H. C. G. Matthew, 'Introduction', *GD*, VII lxviii-lxix; and Sir P. Magnus, *Gladstone* (London, 1954) 199-217.

12. Gladstone to H. A. Bruce, 1 Sep. 1871, *GD*, VIII 29; and Bruce to Gladstone, 3 Sep. 1871, BL, Add MS 44087; on Bradlaugh see F. A. D'Arcy, 'Charles Bradlaugh and the English Republican Movement, 1868-1878', *Historical Journal* [hereafter *HJ*] 25 (Jun. 1982) 367-83.

13. S. Temple (pseud.), *What Does She Do With It?*, Tracts for the Times, no. 1 (London, 1871); 9 Sep. 1871, *GD*, VIII 32, n. 8.

14. *Sir Charles Dilke on the Cost of the Crown* (London, 1871) 23.

15. Gladstone to Lowe, 24 Nov. 1871, BL, Add MS 44540, fol. 176.

16. The queen to Gladstone, 4 Dec. 1871, *Q & G*, 342 [The queen's emphasis].

17. A. Ponsonby, *Henry Ponsonby, Queen Victoria's Private Secretary* (New York, 1943) 98-9.

18. The queen to Gladstone, and Gladstone to the queen, 15 Dec. 1871, *Q & G*, 345.

19. Ponsonby to Granville, 16 and 17 Dec. 1871, Granville Papers, PRO, 30/29/33/299-302.

20. Ponsonby to Gladstone, 17 Dec. 1871, BL, loan 73, vol. 11; partly printed in *Q & G*, 345-6.

21. D. Schreuder, 'Gladstone and the Conscience of the State', *The Conscience of the Victorian State*, P. Marsh (ed.) (Syracuse, 1979) 90.

22. A list of precedents in Gladstone's hand is in BL, Add MS 44618, fols 47-8; Gladstone to Granville, 19 Dec. 1871, *G & G*, II 291.

23. Gladstone to Granville, 25 Dec. 1871, *G & G*, II 293; for his mem see 21 Dec. 1871, *GD*, VIII 81-4.

24. D. W. R. Bahlman, 'Introduction', *The Diary of Sir Edward Walter Hamilton*, idem (ed.) (Oxford, 1972) I xlviii, n. 2; J. P. Parry, *Democracy and Religion, Gladstone and the Liberal Party 1867-1875* (Cambridge, 1986) 63.

25. A. Ramm, 'Gladstone's Religion', *HJ* 28 (Jun. 1985) 328.

26. J. P. Parry, 'Religion and the Collapse of Gladstone's First Government, 1870-1874', *HJ* 25 (Mar. 1982) 76.

27. Quoted in Lord Rendel, *The Personal Papers of Lord Rendel* (London, 1931) 65.
28. D. Edwards, *Leaders of the Church of England 1828–1944* (Oxford, 1971) 164; W. Arnstein, 'Queen Victoria and Religion', in *Religion in the Lives of English Women 1760–1930*, G. Malmgreen (ed.) (Bloomington, 1986) 113.
29. M. Ponsonby, *Mary Ponsonby* (London, 1927) 43.
30. O. Chadwick, *The Victorian Church* (New York, 1966–70) I 159, 165.
31. *GD*, VIII 84.
32. 21 Dec. 1871, *The Letters of Queen Victoria*, A. C. Benson, Lord Esher, and G. E. Buckle (eds), 3 series, 9 vols. (London, 1907–32) [hereafter *LQV*], 2nd ser., II 181.
33. Granville to Gladstone, 28 Dec. 1871, *G & G*, II 293–4.
34. On Wellesley see G. Battiscombe, 'Gerald Wellesley: A Victorian Dean and Domestic Chaplain', *Report of the Society of the Friends of St George's and the Descendants of the Knights of the Garter, Annual Report to 31st December 1963* (Windsor, 1963) 126–35.
35. Wellesley to Gladstone, 8 Jan. 1872, BL, Add MS 44340, fols 1–2.
36. The queen to W. E. Forster and Forster to Gladstone, 8 Jan. 1872, BL, Add MS 44157, fols 43–7 [The queen's emphasis].
37. The queen to Gladstone, 13 Jan. 1872, *Q & G*, 352.
38. Gladstone to Granville, 15 Jan. 1872, *G & G*, II 299.
39. Gladstone to R. W. Church, dean of St Paul's, 19 Jan. 1872, BL, Add MS 44541, fol. 48; to Lord Sydney, lord chamberlain, 19 Jan. 1872, PRO, LC 2/91(4)/9.
40. See the exchange of letters between Gladstone and Ponsonby, 22, 23 and 24 Dec. 1871, *Q & G*, 347–9; Gladstone to Granville, 25 Dec. 1871 and 9 Feb. 1872, *G & G*, II 293, 306. See also 18, 20 Jan., 14 Feb. 1872, *GD*, VIII 95–6, 110.
41. See Sydney to Gladstone, 22 Jan. 1872, BL, Add MS 44318, fols 443–4; Gladstone to Sydney, same date, Add MS 44541, fol. 50; 22, 23 Jan. 1872, *GD*, VIII 97–8.
42. The queen to Gladstone, 22 Jan. 1872, *Q & G*, 356; Gladstone to the queen, 23 Jan. 1872, BL, loan 73, vol. 12 [The queen's emphasis].
43. Gladstone to Sydney, 23 Jan. 1872, BL, Add MS 44318, fol. 447.
44. Gladstone to Wellesley, 31 Jan. 1872, BL, Add MS 44541, fol. 62.
45. Wellesley to Gladstone, 1 Feb. 1872, BL, Add MS 44340, fol. 3; Gladstone to Wellesley, 2 Feb. 1872, Add MS 44541, fol. 63.
46. Wellesley to Gladstone, 9 Feb. 1872, BL, Add MS 44340, fol. 5.
47. The queen to Gladstone, 1 Feb. 1872, BL, loan 73, vol. 12; 2 Feb., *GD*, VIII 105–6; Gladstone to the queen, undated [2 Feb.?], Gladstone to Ponsonby, 2 Feb. [2 letters], Ponsonby to Gladstone, 3 Feb., Gladstone to Sir Charles Biddulph, 23 Feb., all BL, loan 73, vol. 12; see also Gladstone to Ponsonby, 2 Feb., Add MS 44541, fol. 63.
48. S. Ponsonby Fane, 'The Thanksgiving Service at St Paul's', 27 Feb. 1872, RA LC Private Memoranda – Ceremonials; *Parliamentary Debates* (Hansard) [hereafter *PD*] 3rd ser., vol. 209 (1872), col. 144; Francis Knollys, the prince's private secretary, to Henry Ponsonby, 7 Feb., PRO, LC 2/91(4)/97, 107; *The Times*, 5, 7 and 8 Feb., pp. 10, 12 and 9 respectively.

49. Gladstone to the queen, 22 Feb. 1872, BL, loan 73, vol. 12; Ponsonby Fane, 'Thanksgiving Service', RA LC Private Memoranda.
50. Gladstone to the queen, 15 Feb. 1872, BL, loan 73, vol. 12; *The Times*, 13 Feb. 1872, 5.
51. This account is drawn mainly from *The Annual Register: A Review of Public Events at Home and Abroad, for the Year 1872*, new ser. (London, 1873); *The Times*, 28 Feb. 1872; and *The Illustrated London News*, 2 Mar. 1872.
52. The queen to her eldest daughter, 28 Feb. 1872, in *Darling Child, Private Correspondence of Queen Victoria and the Crown Princess of Prussia 1871–1878*, R. Fulford (ed.) (London, 1976) 32.
53. 27 Feb. 1872, *LQV*, 2nd ser., II 194–5.
54. 27 Feb. 1872, *GD*, VIII 117.
55. 'The Thanksgiving', *The Illustrated London News*, 2 Mar. 1872, 203.
56. 'The Queen and the National Thanksgiving', *The Saturday Review*, 2 Mar. 1872, 259.
57. The queen to Gladstone, 23 Mar. 1872, *Q & G*, 367; see also 19 Mar. 1872, *GD*, VIII 128, n. 6.
58. See 9 and 23 Mar. 1876, *GD*, IX 110, 114.
59. *PD*, 3rd ser., vol. 227 (1876) cols. 1737, 1740–2.
60. Ibid., vol. 228 (1876) col. 492.
61. R. Blake, however, thinks the remarks on the empire were made casually rather than with any definite plan in mind; see his *Disraeli* (New York, 1966) 522–4. Two recent assessments of Disraeli's plans are in H. C. G. Matthew, 'Introduction', *GD*, IX xxxv; and M. Pugh, *The Tories and the People 1880–1935* (Oxford, 1985) 71, 74–5.
62. L. A. Knight, 'The Royal Titles Act and India', *HJ* 11 (Sep. 1968) 488–507.
63. Rendel, *Papers of Lord Rendel*, 148.
64. The first article appeared in *The Contemporary Review* when the first issue of the *Church Quarterly Review* was delayed; see *GD*, IX lxxxv, 32, n. 8.
65. William Ewart Gladstone, *Gleanings of Past Years, 1875–78*, 7 vols (New York, 1879) [hereafter *Gleanings*] I 32–3.
66. Matthew, 'Introduction', *GD*, IX lxxxix.
67. *The Works of Hannah More* (1788; reprint, London, 1801) VI 1, 76–7; F. K. Brown, *Fathers of the Victorians* (Cambridge, 1961) 98–104; D. Spring, 'The Clapham Sect: Some Social and Political Aspects', *Victorian Studies*, 5 (Sep. 1961) 36.
68. *Gleanings*, I 98.
69. R. Welby, 'Crown Appanage Fund', Jun. 1888, Welby Papers, PRO, T 250/2/I/332, p. 1.
70. Knollys to E. W. Hamilton, formerly Gladstone's private secretary, 17 June 1889, Hamilton Papers, BL, Add MS 48604, fols 184–5; Hamilton diary, 18 June 1889, Add MS 48651, fol. 17.
71. Quoted in S. Weintraub, *Victoria, An Intimate Biography* (New York, 1987) 461.
72. *PD*, 3rd ser., vol. 338 (1889) col. 1114.
73. Hamilton diary, 13 Jul. 1889, BL, Add MS 48651, fol. 41.
74. Sir M. Havers, E. Grayson and P. Shankland, *The Royal Baccarat Scandal* (London, 1977); Sir P. Magnus, *King Edward the Seventh* (London, 1964) 222–31.

75. Gladstone to Knollys, 18 Jun. 1891, BL, Add MS 44230, fols 206–7.
76. Knollys to Gladstone, 19, 20 Jun. 1891, BL, Add MS 44230, fols 208–11.
77. J. F. A. Mason, 'Lord Salisbury: A Librarian's View', in *Salisbury: The Man and His Policies*, Lord Blake and H. Cecil (eds) (London, 1987) 26–7.
78. Ponsonby, *Mary Ponsonby*, 69, 178 [Ponsonby's emphasis].
79. Rendel, *Papers of Lord Rendel*, 148.
80. *Prime Ministers' Papers*, Brooke and Sorensen (eds), I 174–5 [Gladstone's emphasis]; *LQV*, 3rd ser., III 146.
81. Quoted in E. Longford, *Victoria R. I.* (London, 1964) 551.
82. Rendel, *Papers of Lord Rendel*, 148.
83. Brooke and Sorensen (eds), *Prime Ministers' Papers*, I 169.
84. Mary Ponsonby was one acute observer who saw that the monarchy would not last long if Gladstone chose to 'bare his teeth' on the subject; see Ponsonby, *Mary Ponsonby*, 68.

3 Lord Esher: Empire Theater

1. Although Brett did not succeed his father as second Viscount Esher until 1899, for the sake of clarity and convenience he is referred to here as Esher throughout.
2. 'Lord Esher', *The Times*, 23 January 1930, 17.
3. Esher to the duchess of Sutherland, 18 Apr. 1911, *Journals and Letters of Reginald Viscount Esher*, M. V. Brett and Lord Esher (eds), 4 vols (London, 1934–38) [hereafter *J & L*] III 49. See also Lees-Milne, *The Enigmatic Edwardian: The Life of Reginald 2nd Viscount Esher* [hereafter Lees-Milne] (London, 1986) 228.
4. C. H. Dudley Ward, 'Reginald, Viscount Esher', *The Quarterly Review*, 254 (1930) 252.
5. Lees-Milne, 34.
6. Ibid., 68–9.
7. R. B. Brett, 'From Three Platforms. I. New Policy and Old Failures', *The Fortnightly Review*, 38 n.s. (Oct. 1885) 457.
8. R. Esher, *Cloud Capp'd Towers* (London, 1927) 94.
9. S. Hignett, *Brett* (New York, 1983) 16–17.
10. L. Esher, *Our Selves Unknown: An Autobiography* (London, 1985) 27–8. On Cory, see M. Howard, 'Empire, Race and War in Pre-1914 Britain', in H. Lloyd-Jones, V. Pearl and B. Worden (eds), *History and Imagination: Essays in Honor of H. R. Trevor-Roper* (London, 1981) 341.
11. I. Howe (ed.), 'The Head of the District', *The Portable Rudyard Kipling* (New York, 1982) 100–24.
12. R. B. Brett, *Yoke of Empire: Sketches of the Queen's Prime Ministers* (London, 1896) 32–3.
13. R. B. Brett, *Footprints of Statesmen during the Eighteenth Century in Britain* (London, 1892) 196–7.
14. Brett, *Yoke*, 180–1.
15. R. B. Brett, 'What Are the Ideals of the Masses?' *The Nineteenth Century*, 28 (Oct. 1890) 526–33.
16. Idem, 'The Tyranny of the "Nonconformist Conscience"', *The Nineteenth Century*, 29 (Feb. 1891) 202–13.

17. Ibid., 206.
18. Lees-Milne, 101; on Kensington Palace see letters of Sir A. Bigge to Esher, ESHR 5/7, fol. 161 and *passim*.
19. Sir A. Bigge to the home secretary, Sir M. Ridley, 7 Aug. 1896, *LQV*, 3rd ser., III 60.
20. W. M. Kuhn, 'Queen Victoria's Jubilees and the Invention of Tradition', *Victorian Poetry*, 25 (Autumn–Winter 1987) 112.
21. Bigge note, undated [Oct. 1896?], RA R45/1.
22. Duchess of Sutherland to Esher, 12 Dec. 1893, *J & L*, I 176–7; Knollys to Bigge, 2 Jan. 1897, RA R45/10.
23. Sir S. Ponsonby Fane, comptroller of the Lord Chamberlain's Office, minutes of the committee's first meeting, 2 Feb. 1897, PRO, LC 2/137.
24. Suggested the previous autumn; see Bigge to S. McDonnell, Salisbury's private secretary, 22 Nov. 1896, HHM, 3rd Marquess of Salisbury Papers, 3M/F15.
25. Ponsonby Fane's minutes of meeting on 28 Feb. 1897, PRO, LC 2/137. See also Davidson chapter.
26. Esher to Knollys, 2 Mar. 1897, PRO, WORK 21/11; emphasis added.
27. Knollys to Bigge, 12 Mar. 1897, RA R45/92.
28. Esher to the first lord of the Treasury, A. J. Balfour, 25 Mar. 1897, Balfour Papers, BL, Add MS 49718, fols 10–11.
29. 'Rehearsal for the Service at St Paul's', *The Illustrated London News*, 19 June 1897, 839.
30. On Edwardes and the Empire music hall, see *The Oxford Companion to the Theatre*, P. Hartnoll (ed.), 4th edn (Oxford, 1983) 243, 247. Edwardes is mentioned in a letter of Esher to his son, Maurice Brett, June 1897, *J & L*, I 203. A remark of Edward Hamilton's in 1902, who represented the Treasury on the committees that planned the diamond jubilee in 1897 and the coronation in 1902, suggests that someone from the Empire music hall had been consulted before; see his diary, 23 June 1902, Edward Hamilton Papers, BL, Add MS 48679, fols 111–12.
31. M. R. Booth, *Victorian Spectacular Theatre 1850–1910* (London, 1981), see especially ch. 1, 'The Taste for Spectacle'.
32. P. Hartnoll (ed.), *Oxford Companion to the Theatre*, 838; Booth, *Victorian Spectacular Theatre*, chs 4, 5; H. Pearson, *Beerbohm Tree, His Life and Laughter* (New York, 1956) 116.
33. 'Ritual and Ritualism' (1874), *Gleanings*, VI 133–4.
34. H. C. G. Matthew, 'Introduction', *GD*, IX xc.
35. Lees-Milne, 162; and 174–5, 237, 345.
36. S. Brooke, *Queen of the Headhunters* (New York, 1972) 39.
37. Creighton to the queen, 8 Jul. 1897, RA R46/75.
38. Esher to M. Brett, 6 Feb. 1901, *J & L*, I 280. The sentence beginning 'Not in the Napoleonic manner . . .' was omitted from the published version of the letter; see ESHR 7/14.
39. See E. Hamilton's diary, 21 Jun. 1901, Hamilton Papers, BL, Add MS 48678, fols 66, 75.
40. Sir A. Fitzroy, 15 Jun. 1901, *Memoirs* (London, 1925) I 42. Bigge to Esher, 2 Aug. 1901, ESHR 5/12, fols 119–34.
41. L. V. Harcourt, 'The Next Coronation', *The Nineteenth Century*, 49 (Jun. 1901) 975–87.

42. Esher to Knollys, 11 Jun. 1901, RA W38/6.
43. Esher to M. Brett, 11 Jun. 1901, *J & L*, I 300.
44. D. Spring, 'Land and Politics in Edwardian England', *Agricultural History*, 58 (Jan. 1984) 18.
45. Bigge to Knollys, 20 Jul. 1901, RA Knollys Papers.
46. Knollys to Bigge, 20 Aug. 1901, RA X28/37b; Knollys to Esher, 15 Sep. 1901, ESHR 5/13, fols 28–9; Esher to Knollys, 17 Sep. 1901, RA W38/25.
47. Esher to C. Williamson, 17 Mar. 1901, ESHR 8/3, fol. 168; journal entry, 8 Apr. 1901, *J & L*, I 292.
48. Esher to M. Brett, 23 Oct. 1901, ESHR 7/14.
49. See 29 Oct. 1901, Fitzroy, *Memoirs*, I 62; recommended also by S. Clarke, 'Westminster Abbey and the Coronation', *The Nineteenth Century*, 50 (Sep. 1901) 387–401.
50. Esher to M. Brett, 22 Feb. 1902, *J & L*, I 325.
51. See 6 Jun. 1902, Fitzroy, *Memoirs*, I 89.
52. See report of R. H. Hobart, secretary to the Earl Marshal's Office, AC MS, EM 1863, p. 28.
53. Esher to M. Brett, 11 Jun. 1902, *J & L*, I 333 [Esher's emphasis].
54. See the account of G. W. Kennion, bishop of Bath and Wells, 'Some Memories of the Coronation of Their Majesties at Westminster Abbey, 9th August 1902', 15 Sep. 1902, WAM 58429.
55. Ibid.
56. *The Times*, 11 Aug. 1902, 6; *The Review of Reviews*, 26 (Sep. 1902) 232.
57. Brett, *Footprints*, 17.
58. Esher to Knollys, 28 Aug. and 2 Sep. 1905, *J & L*, II 103–7. The Colonial Office, the War Office and the Foreign Office were all being asked in the new reign to send more information to the king than had lately been their practice under Queen Victoria; see the letter of a private secretary to Chamberlain, 2 Sep. 1901, Joseph Chamberlain Papers, Birmingham University Library, JC 11/12/108 and throughout the JC 11/12 file.
59. Esher and A. C. Benson published the first series of three volumes of *The Letters of Queen Victoria, 1837–1861* in 1907. The next six volumes were published in two more series of three volumes each. They were edited by G. E. Buckle and covered the years between 1861 and 1901. Buckle followed the guidelines already set down by Esher and Benson.
60. See 15–27 Jul. 1903, *J & L*, II 2–6.
61. *The Diary of Arthur Christopher Benson*, P. Lubbock (ed.) (New York, 1926) 68–9.
62. Lees-Milne, 165.
63. Lubbock (ed.), *Benson*, 70.
64. Esher to Benson 25 Jul. [incorrectly dated 25 Aug.] 1905, *J & L*, II 101–2; Benson to Esher, 9 Aug. 1905, ESHR 11/4.
65. *LQV*, 1st ser., I v.
66. Ibid., vii.
67. R. Esher, *The Girlhood of Queen Victoria* (London, 1912) I 21; see also 16, 40.
68. *Queen Victoria's Journals, Some Unpublished Extracts* (London, 1909) 45. Also published in *The Times*, 6 March 1909 and reprinted in Esher's *Today and Tomorrow and Other Essays* (London, 1910).

69. Esher to J. S. Sandars, 30 Nov. 1910, Sandars Papers, Bodleian Library, Oxford, MS Eng. hist. *c*. 762, fols 68–71 [Esher's emphasis].
70. G. Dangerfield, *The Strange Death of Liberal England 1910–1914* (New York, 1935) viii. S. Hynes, *The Edwardian Turn of Mind* (Princeton, 1968) ch. 1.
71. Brett, *Footprints*, 126.
72. Journal entry, 7 May 1910, ESHR 2/12.
73. See correspondence between G. E. Buckle and Esher, 6–9 May 1910, ESHR 5/34, fols 21, 23, 29; and Murray to Esher, 11 May 1910, ESHR 5/34, fol. 38.
74. Reprinted with other essays in R. Esher, *The Influence of King Edward* (London, 1915).
75. Ibid., 41–2, 45.
76. The classic account of this crisis is Dangerfield, *Strange Death*; it is also evoked in Hynes, *Edwardian Turn of Mind*, especially chs 1 and 2.
77. K. Rose, *King George V* (London, 1983) 89.
78. See 10 Sep. 1913, *J & L*, III 128. Lees-Milne, 245.
79. Esher to Bigge, after 1911 Lord Stamfordham, 28 Dec. 1913, *J & L*, III 147–8. Also see H. Nicolson, *King George the Fifth* (London, 1952) 231, n. 1.
80. See the comment of the Austrian ambassador, Count Mensdorff in Nicolson, *King George the Fifth*, 232.
81. Journal entry, 28 Dec. 1916, *J & L*, IV 77–8.
82. Lees-Milne, 309.
83. Ibid., 317.
84. R. Esher, *After the War* (London, 1918) 9.
85. P. Ziegler, *King Edward VIII* (London, 1991) 93.

4 Randall Davidson: Quietness, Compromise and Comprehension

1. G. K. A. Bell, *Randall Davidson: Archbishop of Canterbury*, 3rd edn (London, 1952) [hereafter Bell] 354.
2. Ibid., 608–9.
3. Ibid., 14–15 [Davidson's emphasis].
4. Ibid., 22.
5. Ibid., 30.
6. Ibid., 39.
7. Journal entry, 9 Dec. 1882, *LQV*, 2nd ser., III 368–9.
8. See 6 May 1883, in *The Diary of Sir Edward Walter Hamilton*, D. W. R. Bahlman (ed.) (Oxford, 1972) II 432.
9. Bell, 74.
10. Davidson to his father, 21 Jan. 1883, DP, vol. 4, fol. 1 [Davidson's emphasis].
11. A copy can be found among his collected papers at Lambeth.
12. Bell, 92–5.
13. An independent peer, promoting a book soon to be published on the jubilee idea, tried to persuade Lord Granville early in 1886 that the government should sponsor jubilee celebrations. Granville consulted his colleagues and decided there had not been enough public demand shown for them to move ahead; see Granville Papers, PRO, 30/29/213. Later in 1886 there was enough

pressure from the outside for the queen to release a statement saying she wanted any celebration put off until she had actually completed the fifty years' reign in 1887; see W. M. Kuhn, 'Queen Victoria's Jubilees and the Invention of Tradition', *Victorian Poetry*, 25 (Autumn–Winter 1987) 108–9.

14. See discussion of service and precedent of 1872 in Benson Papers, Lambeth Palace Library, vol. 48, fols 12–13.
15. Davidson to Ponsonby, 29 Mar. 1887, RA F 45/125.
16. E. W. Benson, archbishop of Canterbury, to C. W. Peel, clerk of the Privy Council, 22 Apr. 1887, Benson Papers, Lambeth Palace Library, vol. 48, fol. 69.
17. Ponsonby's comment on Davidson's letter to him, 29 Mar. 1887, RA F 45/125.
18. M. Ponsonby, *Mary Ponsonby* (London, 1927) 146.
19. Davidson to the queen, 29 Jun. 1887, RA F 47/11.
20. Bell, 185.
21. Hamilton note, 16 Jun. 1884, *Diary of Sir Edward Walter Hamilton*, Bahlman (ed.) II 638.
22. See correspondence between Lord Salisbury and the queen, 23, 27 Sep., 3, 7 Oct. 1890, *LQV*, 3rd ser., I 638–40, 644–7.
23. The queen to Davidson, 17 Oct. 1890, *LQV*, 3rd ser., I 649.
24. Salisbury to the queen, 22 Oct. 1896, *LQV*, 3rd ser., III 99.
25. Bigge to McDonnell, 22, 26 Nov. 1896; Bigge to Salisbury, 25 Jan. 1897, HHM. Also McDonnell to Bigge, 24, 25 Nov. 1896, *LQV*, 3rd ser., III 105, 106.
26. Bigge to Salisbury, 22 Feb. 1897, HHM; S. Ponsonby Fane minutes of meetings at Marlborough House, 2, 27 Feb. 1897, PRO, LC 2/137.
27. Davidson to Fleetwood Edwards, 14 Feb. 1897, *LQV*, 3rd ser., III 132.
28. Davidson to Temple, 19 Feb. 1897, Frederick Temple Papers, Lambeth Palace Library, vol. 4, fol. 157.
29. Davidson to Bigge, 1 Mar. 1897, *LQV*, 3rd ser., III 140–2; Bell, 308–10.
30. Quoted in J. Pope-Hennessy, *Queen Mary 1867–1953* (London, 1959) p. 335.
31. M. Reid, *Ask Sir James* (London, 1987) 142.
32. Davidson to the queen, 16 May 1897, DP, vol. 26, fol. 98.
33. The queen's dictated instructions to the Prince of Wales and Princess Beatrice, Oct. 25, 1897, RA F 23/1.
34. Memorandum of events, 19 Jan. to 4 Feb. 1901, DP, vol. 19, p. 16b. See also J. M. Packard, *Farewell in Splendor* (New York, 1995).
35. Reid, *Ask Sir James*, 214.
36. *J & L*, I 276.
37. F. Temple to King Edward VII, 28 Jan. 1901, DP, vol. 506, fols 23–4; on demand for services see Frederick Temple Papers, Lambeth Palace Library, vol. 48, fols 83–196, *passim*.
38. 'The Bishop of Winchester on the Coronation', *The Times*, 2 Jan. 1902, 5.
39. Ibid.
40. R. T. Davidson, 'The Coronation in Prospect' (26 Jan. 1902), *Captains and Comrades in the Faith* (London, 1911) 105–7.
41. *The Times*, 1 Jan. 1902, 7.
42. Davidson, *Captains and Comrades*, 108–18.
43. See F. Knollys to Davidson, 9 Jan. 1902, DP, vol. 278, fols 122–4.

44. 'Canon Armitage Robinson on the Coronation', *The Times*, 1 Apr. 1902, 5. See also 'The New Coronation Service', *The Times*, 5 May 1902, 5.
45. Reid, *Ask Sir James*, 224.
46. See Davidson's 'Personal Memoranda', Easter Week 1913, DP, vol. 12, no. 1; see also his copy of the letter he wrote to the king when he left the yacht, 28 Jul. 1902, vol. 20, fol. 6. He thought the letter did some good: he kept it as a charm in his pocket all his life.
47. Quoted in G. St Aubyn, *Edward VII Prince and King* (New York, 1979) 370-1.
48. G. W. Kennion, 'Some Memories of the Coronation of Their Majesties at Westminster Abbey, 9th August 1902', WAM 58429.
49. St Aubyn, *Edward VII*, 372.
50. The scrolls are still in the library at the Abbey.
51. Sir A. Fitzroy, *Memoirs* (London, 1925) I 99.
52. Kennion, 'Some Memories of the Coronation', 8-10.
53. Fitzroy, *Memoirs*, I 99.
54. Kennion, 'Some Memories of the Coronation', 15.
55. Kennion, 'Some Memories of the Coronation', 13, 14; Bell, 371.
56. Bell, 383-5.
57. Quoted in D. Newsome, *On the Edge of Paradise, A. C. Benson: The Diarist* (London, 1980) 113.
58. Bell, 594-95. The late-Victorian development of the idea that bishoprics were nonpolitical appointments and that bishops did not follow the orders of party whips is traced in O. Chadwick, *The Victorian Church* (New York, 1966-70) II 332-5.
59. Bell, 597, 318. Two years earlier Davidson made a list of social questions in which the bishops had taken decisive legislative action; see E. Norman, *Church and Society in England 1770-1970* (Oxford, 1976) 255.
60. Davidson to Knollys, 24 and 30 Jan. 1910, DP, vol. 5, fols 105-8.
61. Esher to his son and to Balfour, 24 Jan. 1910, *J & L*, II 439-40.
62. See for example John Morley on Davidson as a 'nonpolitical man' in E. Hamilton's diary, Mar./Apr. 1901, Hamilton Papers, BL, Add MS 48678, fol. 24.
63. J. D. Fair, *British Interparty Conferences: A Study of the Procedure of Conciliation in British Politics, 1867-1921* (Oxford, 1980) 75.
64. On Davidson and the House of Lords, see Cosmo Gordon Lang, quoted in Bell, x.
65. 'A General Election' (2 Jan. 1910), Davidson, *Captains and Comrades*, 92.
66. 'Thirteen Hundredth Anniversary, Rochester Cathedral' (30 Nov. 1904), Davidson, *Captains and Comrades*, 193.
67. J. Burrow, *A Liberal Descent: Victorian Historians and the English Past* (Cambridge, 1981) 217.
68. 'The Public Worship Regulation Bill' (1874), *Works*, VII 312.
69. Bell, 606; 23 Apr. 1910 memorandum is in DP, vol. 12, 'Constitutional, etc. 1910', no. 2.
70. Bell, 607.
71. 9, 11 May 1910, RA GV Diary.
72. Davidson to Bigge, 7 May 1910, DP, vol. 326, fol. 5.
73. Davidson to Knollys, 7 May 1910, DP, vol. 326, fol. 7. See also Bell, 609.

74. 'The Death of King Edward', Davidson, *Captains and Comrades*, 121.
75. See O. Bland, *The Royal Way of Death* (London, 1986); on the lying in state of George IV, for example, 142–3.
76. P. S. Fritz, 'From "Public" to "Private": The Royal Funerals in England, 1500–1830', in *Mirrors of Mortality*, J. Whaley (ed.) (New York, 1981) 61–79; O. Bland, *Royal Way of Death*, 169.
77. *Royal Way of Death* states blandly (214) that it was Edward VII's own idea to have a public lying in state; *but* see Davidson's mem., 9 May 1910, DP, vol. 20, fol. 17, p. 8 (partly quoted in Bell, 609–10), which says the idea was George V's.
78. Esher to McDonnell, 9 May 1910, PRO, WORK 21/35/84 [Esher's emphasis].
79. Davidson mem., 10 May 1910, DP, vol. 20, fol. 17, pp. 9–10.
80. Ibid.
81. McDonnell to Bigge, 10 May 1910, PRO, WORK 21/35/95–6.
82. McDonnell to Bigge, 11 May 1910, PRO, WORK 21/35/13–14. This was also approved.
83. Bell, 610–11.
84. 22 May 1910, Queen Mary to grand duchess of Mecklenburg-Strelitz, RA GV CC 25/59.
85. PRO, WORK 21/35/105–6; sample of requests for tickets to opening and closing ceremonies, 21/35/107–51.
86. See minutes of meetings 2 Mar., 11 Apr. 1911, *Coronation (Executive) Committee: List of Members, Memoranda and Minutes of Proceedings* (London, 1911) 28, 32.
87. Davidson to Selby, secretary to the duke of Norfolk, no date [Mar./Apr. 1911], DP, vol. 280, fols 206–7.
88. McDonnell to Davidson, 9 Jun. 1911, DP, vol. 280, fols 303–7.
89. The king's original approval was conditional on Stone's distributing the results of his work to the press and his not photographing reception of the sacrament by the king and queen; see Bigge to Norfolk, 19 May 1911, AC MS, EM 3470. The small retreats are in Davidson to Norfolk, 13 Jun. 1911, DP, vol. 280, fols 315–16; and Bigge to Norfolk, 14 Jun. 1911, AC MS, EM 3472. There is other correspondence related to this controversy in AC MS, EM 3473, EM 3476; and DP, vol. 280, fols 314, 324–5.
90. Davidson to Lord Newton, 10 Jul. 1911, DP, vol. 5, fol. 115 [Davidson's emphasis].
91. Mem. of conversation with Stamfordham, 14 Aug. 1911, DP, vol. 12.
92. Lees-Milne, 244.
93. 'Sept. 28, 1913 – Lambeth – The older generation and change', DP, vol. 12, personal memoranda, no. 2.
94. The anthropologist, Ilse Hayden, reached the same conclusion in her study of the monarchy in the last quarter of the twentieth century; see her *Symbol and Privilege, The Ritual Context of British Royalty* (Tucson, 1987).

5 The Duke of Norfolk: Authenticity, Eccentricity, Absurdity

1. O. Chadwick, *The Victorian Church* (New York, 1966–70) II 402–3. J. M. Robinson, *The Dukes of Norfolk* (Oxford, 1983) [hereafter Robinson] 191–2, 201–2.

2. M. Bence-Jones, *The Catholic Families* (London, 1992) 173.
3. Gwendolen, duchess of Norfolk, *A Duke of Norfolk Notebook* (London, 1917) [hereafter *Notebook*] 47.
4. Ibid., 111.
5. On Bagehot's interest in Newman see R. H. Hutton, 'Memoir of Walter Bagehot', *Works*, XV 93–4; A. Birrell, 'Walter Bagehot', *Works*, XV 198, 200; and N. St John-Stevas, 'Bagehot's Religious Views', *Works*, XV 248–50, 264–5.
6. *Notebook*, 122.
7. W. Ward, *The Life of John Henry Cardinal Newman* (London, 1912) II 348–9.
8. *Notebook*, 38.
9. Norfolk to Gladstone, 29 Aug. 1870, BL, Add MS 44428, fol. 69.
10. Partly quoted in Robinson, 220; G. E. Buckle and W. F. Monypenny, *The Life of Benjamin Disraeli, Earl of Beaconsfield* (London, 1910–20) VI 196.
11. *Notebook*, 68.
12. Ibid., 108.
13. N. Mitford, *Love in a Cold Climate* (London, 1949).
14. W. Ward, *Men and Matters*, reprint (1914; New York, 1968) 52.
15. Quoted in Robinson, 229.
16. D. Quinn, *Patronage and Piety, The Politics of English Roman Catholicism, 1850–1900* (Basingstoke and London, 1993) ch. 7.
17. J. H. Robb, *The Primrose League 1883–1906*, reprint (1942; New York, 1968) 24–5, 47, 51, 87.
18. Robinson, 225.
19. Quoted in ibid.
20. See 12 May 1902, Sir A. Fitzroy, *Memoirs* (London, 1925) I 85–6.
21. Ibid., 96.
22. Ibid., 95–6.
23. E. W. Sheppard, *A Short History of the British Army*, 4th edn (London, 1950) 292; see also Norfolk's remarks in the House of Lords, *PD*, 4th ser. (1904) vol. 136, cols 1207–10.
24. The withdrawal of peers from active politics into a more purely formal, ceremonial role is one of the themes of D. Cannadine's *The Decline and Fall of the British Aristocracy* (New Haven, 1990). A contrary view, that peers remained both dignified and efficient, for example on county councils, right up to the First World War is in A. Adonis, *Making Aristocracy Work, The Peerage and the Political System in Britain 1886–1914* (Oxford, 1993).
25. Quinn, *Patronage and Piety*, 167.
26. See the correspondence between Newman and Norfolk in C. S. Dessain and T. Gornall (eds), *The Letters and Diaries of John Henry Newman* (Oxford, 1975) XXVII 164, 170–1, 177. *Notebook*, 34.
27. See for example *PD*, 4th ser. (1893) vol. 17, cols 59–63.
28. *The Illustrated London News*, 11 June 1898, 853.
29. *PD*, 4th ser. (1902) vol. 116, cols 581–4.
30. *PD*, 4th ser. (1906) vol. 162, col. 966.
31. *PD*, 4th ser., (1903) vol. 124, cols 516–17; (1904) vol. 137, cols 267–75.
32. Quinn, *Patronage and Piety*, 167–9.
33. M. Ward, *The Wilfrid Wards and the Transition* (London, 1934–7) II *passim*.

34. See, for example, M. Girouard, *The Return to Camelot* (New Haven and London, 1981); C. Dellheim, *The Face of the Past* (Cambridge, 1982); J. W. Burrow, *A Liberal Descent* (Cambridge, 1981) and R. J. Smith *The Gothic Bequest* (Cambridge, 1987).
35. 24 Jan. 1901, Fitzroy, *Memoirs,* I 43.
36. Akers-Douglas to his son, 24 Jan. 1901, Chilston Papers, Kent Record Office, U564, C603.
37. Robinson, ch. 1. The earl marshalship was a lifetime appointment until the reign of Charles II who made the title hereditary to the dukes of Norfolk.
38. There were three kings of arms (Garter, Clarenceux, Norroy), six heralds (Lancaster, Chester, York, Richmond, Windsor, Somerset) and 4 poursuivants (Rouge Croix, Bluemantle, Portcullis, Rouge Dragon). Their history is in Sir A. Wagner, *Heralds of England* (London, 1967).
39. Some doubt is cast on the military origins of heraldry in a recent book, which suggests that heraldic devices may have been used by noblemen for vanity and display as much as for identification in battle; see T. Woodcock and J. M. Robinson, *The Oxford Guide to Heraldry* (Oxford, 1988) ch. 1.
40. A. Wagner, *The Records and Collections of the College of Arms* (London, 1952) 4.
41. P. S. Fritz, 'From "Public" to "Private": the Royal Funerals in England, 1500–1830', in J. Whaley (ed.), *Mirrors of Mortality* (New York, 1981) 74.
42. G. Lushington to the lord chamberlain, 18 June 1887, PRO, LC 2/106; also AC MS, EM 2251–7.
43. Sir F. Ponsonby, *Recollections of Three Reigns* (London, 1951) 85.
44. Ibid., 86.
45. 31 Jan. 1901, Fitzroy, *Memoirs,* I 44.
46. Bigge to Knollys, 20 Jul. 1901, RA Knollys Mss.
47. Ponsonby, *Recollections of Three Reigns,* 90.
48. Esher to Knollys, 8 Feb. 1901, *J & L,* I 280–1. The last sentence is omitted from the published letter; see ESHR 5/11, fol. 62 [Esher's emphasis].
49. Lees-Milne, 133.
50. Esher to Knollys, 8 Feb. 1901, *J & L,* I 280–1.
51. 15 Jun. 1901, Fitzroy, *Memoirs,* I 52.
52. Lord Salisbury and the cabinet approved of the idea of *two* coronation committees at the suggestion of the king. See Salisbury to Edward VII, 14 Jun. 1901, PRO, CAB 41/26/13. Esher and Knollys had prompted the king.
53. 10 & 16 Jul. 1901, Fitzroy, *Memoirs,* I 55–6.
54. Hamilton Diary, 31 Jul. 1901, E. W. Hamilton Papers, BL, Add MS 48678, fol. 86.
55. Hamilton Diary, 8 Oct. 1901, Add MS 48678, fols 108–9.
56. 29 Oct. 1901, *J & L,* I 311.
57. Viscount Alverstone, *Recollections of Bar and Bench* (London, 1915) 258–9.
58. *Punch,* 25 Jun. 1902, vol. 122, p. 455.
59. See also the references to the fictional 'claims' of Pierpont Morgan and the actual claim of the marquess of Cholmondely, p. 476.
60. Ibid., 455–6.
61. See for example the relatively solemn retrospective engravings of royal occasions collected together in the *Punch* issue commemorating the reign of Queen Victoria, vol. 120, pp. 73–98.

62. *Punch*, 25 Jun. 1902, vol. 122, p. 456.
63. Knollys to Bigge, 16 Nov. 1896, RA W13/72.
64. Hamilton Diary, 23 Jun. 1902, BL, Add MS 48679, fols 111–12.
65. 6 Aug. 1902, Fitzroy, *Memoirs*, I 96–7.
66. See the earl marshal's circular in WAM 5846.
67. See report of R. H. Hobart, secretary to the Earl Marshal's Office, AC MS, EM 1863, pp. 12, 46.
68. Reminiscences composed after the funeral in the summer of 1910, Brian Godfrey-Faussett Papers, Churchill College, Cambridge, BGGF 1/61, p. 138.
69. K. Rose quoting McDonnell's Diary, *King George V* (London, 1983) 77.
70. McDonnell to Scott-Gatty (garter), 24 May 1910, PRO, WORK 21/35/ 289–90.
71. M. Bonham Carter (ed.), *The Autobiography of Margot Asquith* (1962; London, 1985) 271.
72. Norfolk to McDonnell, 28 May 1910, PRO, WORK 21/35/313.
73. Sandars to Esher, 29 May 1910, ESHR 5/34, fol. 63.
74. *Notebook*, 109.
75. *Oxford English Dictionary* (1989 edn.) vol. 2, p. 1048.
76. *Notebook*, 79.
77. Ibid., 113–14, n.
78. See Asquith to Harcourt, 31 May 1910, Lewis Harcourt Papers, Bodleian Library, Oxford, L. Harcourt Ms. 421, fol. 141.
79. Enclosed in Bigge to Vaughan Nash, 9 Jul. 1910, H. H. Asquith Papers, Bodleian Library, Oxford, Asquith Ms. 2, fols 43–4.
80. McDonnell to Bigge, no date [probably June or Jul. 1910] PRO, WORK 21/ 23/9/4–8. See also 21 Jul. 1910, Fitzroy, *Memoirs*, II 416, on the prime minister's move to disestablish the Earl Marshal's Department 'with its antiquated methods and fancy *cortège* of heralds'.
81. Dawson to Bigge, and McDonnell to Bigge, 22 Jul. 1910, RA Coronation Records (1911) A/I/13–14.
82. See 26 Jul. 1910, in Fitzroy, *Memoirs*, II 416–17, on the contentious first meeting of the Executive Committee. Also see Norfolk's memorandum, stating his preference for supervising a small staff of his own choosing rather than a large central committee; PRO, WORK 21/23/9/12–17; and AC MS, EM 1879–80.
83. Dawson to Bigge, 26 Jul. 1910, RA Coronation Records (1911) A/I/18; see also A/I/19–26.
84. Scott-Gatty to Norfolk, 12, 14 Sep. 1901, AC MS, EM 3627 [Scott-Gatty's emphasis].
85. J. Grigg, *Lloyd George: The People's Champion 1902–1911* (Berkeley and Los Angeles, 1978) 303; B. B. Gilbert, *David Lloyd George: A Political Life* (London, 1987) 446–7.
86. Scott-Gatty to Norfolk, 17 Nov. 1910, AC MS, EM 3627.
87. See Dawson to Norfolk, 25 Mar. 1911; Norfolk to Dawson, 27 Mar. 1911; Bigge to Norfolk, 29 Mar. 1911; all in AC MS, EM 3627.
88. Bigge note of the king's meeting with Norfolk, 3 Aug. 1910, RA Coronation Records (1911) A/I/28; *Coronation (Executive) Committee: List of Members, Memoranda and Minutes of Proceedings* (London, 1911) pp. 5–6.
89. 12 Jan. 1911, Fitzroy, *Memoirs*, II 429.

90. See for example, Norfolk to Bigge, 2 Aug. 1910, RA Coronation Records (1911) A/I/27.
91. *PD* (Lords), 5th ser., vol. 4 (1909) col. 787.
92. J. D. Fair points out the importance of 1869 in setting precedents for future mediation of inter-party conflicts in *British Interparty Conferences* (Oxford, 1980) 6.
93. *Works*, VI 20.
94. 'The Duke of Norfolk at Littlehampton', *The Times*, 8 Jan. 1910, 6.
95. The theory that the Lords had an active duty to refer controversial legislation on which the electorate had not had a chance to pronounce its decision to a popular referendum had its origins in the previous century; see C. C. Weston, 'Salisbury and the Lords, 1868–1895', *HJ* 25 (Mar. 1982) 103–29.
96. See reports of his speeches in *The Times*: 'The Duke of Norfolk at Taunton', 14 Dec. 1909, 7; 'The Duke of Norfolk at Bognor', 4 Jan. 1910, 7.
97. 'The Peers and the Issue', *The Times*, 10 Jan. 1910, 10. Other nobles who took to election platforms in the first election of 1910 also underwent 'peer-baiting'; see N. Blewett, *Peers, the Parties and the People: The General Elections of 1910* (London, 1972) 114–15.
98. 4 Mar. 1910, Fitzroy, *Memoirs*, I 398.
99. *PD* (Lords), 5th ser., vol. 5 (1910) cols 447–9.
100. On the diehards see G. D. Phillips, *The Diehards: Aristocratic Society and Politics in Edwardian England* (Cambridge, Mass., 1979).
101. 11 Aug. 1911, Fitzroy, *Memoirs*, II 459.
102. H. Nicolson, *King George the Fifth* (London, 1952) 199. See also D. Gwynn, *One Hundred Years of Catholic Emancipation* (London, 1929) 258; and I. Colvin, *The Life of Lord Carson*, 3 vols (London, 1934) II 129–30.
103. D. Spring, 'Land and Politics in Edwardian England', *Agricultural History*, 58 (Jan. 1984) 39–40.
104. Lees-Milne, 318.
105. E. P. Thompson, *The Making of the English Working Class* (London, 1963).

Selected Bibliography

MANUSCRIPT SOURCES

Individuals

Asquith Papers, Bodleian Library, Oxford
Bagehot Papers, Sterling Memorial Library, Yale University, New Haven
Balfour Papers, British Library, London
Chamberlain Papers, Birmingham University Library, Birmingham
Chilston Papers, Kent Record Office, Maidstone
Davidson Papers, Lambeth Palace Library, London
Esher Papers, Churchill College, Cambridge
Gladstone Papers, British Library, London
Godfrey-Faussett Papers, Churchill College, Cambridge
Granville Papers, Public Record Office, Kew
Hamilton Papers, British Library, London
Harcourt Papers, Bodleian Library, Oxford
Ponsonby Papers, British Library, London
Salisbury Papers, Hatfield House, Hatfield
Sandars Papers, Bodleian Library, Oxford
Temple Papers, Lambeth Palace Library, London
Welby Papers, Public Record Office, Kew

Offices

Cabinet Letters to the Crown, Public Record Office, Kew
Earl Marshal Papers, Arundel Castle, Arundel
Guildhall Library Manuscripts, London
Lord Chamberlain Papers, Public Record Office, Kew
Office of Works Papers, Public Record Office, Kew
The Royal Archives, Windsor
Treasury Papers, Public Record Office, Kew
Westminster Abbey Muniments, London

SERIALS CONSULTED

The Annual Register
Church Quarterly Review
The Contemporary Review
The Economist
The Fortnightly Review
The Graphic
Hansard Parliamentary Debates
The Illustrated London News

The Nineteenth Century
Punch
The Quarterly Review
The Review of Reviews
The Saturday Review
The Spectator
The Times

OTHER PRINTED PRIMARY SOURCES

Alverstone, Viscount, *Recollections of Bar and Bench* (London, 1915).
Asquith, Margot, countess of Oxford and, *The Autobiography of Margot Asquith*, Maurice Bonham Carter (ed.), reprint (London, 1985).
Bagehot, Walter, *The Collected Works of Walter Bagehot*, Norman St John-Stevas (ed.), 15 vols (London, 1965–86).
Benson, A. C., *The Diary of Arthur Christopher Benson*, Percy Lubbock (ed.) (New York, 1926).
Clarke, Sidney, 'Westminster Abbey and the Coronation', in *The Nineteenth Century*, 50 (September 1901) 387–401.
Coronation Executive Committee: List of Members, Memoranda and Minutes of Proceedings (London, 1911).
Davidson, Randall Thomas, 1st Lord Davidson of Lambeth, *Captains and Comrades in the Faith* (London, 1911).
——, *The Character and Call of the Church of England* (London, 1912).
——, *The Christian Opportunity: Being Sermons and Speeches Delivered in America* (New York, 1904).
——, *Occasions* (London, 1925).
——, *Quit You Like Men* (London, 1915).
——, *The Testing of a Nation* (London, 1919).
——, and William Benham, *Life of Archibald Campbell Tait: Archbishop of Canterbury*, 2 vols (London, 1891).
Dicey, Albert Venn, *Lectures Introductory to the Study of the Law of the Constitution*, 2nd edn (London, 1886).
Dilke, Sir Charles, *Sir Charles Dilke on the Cost of the Crown* (London, 1871).
Edwards, A. G. (archbishop of Wales) *Memories* (London, 1927).
Esher, Reginald Baliol Brett, 2nd Viscount, *Cloud Capp'd Towers* (London, 1927).
——, *Footprints of Statesmen during the Eighteenth Century in Britain* (London, 1892).
——, 'From Three Platforms, I. New Policy and Old Failures', *The Fortnightly Review*, new ser., 38 (October 1885) 453–62.
——, *The Girlhood of Queen Victoria*, 2 vols (London, 1912).
——, *The Influence of King Edward* (London, 1915).
——, *Journals and Letters of Reginald Viscount Esher*, Maurice V. Brett and Oliver, 3rd Viscount Esher (eds), 4 vols (London, 1934–8).
——, *Queen Victoria's Journals: Some Unpublished Extracts* (A Lecture entitled 'Queen Victoria' delivered by Lord Esher at the Royal Institution on Friday March 5, and published in *The Times* of Saturday March 6) (London, 1909).
——, *Today and Tomorrow and Other Essays* (London, 1910).

——, 'The Tyranny of the "Nonconformist Conscience"', *The Nineteenth Century*, 29 (February 1891) 202–13.

——, *The Yoke of Empire: Sketches of the Queen's Prime Ministers* (London, 1896).

Fitzroy, Sir Almeric, *Memoirs*, 2 vols (London, 1925).

Gladstone, William Ewart, *A Chapter of Autobiography* (London, 1868).

——, *Correspondence on Church and Religion of William Ewart Gladstone*, D. C. Lathbury (ed.), 2 vols (London, 1910).

——, *The Gladstone Diaries, 1825–39*, M. R. D. Foot (ed.), 2 vols. *1840–54*, M. R. D. Foot and H. C. G. Matthew (eds), 2 vols. *1855–96*, H. C. G. Matthew (ed.), 10 vols so far (Oxford, 1968–94).

——, *Gleanings of Past Years, 1875–78*, 7 vols (New York, 1879).

——, *Midlothian Speeches 1879*, reprint edn (New York, 1971).

——, *The Political Correspondence of Mr Gladstone and Lord Granville 1868–76*, Agatha Ramm (ed.), Camden third series, vols 81–2 (London, 1952).

——, *The Prime Ministers' Papers Series: W. E. Gladstone*, John Brooke and Mary Sorensen (eds), 4 vols (London, 1971–81).

——, *The Queen and Mr Gladstone*, Philip Guedalla (ed.), 2 vols 1934, reprint edn (2 vols in 1) (London, 1969).

——, *The State in its Relations with the Church*, 1838, rev. edn, 2 vols (London, 1841).

Hamilton, Edward W., *The Diary of Sir Edward Walter Hamilton*, D. W. R. Bahlman (ed.), 2 vols (Oxford, 1972).

Harcourt, Lewis Vernon, 'The Next Coronation', *The Nineteenth Century*, 49 (June 1901) 975–87.

Harrison, Frederic, *Order and Progress*, Martha Vogeler (ed.), 1875, reprint edn, (Cranbury, N. J., 1975).

Kennedy, A. L. (ed.), *My Dear Duchess, Social and Political Letters to the Duchess of Manchester* (London, 1956).

Martin, Sir Theodore, *The Life of His Royal Highness the Prince Consort*, 5 vols (London, 1875–80).

More, Hannah, *The Works of Hannah More*, 1788, rev. edn, 8 vols (London, 1801).

Newman, John Henry, *Apologia Pro Vita Sua*, Maisie Ward (ed.), 1864 (London, 1948).

——, *The Letters and Diaries of John Henry Newman*, Charles Stephen Dessain, Thomas Gornall *et al.* (eds), 31 vols (London and Oxford, 1961–84).

Norfolk, Gwendolen, duchess of, *A Duke of Norfolk Notebook* (London, 1917).

Ponsonby, Magdalen, *Mary Ponsonby* (London, 1927).

Ponsonby, Arthur, Baron Ponsonby of Shulbrede, *Henry Ponsonby, Queen Victoria's Private Secretary: His Life from His Letters* (New York, 1943).

Ponsonby, Frederick, Baron Sysonby, *Recollections of Three Reigns* (London, 1951).

Rendel, Stuart Rendel, Baron, *The Personal Papers of Lord Rendel* (London, 1931).

Stanley, Lady Augusta, *Later Letters of Lady Augusta Stanley 1864–76*, the dean of Windsor [Albert V. Baillie] and Hector Bolitho (eds) (New York, 1929).

Temple, Solomon (pseud.), *What Does She Do With It?* Tracts for the Times, no. 1 (London, 1871).

Victoria, Queen, *Darling Child: Private Correspondence of Queen Victoria and the Crown Princess of Prussia 1871–8*, Roger Fulford (ed.) (London, 1976).

——, *The Letters of Queen Victoria, 1837–61*, Arthur C. Benson and Viscount Esher (eds), 1st ser., 3 vols (London, 1907). *1862–85*, George E. Buckle (ed.),

2nd ser., 3 vols (London, 1926–8). *1886–1901*, George E. Buckle (ed.), 3rd ser., 3 vols (London, 1930–2).

Vincent, John (ed.), *Disraeli, Derby and the Conservative Party: Journals and Memoirs of Edward Henry, Lord Stanley 1849–69* (New York, 1978).

Ward, Wilfrid, *The Life of John Henry Cardinal Newman*, 2 vols (London, 1912).

SECONDARY SOURCES

Adonis, Andrew, *Making Aristocracy Work: The Peerage and the Political System in Britain 1886–1914* (Oxford, 1993).

Altick, Richard D., *The English Common Reader* (Chicago, 1957).

Arnstein, Walter L., 'Queen Victoria and Religion', in Gail Malmgreen (ed.), *Religion in the Lives of English Women, 1760–1930* (London, 1986).

——, 'Queen Victoria Opens Parliament: The Disinvention of Tradition', *Historical Research*, 63 (June 1990) 178–94.

Baillie, Albert V., *My First Eighty Years* (London, 1951).

Battiscombe, Georgina, 'Gerald Wellesley: A Victorian Dean and Domestic Chaplain', *Report of the Society of the Friends of St George's and the Descendants of the Knights of the Garter: Annual Report to 31st December 1963* (1963) 126–35.

Beales, Derek E. D., *History and Biography (An Inaugural Lecture)* (Cambridge, 1981).

Bell, George K. A., *Randall Davidson: Archbishop of Canterbury*, 3rd edn (London, 1952).

Bence-Jones, Mark, *The Catholic Families* (London, 1992).

Bentley, James, *Ritualism and Politics in Victorian Britain: The Attempt to Legislate for Belief* (Oxford, 1978).

Blake, Robert, Lord, *Disraeli* (New York, 1966).

——, *Gladstone, Disraeli and Queen Victoria (The Centenary Romanes Lecture)* (Oxford, 1993).

Bland, Olivia, *The Royal Way of Death* (London, 1986).

Blewett, Neal, *The Peers, the Parties and the People: The General Elections of 1910* (London, 1972).

Booth, Michael R., *Victorian Spectacular Theatre 1850–1910* (Boston, 1981).

Brooke, Hon. Sylvia Leonora Brett, Lady (Rani of Sarawak), *Queen of the Headhunters: The Autobiography of H. H. the Hon. Sylvia Lady Brooke* (New York, 1972).

Brown, Ford K., *Fathers of the Victorians* (Cambridge, 1961).

Buckle, George E. and W. F. Monypenny, *The Life of Benjamin Disraeli, Earl of Beaconsfield*, 6 vols (London, 1910–20).

Burrow, John W., *A Liberal Descent: Victorian Historians and the English Past* (Cambridge, 1981).

——, 'Sense and Circumstances: Bagehot and the Nature of Political Understanding', in *That Noble Science of Politics*, Stefan Collini, Donald Winch and Burrow (eds) (Cambridge, 1983).

——, *Whigs and Liberals: Continuity and Change in English Political Thought* (Oxford, 1988).

Butler, Perry, *Gladstone: Church, State and Tractarianism* (Oxford, 1982).

Cannadine, David, 'The Context, Performance and Meaning of Ritual: The British Monarchy and the "Invention of Tradition," *c.* 1820–1977', in *The Invention of Tradition*, Eric Hobsbawm and Terence Ranger (eds) (Cambridge, 1983).

——, *The Decline and Fall of the British Aristocracy* (New Haven and London, 1990).

——, 'Introduction: Divine Rights of Kings', in *Rituals of Royalty*, Cannadine and Simon Price (eds), (Cambridge, 1987).

——, 'The Last Hanoverian Sovereign? The Victorian Monarchy in Historical Perspective, 1688–1988', in *The First Modern Society: Essays in English History in Honour of Lawrence Stone*, A. L. Beier, Cannadine and J. M. Rosenheim (eds) (Cambridge, 1988).

——, *Lords and Landlords: The Aristocracy and the Towns, 1774–1967* (Leicester, 1980).

——, *The Pleasures of the Past* (London, 1989).

Cannon, John, *The Modern British Monarchy: A Study in Adaptation (The Stenton Lecture)* (Reading, 1987).

——, 'The Survival of the British Monarchy: The Prothero Lecture', *Transactions of the Royal Historical Society*, 5th ser., no. 36 (1986) 143–64.

—— and Ralph Griffiths, *The Oxford Illustrated History of the British Monarchy* (Oxford, 1988).

Chadwick, Owen, 'Church and State in Victorian Times', in *Church, State and Society in the Nineteenth Century: An Anglo-German Comparison*, Adolf M. Birke and Kurt Kluxen (eds) (Munich, 1984).

—— (ed.), *The Mind of the Oxford Movement* (Stanford, 1960).

——, *The Victorian Church*, 2 vols (New York, 1966–70).

Clark, Jonathan C. D., *English Society 1688–1832: Ideology, Social Structure and Political Practice during the Ancien Regime* (Cambridge, 1985).

Cohn, Bernard S., 'History and Anthropology: The State of Play', *Comparative Studies in Society and History*, 22 (April 1980) 198–221.

——, 'Representing Authority in Victorian India', in *The Invention of Tradition*, Eric Hobsbawm and Terence Ranger (eds) (Cambridge, 1983).

Colley, Linda, 'The Apotheosis of George III: Loyalty, Royalty and the British Nation 1760–1820', *Past and Present*, no. 102 (February 1984) 94–129.

——, *Britons: Forging the Nation 1707–1837* (New Haven and London, 1992).

——, 'Whose Nation? Class and National Consciousness in Britain 1750–1830', *Past and Present*, no. 113 (November 1986) 97–117.

Collini, Stefan, 'A Place in the Syllabus: Political Science at Cambridge', in *That Noble Science of Politics*, Collini, Donald Winch and John Burrow (eds) (Cambridge, 1983).

Colvin, Ian, *The Life of Lord Carson*, 3 vols (London, 1934).

Curtis, Lewis P. Junior, 'The Queen's Two Bonnets', *Victorian Studies*, 9 (March 1966) 259–92.

D'Arcy, Feargus A., 'Charles Bradlaugh and the English Republican Movement, 1868–78', *Historical Journal*, 25 (June 1982) 367–83.

Dangerfield, George, *The Strange Death of Liberal England 1910–14* (New York, 1935).

Dark, Sidney, *Archbishop Davidson and the Church of England* (London, 1929).

Dellheim, Charles, *The Face of the Past: The Preservation of the Medieval Inheritance in Victorian England* (Cambridge, 1982).

Dessain, Charles Stephen, *John Henry Newman* (London, 1966).

Edwards, David L., *Leaders of the Church of England 1828–1944* (Oxford, 1971).

Emerson, Sir Harold, *The Ministry of Works* (London, 1956).

Esher, Lionel Brett, 4th Viscount, *Our Selves Unknown: An Autobiography* (London, 1985).

Fair, John D., *British Interparty Conferences* (Oxford, 1980).

Fraser, Peter, *Lord Esher: A Political Biography* (London, 1973).

Fritz, Paul S., 'From "Public" to "Private": The Royal Funerals in England, 1500–1830', in *Mirrors of Mortality*, Joachim Whaley (ed.) (New York, 1981).

Geertz, Clifford, *The Interpretation of Cultures* (New York, 1973).

——, *Negara: The Theatre State in Nineteenth-Century Bali* (Princeton, 1980).

Gilbert, Bentley Brinkerhoff, *David Lloyd George: A Political Life: The Architecture of Change 1863–1912* (London, 1987).

Girouard, Mark, *The Return to Camelot: Chivalry and the English Gentleman* (New Haven and London, 1981).

Gossman, Norbert, 'Republicanism in Nineteenth-Century England', *International Review of Social History*, 7 (1962) 47–60.

Grigg, John, *Lloyd George: The People's Champion 1902–1911* (Berkeley and Los Angeles, 1978).

Gwynn, Stephen, and Gertrude M. Tuckwell, *The Life of the Rt. Hon. Sir Charles Dilke*, 2 vols (London, 1918).

Gwynn, Denis, *A Hundred Years of Catholic Emancipation (1829–1929)* (London, 1929).

Harcourt, Freda, 'Gladstone, Monarchism, and the "New" Imperialism, 1868–74', *Journal of Imperial and Commonwealth History*, 14 (October 1985) 20–51.

Hardie, Frank, *The Political Influence of the British Monarchy, 1868–1952* (London, 1970).

Hardie, Frank, *The Political Influence of Queen Victoria, 1861–1901* (London, 1935).

Hartnoll, Phyllis (ed.), *The Oxford Companion to the Theatre*, 4th edn (Oxford, 1983).

Havers, Sir Michael, Edward Grayson and Peter Shankland, *The Royal Baccarat Scandal* (London, 1977).

Hayden, Ilse, *Symbol and Privilege: The Ritual Context of British Royalty* (Tucson, 1987).

Hibbert, Christopher, *The Illustrated London News* (London, 1975).

Hignett, Sean, *Brett: From Bloomsbury to New Mexico: A Biography* (London, 1984).

Hitchens, Christopher, *The Monarchy* (London, 1990).

Hobsbawm, Eric, 'Mass Producing Traditions: Europe, 1870–1914', in *The Invention of Tradition*, Hobsbawm and Terence Ranger (eds) (Cambridge, 1983).

Howard, Michael, 'Empire, Race and War in Pre-1914 Britain', in *History and Imagination: Essays in Honour of H. R. Trevor-Roper*, Hugh Lloyd-Jones, Valerie Pearl and Blair Worden (eds) (London, 1981).

Howe, Irving (ed.), *The Portable Rudyard Kipling* (New York, 1982).

Hudson, Derek, *Martin Tupper* (London, 1949).

Hull, Isabel V., *The Entourage of Kaiser Wilhelm II, 1888–1918* (Cambridge, 1982).

——, 'Prussian Dynastic Ritual and the End of the Monarchy', in *German Nationalism and the European Response, 1890–1945*, Carole Fink, Hull and MacGregor Knox (eds) (Norman, Oklahoma, 1985).

Hynes, Samuel, *The Edwardian Turn of Mind* (Princeton, 1968).

Jenkins, Sir Roy, *Sir Charles Dilke* (London, 1958).

Kent, Christopher, *Brains and Numbers: Elitism, Comtism and Democracy in Mid-Victorian England* (Toronto, 1978).

Knight, L. A., 'The Royal Titles Act and India', *Historical Journal*, 11 (1968) 488–507.

Kuhn, William M., 'Ceremony and Politics: The British Monarchy, 1871–2', *Journal of British Studies*, 26 (April 1987) 133–62.

——, 'Ceremony and Politics: The Management of British Royal Ceremonial, 1861–1911', PhD thesis, Johns Hopkins, 1990.

——, 'Queen Victoria's Civil List: What Did She Do With It?' *Historical Journal*, 36 (September 1993) 645–65.

——, 'Queen Victoria's Jubilees and the Invention of Tradition', *Victorian Poetry*, 25 (Autumn–Winter 1987) 107–14.

Lee, Sir Sidney, *King Edward VII: A Biography*, 2 vols (New York, 1925–7).

Lees-Milne, James, *The Enigmatic Edwardian: The Life of Reginald 2nd Viscount Esher* (London, 1986).

——, *Harold Nicolson*, 2 vols (London [U.K.] and Hamden, Connecticut, 1980–4).

Longford, Elizabeth, countess of, *Elizabeth R.: A Biography* (London, 1983).

——, *Victoria R. I.* (London, 1964).

Magnus, Sir Philip, *Gladstone* (London, 1954).

——, *King Edward the Seventh* (London, 1964).

Marsh, Peter T., *The Victorian Church in Decline* (London, 1969).

Mason, J. F. A., 'Lord Salisbury: A Librarian's View', in *Salisbury: The Man and His Policies*, Lord Blake and Hugh Cecil (eds) (London, 1987).

Matthew, Henry C. G., *Gladstone 1809–1874* (Oxford, 1986).

——, *The Liberal Imperialists: The Ideas and Politics of a Post-Gladstonian Elite* (London, 1973).

Mitford, Nancy, *Love in a Cold Climate* (New York, 1949).

Morley, John, *The Life of William Ewart Gladstone*, 3 vols (London, 1903).

Morris, Marilyn A., 'Monarchy as an Issue in English Political Argument during the French Revolutionary Era', PhD thesis, London, 1988.

Murray, Bruce K., *The People's Budget 1909–10: Lloyd George and Liberal Politics* (New York, 1980).

Nairn, Tom, *The Enchanted Glass: Britain and its Monarchy* (London, 1988).

Newsome, David, *On the Edge of Paradise: A. C. Benson: The Diarist* (London, 1980).

Nicolson, Hon. Sir Harold, *King George the Fifth: His Life and Reign* (London, 1952).

Norman, Edward, *Church and Society in England, 1770–1970* (Oxford, 1976).

Packard, Jerrold M., *Farewell in Splendor: The Passing of Queen Victoria and Her Age* (New York, 1995).

Parry, Jonathan P., *Democracy and Religion: Gladstone and the Liberal Party 1867–75* (Cambridge, 1986).

——, 'Religion and the Collapse of Gladstone's First Government, 1870–4', *Historical Journal*, 25 (March 1982) 71–101.

Pearson, Hesketh, *Beerbohm Tree: His Life and Laughter* (New York, 1956).

Pearson, John, *The Ultimate Family: The Making of the Royal House of Windsor* (London, 1986).

Phillips, Gregory D., *The Diehards: Aristocratic Society and Politics in Edwardian England* (Cambridge, Massachusetts, 1979).

Pinto-Duschinsky, Michael, *The Political Thought of Lord Salisbury, 1854–68* (London, 1967).

Poovey, Mary, *Uneven Developments: The Ideological Work of Gender in Mid-Victorian England* (London, 1989).

Pope-Hennessy, James, *Queen Mary 1867–1953* (London, 1959).

Pugh, Martin, *The Tories and the People 1880–1935* (Oxford, 1985).

Pugh, Ralph Bernard, *The Crown Estate: An Historical Essay* (London, 1960).

Quinn, Dermot, *Patronage and Piety, The Politics of English Roman Catholicism, 1850–1900* (Basingstoke and London, 1993).

Ramm, Agatha, *Gladstone as Man of Letters (James Bryce Memorial Lecture)* (Oxford, 1981).

——, 'Gladstone's Religion', *Historical Journal*, 28 (June 1985) 327–40.

Reid, Michaela, *Ask Sir James: Sir James Reid, Personal Physician to Queen Victoria and Physician in Ordinary to Three Monarchs* (New York, 1990).

Robb, Janet Henderson, *The Primrose League 1883–1906* (New York, 1942).

Robinson, John Martin, *The Dukes of Norfolk* (Oxford, 1983).

Röhl, John C. G. and Nicolaus Sombart (eds), *Kaiser Wilhelm II, New Interpretations: The Corfu Papers* (Cambridge, 1982).

Rose, Kenneth, *King George V* (London, 1983).

Rotberg, Robert I., with the collaboration of Miles F. Shore, *The Founder: Cecil Rhodes and the Pursuit of Power* (New York, 1988).

Rowell, Geoffrey, *The Vision Glorious: Themes and Personalities of the Catholic Revival in Anglicanism* (Oxford, 1983).

St Aubyn, Giles, *Edward VII Prince and King* (New York, 1979).

Schreuder, Deryck, 'Gladstone and the Conscience of the State', in *The Conscience of the Victorian State*, Peter Marsh (ed.) (Syracuse, 1979).

Slack, Kenneth, *George Bell* (London, 1971).

Smith, R. J., *The Gothic Bequest: Medieval Institutions in British Thought 1688–1863* (Cambridge, 1987).

Spring, David, 'The Clapham Sect: Some Social and Political Aspects', *Victorian Studies*, 5 (September 1961) 35–48.

——, 'Land and Politics in Edwardian England', *Agricultural History*, 58 (January 1984) 17–42.

St John-Stevas, Norman, 'Bagehot as a Writer and Literary Critic', in *The Collected Works of Walter Bagehot*, St John-Stevas (ed.) vol. 15 (London, 1986).

——, 'Bagehot and the Monarchy', in *The Collected Works of Walter Bagehot*, St John-Stevas (ed.) vol. 15 (London, 1986).

——, 'Bagehot's Religious Views', in *The Collected Works of Walter Bagehot*, St John-Stevas (ed.) vol. 15 (London, 1986).

——, *Walter Bagehot* (London, 1959).

Shedell, James, 'Emperor, Church, and People: Religion and Dynastic Loyalty during the Golden Jubilee of Franz Joseph', *Catholic Historical Review*, 76 (January 1990) 71–92.

Sinclair, David, *Two Georges: The Making of the Modern Monarchy* (London, 1988).

Tollemache, Lionel, *Talks with Mr. Gladstone*, 3rd edn (London, 1903).

Wagner, Sir Anthony, *Heralds of England* (London, 1967).

——, *The Records and Collections of the College of Arms* (London, 1952).

Ward, Maisie, *The Wilfrid Wards and the Transition*, 2 vols (London, 1934–7).

Weintraub, Stanley, *Victoria: An Intimate Biography* (New York, 1987).

Weston, Corinne C., 'Salisbury and the Lords, 1868–95', *Historical Journal*, 25 (March 1982) 103–29.

Whyte, Frederick, *The Life of W. T. Stead*, 2 vols (New York, 1925).

Williams, P. R., 'Public Discussion of the British Monarchy, 1837–87', PhD thesis, Cambridge, 1988.

Wilson, Edgar, *The Myth of the British Monarchy* (London, 1989).

Woodcock, Thomas and John Martin Robinson, *The Oxford Guide to Heraldry* (Oxford, 1988).

Wortman, Richard, *Scenarios of Power, Myth and Ceremony in Russian Monarchy*, 1 vol. so far (Princeton, 1995).

Ziegler, Philip, *King Edward VIII* (London, 1991).

Index

accession declaration, royal, 121
Akers-Douglas, Alfred, 122
Albert, Prince (The Prince Consort),
   27–8, 55, 61, 73–4
   aristocracy, 41
   death of, 10–11, 36, 39
   Disraeli, Benjamin (Lord
     Beaconsfield), 27
   economies, 37
   Gladstone, William Ewart, 35
   industrialism, 3
   Martin, Theodore, 49
   middle class ideals, 10
   monarchy, popularity of, 28, 35,
     49–50
   political influence, 10, 27, 73, 75,
     80
Albert Victor, Prince, 45
Alexandra, Queen, 45, 91, 101–2
Arundel, 116, 134
Arundel Castle, 118–19, 138
Arundel Cathedral, 121
Asquith, H. H., 51, 131, 133
Asquith, Margot, 129

Bagehot, Eliza Wilson, 18, 30
Bagehot, Walter, 12, 48, 55, 71–2, 79,
   98–100, 133, 142
   Albert, Prince (The Prince Consort),
     27–8, 56, 61
   aristocracy, 23–5
   Cavaliers, 16–17
   Crystal Palace Exhibition, 17
   Edinburgh Review, 25
   educated and uneducated men, 19–20,
     22
   Eldon, Lord, 25
   Empress of India, 7, 20–1
   English Constitution, The, 15, 18–31,
     56, 61
   Gibbon, Edward, 24
   Gladstone, William Ewart, 24, 33
   Hobsbawm, Eric, 2
   influence of, 15
   Irish Church Bill, 135
   Lords, House of, 19, 21, 23, 135–6

Macaulay, T. B., 16–17, 30
monarchy: ambivalence toward,
   23–7, 30; Bank of England, 25;
   disguise, 22; intelligibility of, 19;
   morality, 21–2; power of, 78;
   public liking for state and show,
   47–8; sacred, 20–1; secrecy, 143;
   separate spheres, 28–9, 30–1;
   society, 21–2; wife, middle-class,
   28–9, 30–1; working classes, 65
mysticism, 25
Newman, John Henry, 115
Physics and Politics, 20
Public Worship Regulation Bill,
   25–6, 100
religious views, 25–6
republicanism, 21
Roman Catholic Church, 26
Tories, 16, 17, 30–1
upbringing, 15–16
see also thanksgiving for the recovery
   of the Prince of Wales (1872)
Balfour, A. J., 97, 99, 130
Bank of England, 25
Beaton, Cecil, 143
Beatrice, Princess, 45, 91
Benson, A. C., 73–5, 97–8
Bessborough, Lord, 37
Bigge, Arthur (Lord Stamfordham),
   70, 79, 88, 90, 127, 131, 133,
   138
Bismarck, Otto von, 39
Blenheim Palace, 136
Bloomsbury, 138
Boer War, 93, 102, 119
Bradlaugh, Charles, 37
Brett, Hon. Maurice, 62, 67, 79
British Covenant, 136–7
Brompton Oratory, 116, 121
Brooke, Sylvia, 67
Brown, John, 87
Buckingham Palace, 42, 45, 79, 83, 94,
   136
budget (1909), 77, 98, 109, 134–5,
   137
Burke, Edmund, 100

Cadogan, Lady, 125
Caernarvon Castle, 131
Cambridge, duke of, 38, 53
Cannadine, David, 1–9
Cannon, John, 5, 15
Canterbury Cathedral, 99
Caroline, Queen, 76
Carson, Edward, 136
Cavaliers, 16–17
Cawston, Richard, 86
Chamberlain, Joseph, 7, 58–9, 63, 65,
    68
Chapel Royal, St James's Palace, 42
Charles I, 103
Charles, Prince of Wales, 15
Charlotte, Princess, 29
Church of England, 25–6, 33–4, 41–2,
    54, 82, 84–5, 87–90, 92–4, 97–8,
    107, 108–10, 141, 143
Church, Irish, 36, 53, 135
Church, R. W. (dean of St Paul's), 43
Church, Welsh, 78, 99
civil list, 20, 36–7, 47, 50–1, 55, 124
Civil Service, 124–6, 128, 131–3
Civil War, 139
Clarendon, Lord, 27–8
Clark, J. C. D., 33
College of Arms, 123–5, 127–32, 136
Colley, Linda, 3–4, 29
Columbus, Christopher, 9
Commons, House of, 24, 73, 135, 140
Commune, Paris, 46
conservative party, 7–8, 49, 54, 58–9,
    77–8, 99, 101, 116–21, 128,
    135–7
Corn Laws, 18
coronation of King Edward VII and
    Queen Alexandra (1902), 11, 56–7,
    70, 97, 102, 106, 110
  Abbey decorations, 71
  Abbey seating, 71–2
  abbreviated, 71, 94
  bishop's consecration, parallel to,
    94
  committee, 71, 125–6, 128
  Court of Claims, 127
  Davidson, Randall, 92–7
  disputes at, 128
  divinity and imperfection, 96
  earl marshal (duke of Norfolk), 113,
    125, 127–8

electric lighting, 96
exclusivity, 71–2
Esher, Lord, 71–2, 125–7
  mishaps at, 95–7
  Punch, 127
  oath, 96
  regalia, 96
  rehearsals, 71, 128
  research for, 94
  revival of old ceremonies, 127
  scrolls printed with form of service,
    95–6
  Westminster School, 95
  Zadok the Priest, 96
coronation of King George V and
    Queen Mary (1911), 11, 92, 110
  committee, 131–2, 137
  Davidson, Randall, 92, 106
  disputes at, 131–4
  earl marshal (duke of Norfolk),
    106–7, 113, 131–4, 137
  photography, 106–7
coronation of King George VI and
    Queen Elizabeth (1937), 143
coronation of Queen Victoria (1838),
    33, 70
coronation service, 33
Court of Claims, 127
Creighton, Mandell (bishop of London),
    67–8
crowds, 46–7, 55, 88–9, 92
Cumberland, duke of, 53

Davidson, Edith (Edith Tait), 84
Davidson, Randall Thomas, 12, 76
  Bagehot, Walter, 99–100
  bishops, political influence of, 98
  Boer War, 93
  broad church views, 84–5, 93
  Canterbury, archbishop of, 97
  Dartford, 84
  education legislation, 93, 99
  Edward VII, King, 94, 101–2
  Esher, Lord, 98
  George V, King, 79, 110, 142
  Gladstone, William Ewart, 93
  Harrow, 83
  imperialism, 93
  Lloyd George, David, 109
  mediator, 98–9, 108–9

Davidson, Randall Thomas – *continued*
  monarchy: accessibility of, 91, 107,
    110; adapted to democratic
    conditions, 98, 101–2, 107;
    ambivalence toward, 110; conduct
    of royal family, 95; prestige of
    government service, 110; religion
    and, 82, 87, 89–90, 92–7, 105,
    110; showiness and, 88
  marriage, 84
  non-partisanship, 98–9
  ordination, 84
  Oxford, 84
  Parliament Bill, 108–9
  personality, 82–4, 89
  politics of, 93–4, 98–100, 108–9
  public demand for ceremonial, 87
  queen mother, title, 101–2
  Rochester, bishop of, 89
  Rochester Cathedral, 99–100
  sycophancy, 87, 91
  Tait, A. C., 84–5
  Tait, Craufurd, 84
  Temple, Frederick, 97
  upbringing, 83
  Victoria, Queen, 85–7, 91
  Welsh Church, 99
  Winchester, bishop of, 89
  Windsor, dean of, 85
  see also coronation of King Edward
    VII and Queen Alexandra (1902);
    coronation of King George V and
    Queen Mary (1911); jubilee,
    diamond (1897); jubilee, golden
    (1887); lying in state of King
    Edward VII (1910)
Dawson, Sir Douglas, 131
democratic royalism
  absurdity as part of monarchy's
    appeal, 128
  ambivalence in, 30–1, 54–5, 80–1,
    110
  antiquity, 113, 138
  argument for retaining monarchy,
    12–13, 140–3
  Bagehot, Walter, 30–1, 98
  Davidson, Randall, 82, 98, 102, 107,
    110–11
  entertainment value, 80, 113
  Esher, Lord, 80–1, 98
  expanded franchise, safety of, 56

Gladstone, William Ewart, 54–6, 98
  non-partisanship, monarchy's
    reputation for, 56
Norfolk, duke of, 110–14, 120, 128,
  138
paired opposite ideas, 30, 113
photography, 107
prestige of government service, 110
pride dampened by dwelling on
  problems, 110
religious services, convey rationale
  for monarchy, 54, 82
reverence and resentment, 80–81
royal family occupies 'representative
  home', 102
service, self-sacrifice and ceremonial
  roles, 54, 120
silliness and seriousness, 114
unifying impulse of, 54, 110
Derby, 15th earl of (Lord Stanley), 28
Dilke, Sir Charles, 61
  civil list enquiry, 47
  Gladstone, William Ewart, 39–40, 54
  Greater Britain beyond the Seas, 59,
    70
  imperialism, 7, 58–9
  Newcastle speech (1871), 37, 65, 103
  Victoria, Queen, 38
Disraeli, Benjamin (Lord Beaconsfield),
  48
  Albert, Prince (The Prince Consort),
    27
  Empress of India, 7, 20, 48–9, 54
  Hobsbawm, Eric, 2
  monarchy, influence on exaggerated,
    8, 31, 55
  Norfolk, 15th duke of, 116
  Primrose League, 118
  royal ceremony, 7
  showiness, 7–8, 117
durbar, Delhi (1877), 88
durbar, Delhi (1911), 132–3, 142

Ecclesiastical Titles Bill, 114
Economist, The, 1, 18, 20, 24, 30
Education Bill (1906), 99, 121
Edward VII, King, 48, 50, 53
  annuity to children of, 50–1
  ceremonial, liking for, 69, 142
  character of, 77
  coronation oath, 96

Edward VII, King – *continued*
death of, 76, 83, 101–2, 128
illness of (1871–2), 38, 46, 95
illness of (1902), 71, 94–5, 128
income, 43
Ireland, 36, 43
precedent, 69
scandals, 36, 43, 51–2, 61, 95
Victoria, Queen, 72, 82, 91
see also coronation of King Edward
VII and Queen Alexandra (1902);
funeral of King Edward VII
(1910); funeral of Queen Victoria
(1901); jubilee, diamond (1897);
lying in state of King Edward VII
(1910); thanksgiving for the
recovery of the Prince of Wales
(1872)
Edward VIII, King, 131–2
Edwardes, George, 66
Edwards, A. G. (bishop of St Asaph), 8,
132
Empire music hall, 66
Elizabeth II, Queen, 1, 14, 15
Elizabeth, Queen (The Queen Mother),
143
Ellis, Arthur, 125
English Constitution, The, 15, 18–31,
56, 61
Esher, Eleanor, Lady, 59
Esher, Lionel Gordon Baliol Brett, 4th
Viscount, 59
Esher, Reginald Baliol Brett, 2nd
Viscount, 12, 56, 98, 130, 133
After the War, 79
ages, 76
Albert, Prince (The Prince Consort),
61
aristocracy, 58, 69–70
Bagehot, Walter, 61, 78
Brett, Hon. Maurice, 62
ceremony, authority on, 57, 69
Chamberlain, Joseph, 58
College of Arms, 125–6
courtier, as, 58–9
Davidson, Randall, 98–9
democracy, 61, 75
Dilke, Sir Charles, 58
Edward VII, King, 58, 61, 63,
69–73, 76–8
Eton, 59

Footprints of Statesmen, 60
French Revolution (1789), 69
George V, King, 79, 142
Girlhood of Queen Victoria, The, 75,
77
Gladstone, William Ewart, 61
imperialism, 7, 59–61, 80
Irish Home Rule, 78
Letters of Queen Victoria, The, 73–7,
80
liberal party, 58
masses, 61
monarchy: ambivalence toward, 57,
65, 71, 80–1; character and, 74,
77, 80; critical of, 59; empire and,
61, 80, 143; history, 72–3;
homosexuals and, 73–4; power,
72–3; representative government
and, 80; theater, 68–9, 71–2, 75,
80, 82, 88, 143; working classes
and, 80
Newman, John Henry, 75, 115
Nonconformists, 61
Norfolk, duke of, 71
precedent, 69–70
Queen Victoria's Journals, 75, 77
radicalism, 58
Royal Archives, 72
royalty, fascination with, 57
Somerset, Lord Arthur, 62
theater, 66–7
Victoria, Queen, 70, 73–7, 80, 122
Works, Office of, 62
World War I, 79, 138
Yoke of Empire, 60–1, 63, 73
Esher, William Baliol Brett, 1st
Viscount, 58
Eugénie, Empress, 45

Fitzalan Chapel, Arundel, 118
Fitzroy, Almeric, 95, 118–19, 122, 128,
132
Franco-Prussian War, 36, 43
Frederick, Empress, 8, 53
French Revolution (1789), 69
Frogmore, 92
funeral of King Edward VII (1910),
105
earl marshal (duke of Norfolk), 113,
128–9
mishaps, 128–31

funeral of Queen Victoria (1901), 55,
   57, 102
   crowds, 92
   dispute over right to manage, 122, 124
   earl marshal (duke of Norfolk), 113,
      122, 124–5, 133
   Edward VII, King, 122, 124
   Esher, Lord, 57, 122
   instructions for, Queen Victoria's, 91
   mistakes, 125
   public demand for ceremonial, 92
   procession, 92
   Windsor, 124–5

Geertz, Clifford, 4–5
George I, King, 22
George II, King, 22
George III, King, 3–4, 22, 39, 41, 44,
   50, 53
George IV, King, 4, 10, 22, 61, 70
George V, King
   Bagehot, Walter, 15
   court, 57, 142
   Edward VII, King, 83, 101–3
   India, 132–3, 142
   Irish Home Rule, 78
   Parliament Bill, 108, 110
   Prince of Wales, 70
   Victoria, Queen, 75
   World War I, 142
   see also coronation of King George V
      and Queen Mary (1911); lying in
      state of King Edward VII (1910)
Gibbon, Edward, 24
Gladstone, Catherine, 52–3
Gladstone, William Ewart, 12, 31, 71–2,
   76, 79, 98
   Albert, Prince (The Prince Consort),
      35, 43, 49–50, 54, 56, 61
   Bagehot, Walter, 24–5, 33
   Church Quarterly Review, The, 49
   Davidson, Randall, 85, 89
   Edward VII, King, 36–7, 39–41, 43,
      48, 50–2
   Eton, 35, 42
   funeral of, 120, 123
   Gleanings of Past Years, 49
   imperial triumphalism, 48–9, 52,
      54–5, 61
   Irish Church, 135
   Irish Home Rule, 50

lying in state of, 103
Martin, Theodore, 49–50, 54
monarchy: Albertine, 49–50, 55–6,
   58; aristocracy and, 41, 50; Bible
   supports, 34; ceremonial, public
   taste for, 47, 55; French influence
   on, 40–1; Irish plan, 36–7, 43, 48,
   54; precedent renewed, 47;
   relations with queen affect, 33, 55;
   reverence for, 52, 56; royalty
   question, 39, 54; symbolism, 33,
   40, 54; silence on, 50–1, 55; tory
   party, 88
More, Hannah, 50
national acts of religion, 39–40, 48,
   54–5, 93
Newcastle, duke of, 35
Newman, John Henry, 115
   religious views, 41–2, 50, 54
Royal Titles Bill, 48
*State in Its Relations with the
   Church, The*, 33
Victoria, Queen, 11, 32–3, 35–6,
   39–41, 48, 50, 53, 55
Wellesley, Gerald Valerian (dean of
   Windsor), 42–3
see also coronation of Queen Victoria
   (1838); jubilee, diamond (1897);
   jubilee, golden (1887); thanksgiving
   for the recovery of the Prince of
   Wales (1872)
Godfrey-Faussett, Bryan, 128–9
Gordon, General, 53, 60
Granville, Lord, 39, 42–3
Graphic, The, 46
Grey, Albert, 58
Grigg, John, 1

Haig, Douglas, 74
Halsbury, Lord, 136
Hamilton, E. W., 51, 85, 126, 128
Handel, George Frederick, 88
Hanover, queen of, 53
Harcourt, Lewis, 131
Hardie, Frank, 5
Hartington, Lord, 56, 58–9
Hawarden, 32, 52
Herbert, Auberon, 47
Hervey, Lord, 74
Hitchens, Christopher, 5
Hobsbawm, Eric, 2

Home Office, 37
Household, Royal, 123–5, 131–3
Hutton, Richard Holt, 26

Illustrated London News, The, 44, 46, 66, 106–7, 120
imperialism, 7, 20–1, 58–61, 63, 65, 68, 93, 95, 112, 118, 132, 138, 143
investiture of the Prince of Wales (1911)
    College of Arms, 131–2
    conspiracy to defraud the people, not a, 8
    Lloyd George, 8, 131–3
    medieval precedents, legitimate, 8
Irish Home Rule, 50, 53, 78–9, 120, 136–9
Irish Nationalists, 136
Irving, Henry, 66

John Brown's Legs, 87
Johnson, William (William Cory), 59, 62
jubilee, diamond (1897), 11, 31, 71, 81, 102
    audience, 65–6
    City officials, 64–5
    colonial premiers, 68
    colonial troops, 68
    committee, 57, 63
    Davidson, Randall, 63, 90
    Edward VII, King, 63
    Esher, Lord, 64–5, 68, 71
    Gladstone, William Ewart, 48, 52–3, 55
    imperial coronation, 68
    imperial federation, 68
    origins, 62–3
    planning for, 90
    procession, 65–6, 90, 103, 127
    public demand for celebration, 89
    rehearsals, 66
    religion as antidote to triumphalism, 90
    Salisbury, Lord, 62–3
    scene in front of St Paul's, 67–8
    semi-state, 123
    service at St Paul's, 90
jubilee, golden (1887), 11, 31, 48, 52–3, 54–6, 102
    Abbey seating, 71
    Davidson, Randall, 88
    expense, 62

form of service, distribution, 87–8
Gladstone, William Ewart, 52
herald caught trying to hawk ticket, 124
origins of, 87, 142
semi-state, 123
supported by custom, 52

Karim, Abdul, 91
Kennion, George Wyndham (bishop of Bath and Wells), 72, 95–7
Kensington Palace, 62
Kipling, Rudyard, 51, 60
Kitchener, Lord, 60
Knollys, Francis, Viscount, 38, 50–1, 64, 70, 98–9, 125–7

Leaves from the Journal of Our Life in the Highlands, 86–7
Leopold I, King, 27
Letter to the Duke of Norfolk, 120
Lloyd George, David, 8, 75, 77, 98, 109, 131–6
Longford, Elizabeth, countess of, 143
Lord Chamberlain's Office, 122–4, 131, 133–4, 141
Lord Mayor's Show, 127
Lord Steward's Office, 124
Lords, House of, 8, 19, 21, 23, 78, 98–101, 106–10, 124, 134–9
Louise, Princess, 38
Lowe, Robert, 37
lying in state of King Edward VII (1910), 92, 102–6
    attendance figures, 105
    contrasted with funeral, 105
    Davidson, Randall, 102–5
    Esher, Lord, 103
    George V, King, 101–3
    middle classes, 105–6
    photography, 104
    political compromise, 106
    procession, 104
    religious character, 103
    return to early-modern spectacle, 103
    sermon, 104–5
    upper classes, 104–6
    working classes, 103–6

Macaulay, T. B., 16–17, 30, 33
Major, John, 1

Manchester, duchess of, 27
Marlborough House, 46, 58, 80
Martin, Theodore, 49–50
Mary, Queen, 57, 79, 90, 105–6
Master of the Horse's Office, 124
McDonnell, Hon. Schomberg, 90,
    103–4, 107, 126, 129, 131, 133
Mecklenburg-Strelitz, Augusta, grand
    duchess of, 90, 105
Melbourne, Lord, 47
Mitford, Nancy, 117
More, Hannah, 50–1, 54
*More Leaves from the Journal of a Life
    in the Highlands*, 86–7
Morris dancing, 139
Mountbatten, Lord, 143
Murray, John, 77

Nairn, Tom, 5, 15
Napoleon III, Emperor, 27, 36, 45
National Trust, 3
Newman, John Henry, 75, 114–16,
    120
Nicholas II, Tsar, 79–80
Nicolson, Harold, 74, 143
Norfolk Commission, 119–20
Norfolk, Bernard Marmaduke Fitzalan-
    Howard, 16th duke of, 138, 143
Norfolk, Flora, duchess of (Lady Flora
    Hastings), 116
Norfolk, Gwendolen, duchess of, 130
Norfolk, Henry Charles Howard, 13th
    duke of, 114
Norfolk, Henry Granville Fitzalan-
    Howard, 14th duke of, 114
Norfolk, Henry Fitzalan-Howard, 15th
    duke of, 12, 71
  aristocracy, 120
  Arundel Castle, 112, 118–19, 138
  Blenheim Palace, speech at, 136
  Boer War, 119
  Bognor, speech at, 135
  British Covenant, 136–7
  Brixton, speech at, 135–6
  budget (1909), 134–5
  Carson, Edward, 136
  ceremony, aversion to, 130
  church building, 121
  Court of Claims, 127
  Disraeli, Benjamin (Lord
    Beaconsfield), 116

earl marshal, 113, 118, 122–6,
    129–34, 136
education legislation, 117, 121
extremism, 137
family, 114, 123
hereditary right, insistence on, 126,
    130, 133–7
independence, 120–2
Ireland, 114, 117, 120–1, 136–9
Letter to the Duke of Norfolk, 120
Littlehampton, speech at, 135
Lloyd George, David, 136
Lords, House of, 134–9
marriage to Lady Flora Hastings, 116
medievalism, 118–19, 121–2
military training, views on, 119–20
monarchy: age of, 113, 138; appeal
    of, 114; authenticity of, 138;
    entertainment value, 112–13, 127,
    137; mystery, 116; national history,
    116; ridicule, 127, 137–9;
    symbolism of, 112–13
Newman, John Henry, 114–16
Oratory School (Birmingham), 114,
    116
personality, 114, 117, 119, 127
postmaster general, 117
precedence, 129, 138–9
Primrose League, 118
Roman Catholic Church, 111,
    113–14, 117, 119–22, 127, 138
Salisbury, Lord, 117–18, 121
Sheffield, 117, 134
showiness, 116
Taunton, speech at, 135
Ulster Protestants, 136
Vatican, 121–2, 130
Victoria, Queen, 117
see also coronation of King Edward
    VII and Queen Alexandra (1902);
    coronation of King George V and
    Queen Mary (1911); funeral of
    King Edward VII (1910); funeral
    of Queen Victoria (1901);
    investiture of the Prince of Wales
    (1911)
Norwich Cathedral, 121–2

Oratory School (Birmingham), 114,
    116
Osborne, 86

Paine, Tom, 6
Parliament Bill, 78, 106–10, 136–9
Parnell, Charles Stewart, 61
Peel, Sir Robert, 33
Pius IX, Pope, 121
photography, 104, 106–7
Ponsonby, Frederick, 124–5
Ponsonby, Henry, 38–9, 59, 87–8,
    123
Ponsonby, Mary, 52, 88
Ponsonby-Fane, Spencer, 125
Pope-Hennessey, James, 74
Primrose League, 118
Public Worship Regulation Bill, 25–6,
    84, 100
Punch, 127–8

Quarterly Review, The, 77
queen mother, title, 101–2

Reform Bill, First, 34
Reform Bill, Second, 18, 24–30
Reid, Sir James, 82, 91
Rendel, Lord, 52, 54
republicanism, 21, 36–7, 47, 55
Review of Reviews, The, 72
Rhodes, Cecil, 60
Robinson, John Martin, 112, 118
Rochester Cathedral, 99
Roman Catholic Church, 26, 111,
    113–14, 117, 119–22, 127, 138
Rose, Kenneth, 129
Rosebery, Lord, 62, 78
Royal Titles Bill, 7, 20–1, 48–9
Russell, Lord John, 114

Salisbury, Lady, 118
Salisbury, Lord, 27–8, 50, 52, 62–3, 65,
    69, 88–90, 117–18, 121
Sandars, J. 75, 130
Sandringham, 38
Saturday Review, The, 46
Scott, Sir Walter, 31
Scott-Gatty, Sir Alfred, 131–2
separate spheres, 28–9, 30–1, 142–3
Sheffield, 117, 134
Shils, Edward, 13–14
Snowdon, Lord, 143
Society for the Promotion of Christian
    Knowledge, 88
Somerset, Lord Arthur, 62

Somerset, duke of, 117
Spencer, Lady Diana (Princess of
    Wales), 138
St George's Chapel, 42, 92, 125, 129
St James's Palace, 131
St Paul's Cathedral, 11, 30, 39, 41–7,
    50, 54–5, 63–8, 81, 90–1, 103,
    141
Stead, W. T., 72
Stockmar, Lord, 59
Stone, Sir Benjamin, 106–7
Strachey, Lytton, 77
Stuart, Charles Edward, 139
Sussex Imperial Yeomanry, 119
Sydney, Lord, 43

Tait, A. C., 84
Tait, Craufurd, 84
taxation, 37
Te Deum, 45, 63–5, 67, 88, 91
Temple, Frederick, 67, 90, 95, 97
thanksgiving for the recovery of the
    Prince of Wales (1872), 11, 30,
    39–48, 54–5, 88–9, 93
    Bagehot, Walter, 30
    crowds, 46, 88
    Gladstone, William Ewart, 39–48
    illuminations, 45–6
    jubilees, as re-enactments of
        thanksgiving (1872), 48
    length of service, 43–4
    monarchy, turning point for, 47
    national act, 40
    origins of, 39
    prayer, 45
    precedent for, 39, 41, 45, 47
    press, 44, 46–7
    procession, 44–5
    religion allied to pomp, queen's
        objections to, 40, 42–4, 47
    semi-state, 43–4, 123
    Victoria, Queen, 39–48
    Wellesley, Gerald Valerian (dean of
        Windsor), 42–4
Thompson, E. P., 138
Times, The, 44, 57, 72, 77, 92–3, 130
Toryism, 16–17, 31
Tranby Croft, 51, 61
Transvaal, 53
Tree, Herbert Beerbohm, 66
Trevelyan, G. O., 37

Ulster Protestants, 136
utilitarians, 34

van de Weyer, Sylvain, 59
Vatican, 121–2, 130
Vaughan, Father Bernard, 115
Victoria, Queen, 31, 48, 59, 61, 140
 Albert, Prince (The Prince Consort),
  85
 aristocracy, 41
 Bagehot, Walter, 142
 Balmoral, 1
 ceremonial, public demand for, 55,
  62
 Chamberlain, Joseph, 63
 constitutional behavior, 61
 Davidson, Randall, 89
 death of, 82,
 Dilke, Sir Charles, 38
 domesticity, 86
 Edward VII, King, 38–40
 Girlhood of Queen Victoria, The, 75,
  77
 Gladstone, William Ewart, 53
 Indian servants, 57, 91
 industrialism, 3
 Letters of Queen Victoria, The, 73–5,
  77, 80
 morbidity, 36, 85
 myth of, 9, 56
 national days of prayer, 87
 political influence, 11, 80
 Queen Victoria's Journals, 75, 77
 religious views, 40–3, 85–6
 reign, length of, 62
 Royal Titles Bill, 7, 20–1, 48–9
 Scotchmen, liking for, 85

seclusion, 27–8, 36, 86
Sheffield, 117
Norfolk, 15th duke of, 117
unpopularity, 4
see also coronation of Queen Victoria
  (1838); funeral of Queen Victoria
  (1901); jubilee, diamond (1897);
  jubilee, golden (1887); thanksgiving
  for the recovery of the Prince of
  Wales (1872)
Vincent, John, 28

Walpole, Horace, 74
Walpole, Sir Robert, 76
Ward, Wilfrid, 115, 121
Wellesley, Gerald Valerian (dean of
  Windsor), 42–3
Wellington, duke of, 123
Westcott, B. F., 83
Westminster Abbey, 11, 33–4, 41, 47,
  55, 62, 70–1, 87–8, 93–6, 101–3,
  106–7, 127, 141
Westminster Cathedral, 121
Westminster, Palace of, 102–5
Westminster School, 95
What Does She Do with It?, 37
Whippingham, 86
Wilhelm II, Kaiser, 82, 91
William IV, King, 4, 10, 22
Williams, P. R., 4
Wilson, James, 18
Windsor Castle, 42, 62
Works, Office of, 62, 122, 131, 133
World War I, 76, 79, 109, 137–8
World War II, 143

Young, Michael, 13–14